BREAKING AND SHAPING BEASTLY BODIES

D1602086

Breaking and Shaping Beastly Bodies

Animals as Material Culture
in the Middle Ages

Edited by

Aleksander Pluskowski

Oxbow Books

Published by
Oxbow Books, Oxford, UK

ISBN 978 1 84217 218 6

This book is available direct from
Oxbow Books, Oxford, UK
(Phone: 01865-241249; Fax: 01865-794449)

and

The David Brown Book Company
PO Box 511, Oakville, CT06779
(Phone: 860-945-9329; Fax: 860-945-9468)

or

from our website
www.oxbowbooks.com

*Cover image: Louis Malet (1441–1516) Seigneur de Graville,
hunting wild boar, from the 'Terrier de Marcoussis', 1491–93 (vellum).
French School, The Bridgeman Art Library, Getty Images.*

Printed in Great Britain by
The Information Press
Eynsham, Oxford

Contents

Contents

Chapter 1

Thinking About Beastly Bodies

Terry O'Connor

People's attitudes to animal bodies go right to the heart of the business of being human. Our increasingly detailed, yet spectacularly incomplete, knowledge of the behavioural complexity of other species has serially quashed many of the claims that have been made for human uniqueness. We use the manufacture of simple artefacts as a proxy indicator of human-like behaviour amongst early hominins, yet Man the Tool-Maker shares that skill with, amongst others, chimpanzees, crows and sea-otters (Boesch 2003). Similarly, as the fossil record pushes upright walking further back into the Pliocene, Man the Biped no longer looks quite so clever (Harcourt-Smith and Aiello 2004). Is there anything, apart from industrialised warfare and cricket, which our species is uniquely good at?

An important human trait is our inclination to develop complex relationships with numerous other species. In its simplest form, this is not unique. Mutualism exists throughout the biosphere, with some pairs of species, such as ants and aphids, evolving elaborate and highly successful relationships to mutual benefit (De Mazancourt *et al.* 2005). In the great majority of cases, however, these mutualistic relationships involve a pair of species, whose co-evolution has been achieved through behavioural adaptation driving positive selection pressures. Humans go a step further, opportunistically and, it sometimes seems, almost arbitrarily elaborating our relationships with many other species, whether through domestication, pet-keeping, taming for menageries, fetishising, deifying, anthropomorphising, exterminating vermin, conserving iconic species, or recruiting as mascots (what is it about military regiments and goats?). That complex web of relationships extends after the death of the animal, ranking some animal foods or particular skins and furs above others. In some instances, we can argue that these rankings reflect availability or some particular functional attribute of a raw material. A well-known example is the selection of reindeer and wolverine fur for different components of the traditional Inuit parka, making optimal use of the different insulating properties of two readily-available animal resources (Cotel *et al.* 2004). In other instances, restricted availability may cause a raw material to be ranked more highly than one of almost indistinguishable appearance and working properties. Thus, a *netsuke* figure carved from the upper incisor tooth of an elephant will be prized over one carved from a tangua nut, which in turn outranks one cast from plastic (fig. 1.1). Human attitudes to other animals, it

Terry O'Connor

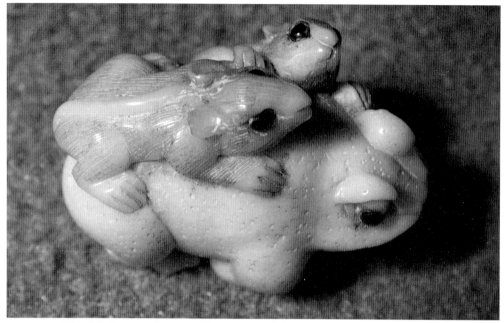

Fig. 1.1. Frog and mouse figure, carved in tangua nut to mimic ivory.

seems, are characteristically complex and range from the strictly utilitarian to the highly conceptualised and culture-specific. When we consider medieval attitudes to animals before and after death, therefore, we are tackling a fundamentally human, and distinctly idiosyncratic, behavioural trait.

A zooarchaeological perspective

Those of us who approach medieval animals primarily through the zooarchaeological record of old bones have to balance three strands of investigation. The bones are the fossils of long-dead animals, which had their own distinctive biology and ethology. Their death assemblage, and therefore the recovered assemblage that we study, will to some degree reflect that biology and ethology. For example, bones of frogs are occasionally very abundant in medieval archaeological deposits (e.g. O'Connor 1988, 106–7, 113). We do not need to postulate mysterious anuran cults to explain this phenomenon: frog behaviour and ecology lead them to be locally abundant in life and particularly susceptible to catastrophic death *en masse*. The same does not apply to cats, so a concentration of cat bones in a medieval pit would require a different form of explanation (Luff and Moreno-Garcia 1995). The bones are also sediment clasts, sometimes the most abundant large particles in an archaeological sediment (Wilson 1996). A range of familiar geomorphic processes, such as downslope colluviation and hydrodynamic sorting, will cause the differential movement of different particle sizes, and may thus bring about patterning in the distribution of bones in the archaeological record. Although the world of medieval archaeology may seem somewhat removed from the more familiar terrain of geomorphology, those same processes will be acting on dumps and yard surfaces and in pitfills. We need a taphonomic analysis of our medieval material just as much as we would for a Lower Palaeolithic assemblage, in order to identify the signature that the processes of death, biostratinomy and diagenesis have left on our assemblage. Finally, of course, the bones are the residue of past human activity, susceptible to archaeological study, and reflecting the decisions and pre-occupations of people of a particular time and place. That decision-making will have influenced the composition of the life-assemblage from which our archaeological sample derives (e.g. by deciding that a particular species shall be excluded from the diet), and it will have affected the post-mortem taphonomy of the bones (e.g. by imposing rules regarding the disposal of organic refuse). As zooarchaeologists, our distinctive challenge is to understand bones as fossils and clasts, in order to understand them all the more clearly as evidence of that decision-making, and thus as archaeology.

Attitudes to animals

Like charity, ethnography begins at home. Our own attitudes to animals as food, labour, clothing and symbol make a useful starting point for discussing medieval beasts. Even the familiar role of animals as food is richly complex and contentious. In some contemporary societies, many individual people and certain religious sects contend that the use of animals for food is essentially immoral. The time-depth of vegetarianism on moral precepts is unknown, and this is not the place to plumb that particular abyss. We should note, however, that intermittent avoidance of meat on fast days has long been a feature of western Christendom, and thus of medieval Europe. How far that avoidance was driven by a sense of moral obligation towards the beasts, and how far by the need to manifest social identity by the imposition of consumption laws, is a matter for debate. Even the decision to eat or to avoid meat is tempered by pragmatism or indecision. In early 21st-century Britain, some 'vegetarians' will consume fish and shellfish, thus apparently making a distinction between endothermic and ectothermic animals, with a lessened moral obligation towards the latter. Others will even eat poultry whilst avoiding 'red' meats such as beef or lamb, implying a yet more subtle categorisation that owes little to biological taxonomy. Similar decisions are made by omnivores, too: the writer of this paper will cheerfully eat rabbit or horse, but not veal.

   The avoidance of some foods on ethical or religious grounds (and the followers of a religion will generally assert that their practices *are* grounded in ethics) is sufficiently well-known to have had some archaeological investigation (Daroczi-Szabo 2004). A good example is Ijzereef's work in Amsterdam (Ijzereef 1989). From an analysis of pit-fills from tenements in a neighbourhood known to have had a substantial Jewish population, Ijzereef was able to show that some refuse assemblages lacked bones of pork and eel, both of which are forbidden by Jewish dietary prohibitions (*Leviticus* chap. 11; *Deuteronomy* chap. 14). Species-specific prohibition is thus identifiable in the zooarchaeological record, at least given high context integrity and excellent standards of archaeological recovery. Fast-day avoidance of all meat would seem to be logically impossible to detect, but for the helpful fact that Christianity not only does not classify the flesh of fishes as 'meat', but goes a step further by grouping a number of marine birds and mammals as honorary fish. This raises the intriguing possibility that the refuse of particularly observant Christian households or communities would occasionally include assemblages rich in the bones of fish, barnacle geese, and maybe the odd beaver. But could we recover and recognise such assemblages? The taphonomic trajectory would be crucial, as any time-averaging or spatial mixing of refuse before or during final deposition would blur the distinctive attributes of the original refuse assemblages. The debris of religious houses would seem to offer the best chance of finding such examples. However, even the Dominican Friary at Beverley, East Yorkshire, failed to give an unambiguous 'Christian fast' assemblage, despite excellent context integrity and excavations in and around the kitchens (Gilchrist and O'Connor 1996). Ironically, it may be that dedicated adherence to a religious ethic is to blame, with 'meat' meals being prepared for charitable distribution even while the brothers were making do with salt herring. In short, were it not for the historical record, the adherence of medieval Christianity to Lenten and Friday fasts would not be inferred from the zooarchaeological record alone.

Apart from religious and ethnic identity, animals as food serve to signify other, often subtle, distinctions of region, wealth and status (which may or may not be the same as wealth). The regional associations of certain foodstuffs are familiar enough. Within England, the bovine stomach – tripe – is generally associated with the urban north, as part of a cultural package that includes whippets, flat caps and rugby league. The fact that all of those 'northern' attributes are to be found fairly generally throughout the country has done little to weaken the association. In fact, there are two quite different aspects to regionalisation in animal foods, both of which have the potential to be recognised archaeologically. First, there is the simple matter of some parts of a larger region favouring certain joints of meat or particular edible offal, leading to the possibility that bones butchered in a distinctive way will be encountered commonly in one region but not in another. This has interesting ramifications for the academic process: it is common for colleagues working on assemblages that originated in sites many miles apart to meet up at conferences and workshops to discuss the detail of their old bones. Evidence of regional identities in butchery may show up at such discussions in the form of cut-marks or element distributions that are familiar to one zooarchaeologist but quite unfamiliar to others working on material of similar date. We return to an example of distinctive butchery below.

The second aspect of food regionalisation is familiar from the present day, yet lacks serious archaeological analysis. When people migrate from their 'homeland' into an unfamiliar host culture, they tend to retain some familiar cultural attributes from that homeland, and food is often an expression of that retention (Wikkramatileke and Singh 1970; Sheikh and Thomas 1994; Wyke and Landman 1997). Present-day North American cuisine (salt beef, bagels, burgers, tacos) reflects the origins of many of the groups that have colonised that continent, and the assimilation of the South Asian curry into the

British diet, although in part a hang-over from Imperial times, is largely a consequence of immigrant groups retaining something familiar from home. The archaeology of this process is seriously under-studied, perhaps because the topic of migration is seen as a relic of a culture-historical paradigm which archaeology would like to think it has outgrown. However, we know for a plain historical fact that people moved around Europe between the 8th and 16th centuries, and there is at least the possibility of investigating the movement of regionally-distinctive foods and means of food preparation. Urban assemblages from eastern England rarely show much of a change in animal utilisation across the mid-11th century, suggesting that the Norman Conquest involved comparatively small numbers of influential people, rather than the substantial migration that might have brought a distinctive cuisine in its wake. However, this association of an altered cuisine with a migrating people may itself be too simplistic. Recent European history shows that cultural influences from one region to another, without substantial migration, may trigger different gastronomic responses in those keen to adopt the new influences and those who wish to conspicuously reject them. Le Blanc (1999) discusses the subject in the context of mid-19th century Russia, showing how food choices became a means of showing one's acceptance or rejection of the pervasive French influence, to such an extent that the food choices of fictional characters could be used to signal their cultural attitudes. At times of cultural change or exogenous influence, here is another potential cause of intra-site variation in the use of beastly bodies.

Other attitudes to animals may be susceptible to change across regions and through quite short periods of time. Within this writer's lifetime, the wearing of fur has moved from being a luxury to which to aspire to becoming a highly contentious act that invites forceful objection. This change in attitude has been rapid, and its archaeological correlates have been few and often distant from the craft itself. A future zooarchaeologist noting the sharp decline of water vole (*Arvicola terrestris*) in the late-20th century would be unlikely to make the link with a decline in the wearing of fur. However, large numbers of mink have been 'liberated' from fur-producers into the surrounding countryside by anti-fur activists. Mink are highly effective predators of water voles, and their impact on vole populations is likely to be one of the most visible and long-lasting effects of the change in attitudes to wearing fur. Over a similarly short period of time, attitudes to the use of animals for labour have changed. In the early-20th century, ponies worked in mines, horses hauled carts and ploughs, and mules moved field artillery around the battlefield. By the end of the century, attitudes in northern Europe had changed to such an extent that attempts were commonly made to export that same level of concern for equine welfare to parts of the world where horses and donkeys were still a vital source of haulage. An interesting footnote to this change of attitude lies in our zoological museums. Across Europe and North America through the later 19th and 20th centuries, hundreds of thousands of mules were used and died, yet only a handful of their skeletons persist in museums, far fewer than, say, the skeletons of gorillas. Peculiar attitudes to dead beasts persist even in modern scientific institutions!

The medieval period: does familiarity breed disrespect?

None of the above is altogether surprising. We know from our own lives and experiences that attitudes to animals, live and dead, are regionally-specific and subject to rapid change. Why is it, then, that we so often transfer contemporary value-judgements (prime meat joints, waste, high-status foods) onto the medieval world?

Maybe the problem is that the medieval period is too recent, too familiar, too nearly contiguous with our own. In England, we are dealing with a period that is deceptively familiar from the survival of medieval buildings, from school history lessons, from more-or-less authentic period reconstructions, and from the survival of later medieval texts that are in something almost recognisable as English. The medieval period is a part of our modern world, most obviously in towns such as York or Chester, and it is so very easy to project onto that world our own attitudes and values. There is a major problem, too, with the casual way that we refer to 'the medieval period' to encompass some eight centuries of cultural upheaval and social change. To a zooarchaeologist with an interest in this island's natural history, the landscape of Tudor England seems quite familiar, whereas the patterns of land-use and the flora and fauna of 9th century England would probably have looked very unfamiliar. 'The medieval period' is the time in which all of that changed, and during which many of the introductions and extinctions that made our contemporary natural history happened.

Apart from differences in farming strategies and wildlife, our transference of values into the medieval centuries assumes a familiarity with the medieval mind that we would not assume for prehistoric periods. Is that justifiable? This is where we need all of the other disciplines that study the medieval world. Do the plot-lines of medieval romances suggest similar minds at work? Does the art speak to us as it presumably did to its contemporary audience? In the latter case, probably not, as the apparent weirdness of thought portrayed by artists such as Hieronymus Bosch (*c*.1450–1516) may have more to do with our inability to decode an imagery unfamiliar to us. Even a brief acquaintance with Chaucer or with the exuberant gargoyles of some medieval churches is a reminder of an earthy attitude to life, sex and faeces, far removed from our own rather precious times. Documents, art, and iconography only rarely contribute directly to the archaeological study of the medieval period, but they are essential for what they show us of minds that are only superficially familiar, and thus capable of making decisions that we would not expect or regard as 'rational'.

Butchery marks observed on animal bones from medieval deposits are a case in point. The basic anatomy of cattle and pigs means that there are considerable constraints on butchering procedures, and it is little surprise that we find concentrations of chopping-marks in predictable places, around joints and at the insertions of major muscles. In the smaller details, however, we sometimes see things that are more difficult to explain. The Castle Mall site in Norwich yielded an intriguing assemblage of chopped-up cattle rib fragments, reduced to fragments between 5cm and 10cm in length by a 'chop and crack' method (fig. 1.2). What does this represent? The simple, 'rational' explanation would be that these bones were being reduced in length in order to pack many of them into a container, perhaps to boil up for stock or some similar product. That would be a satisfactory explanation today, but in the context of medieval Norwich it is quite possible that the bones would be recognised as deriving from a 'breast of beef' joint of a cut no longer utilised. Maybe there was some specific etiquette surrounding that particular place of disposal, such that long, conspicuous bones such as ribs had to be reduced to smaller fragments before disposal? Or maybe the two explanations can be combined. Suppose that beef ribs were perceived to be a 'cheap' cut of meat: perhaps a household with social aspirations ensured that such a downmarket joint was not conspicuous amongst their refuse? All of that is speculation, but it is not inconsistent with what we know of human behaviour in respect of food and animal body parts.

Fig. 1.2. *Cattle rib fragments from castle Mall, Norwich, showing a distinctive 'cut and crack' reduction to short lengths. Original photograph courtesy of Rebecca Nicholson.*

Fig. 1.3 shows the tarsometatarsus of a crane (*Grus grus*) from medieval Lincoln. There are several fine cut-marks around the distal end, consistent with removal of the toes (i.e. the bird's foot) from the metatarsus. This would appear to indicate something about the way that a crane carcass was 'dressed', but in strictly rational terms it makes little sense. Why remove the toes, yet retain the tarsometatarsus, which carries little or no meat? Clearly there is something particular and non-functional about preparing a crane in this way, perhaps leaving the long tarsometatarsals attached to the dressed bird in order to signify the identity of the bird. That, at least, was the interpretation originally offered for this specimen. However, in the discussion of this paper at the *Beastly Bodies* conference, Marsha Levine helpfully pointed out that chicken's feet are a delicacy in

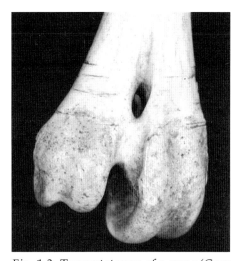

Fig. 1.3. *Tarometatarsus of a crane (Grus grus) from Flaxengate, Lincoln, showing repeated fine cut-marks around the distal end.*

China. Perhaps the tarsometatarsus was 'waste', from which the foot was removed because it constituted a particular delicacy? This is the point at which documentary historians have to take over, searching for references to crane's feet served at banquets.

Other forms of disposal hint at the complexity of medieval behaviour. Where do

you bury a dead cat? In medieval contexts, we encounter cats most often as disarticulated bones dispersed among occupation debris, sometimes as discrete individual burials, occasionally as mass 'kills' such as that at Benet Court (above), or even as foundation burials inserted into foundations and wall-spaces. Each of those forms of disposal indicates a quite different attitude to this most familiar of co-habitees. Some medieval cats merited individual burial, whilst most, one suspects, lived more or less feral lives and constituted part of the background fall-out of corpses. Whether or not the occasional mass kills are evidence of the systematic exploitation of cats for fur is a matter for debate (e.g. McCormick 1997), but whether they represent the cropping of fur or simply the disposal of feline vermin, the attitude differs markedly from that evidenced by individual burial. Then there is the mystical, symbolic aspect of cats, represented in foundation burials, and conspicuous in medieval literature and iconography. This writer has encountered cats in un-ambiguous foundation burials on two occasions, both of them under ecclesiastical buildings, reminding us that the medieval church was not free from the occasional non-liturgical superstition. We see the association of cat and Church at its closest and most charming in the 9th century Irish poem *Pangur Bán*, in which the writer, a scribe, compares his activity with the cat's. In translation, the first stanza runs:

> "I and Pangur Bán my cat/'Tis a like task we are at;/Hunting mice is his delight,/Hunting words I sit all night."

The poem shows what the zooarchaeological record cannot: that a medieval cat could be named, owned, and identified with. Cats may sometimes have been vermin; mice and other commensal animals often so, yet the precise status of some such species can be hard to define, and one suspects that it was sometimes shifting and ambiguous. A good example is the red kite (*Milvus milvus*), a bird quite often represented in medieval assemblages, and arguably a well-adapted urban scavenger (Mulkeen and O'Connor 1997). If we accept that niche for them, we may still ask whether kites were encouraged or merely tolerated. By the end of the medieval period, documents hint at some degree of protection for urban kites, suggesting the former (Gurney 1921). Does that indicate a difference in attitude towards kites rather than other urban scavengers such as crows and jackdaws (*Corvus corone, C. monedula*)? Our distinctively human tendency to acculturate our relationship with other species, discussed at the start of this paper, really comes to the fore with birds. Medieval art and iconography hints at symbolic roles for many bird species, not least the goldfinches that in gigantic form stalk Bosch's nightmare scenes, yet take quite a different role in Raphael's near-contemporary *Our Lady of the Goldfinch* (*ca.* 1506). A similar (though not necessarily the same) diversity of attitude comes through to the present day. One simple example: many species of small bird underwent a sharp population decline in Britain during the last decades of the 20th century (Gregory *et al.* 2004), yet only the house sparrow (*Passer domesticus*) has really caught the attention of public and media. To a biologist, the collapse in corn buntings (*Miliaria calandra*) is more serious and dramatic, but that species is 'out there' in the wild, not so close to our homes and to our attention. Which birds filled the 'close to home' niche in medieval England?

Understanding beastly bodies

Medieval zooarchaeology has made considerable progress over the last couple of decades, at least with regard to broad, general questions of animal husbandry and utilisation. The challenge that still confronts us is the more slippery and complex one of understanding attitudes to animals, live and dead, and of doing so without simply transferring the preoccupations of our own times and culture back into the medieval world. We have to consider the biology and ethology of the animals themselves. Much as we may wish to think of them as 'material culture', living animals were not passive objects, and had their own objectives and motivation (food and sex, much the same as their human compatriots). We have to take those biotic factors into account, and then to understand the circumstances of their deposition and taphonomy during and after death. Much of what we wish to understand about human attitudes to those animals will be tied up in the post-mortem transport of carcasses and parts thereof, including the working of bone, antler, ivory, horn and skin into artefacts. The archaeological study of medieval animals cannot therefore be totally divorced from the taphonomic or palaeobiological study of their material remains: the challenge lies in integrating all of those approaches to ask new questions.

Acknowledgements

This is an opportune place to thank the many colleagues who have discussed medieval animals with me over the years, in particular those who made *Breaking and Shaping Beastly Bodies* such a lively and enjoyable conference. I am grateful to Dr. Rebecca Nicholson for permission to use fig. 1.2.

Bibliography

Boesch, C. (2003) Is culture a golden barrier between human and chimpanzee? *Evolutionary Anthropology* 12, 82–91.

Cotel, A. J. Golingo, R., Oakes, J. E. and Riewe, R. R. (2004) Effect of ancient Inuit fur parka ruffs on facial heat transfer. *Climate Research* 26(1), 77–84.

Daroczi-Szabo, L. (2004). Animal bones as indicators of *kosher* food refuse from 14th century Buda, Hungary. In S. Jones O'Day, W. van Neer and A. Ervynck (eds.) *Behaviour Behind Bones*, 252–261. Oxford, Oxbow Books.

De Mazancourt, C., Loreau, M. and Dieckmann, U. (2005) Understanding mutualism when there is adaptation to the partner. *Journal of Ecology* 93(2), 305–314.

Gilchrist, R. and O'Connor, T. P. (1996) The animal bones. In M. Foreman *Further Excavations at the Dominican Priory, Beverley, 1986–89*, 213–228. Sheffield, Sheffield Excavation Reports 4.

Gregory, R. D. Noble, D. G. and Custance, J. (2004) The state of play of farmland birds: population trends and conservation status of lowland farmland birds in the United Kingdom. *Ibis* 146 (Suppl. 2), 1–13.

Gurney, J. H. (1921) *Early Annals of Ornithology*. London, H.F. and G. Witherby.

Harcourt-Smith, W. E. H. and Aiello, L. C. (2004) Fossils, feet and the evolution of human bipedal locomotion. *Journal of Anatomy* 204, 403–416.

Ijzereef, G. F. (1989) Social differentiation from animal bone studies. In D. Serjeantson and T. Waldron (eds.) *Diet and Crafts in Towns. The Evidence of Animal Remains from the Roman to the Post-Medieval Periods*, 41–53. Oxford, British Archaeological Reports British Series 109.

Le Blanc, R. R. (1999). Food, orality and nostalgia for childhood: gastronomic slavophilism in mid-nineteenth century Russian fiction. *The Russian Review* 58, 244–67.

Luff, R. M. and Moreno-Garcia, M. 1995. Killing cats in the medieval period. An unusual episode in the history of Cambridge, England. *Archaeofauna* 4, 93–114.

McCormick, F. (1997) The animal bones In M. F. Hurley, O. M. B. Scully and S. W. J. McCutcheon (eds.) *Late Viking Age and Medieval Waterford*, 819–853. Waterford, Waterford Corporation.

Mulkeen, S. and O'Connor, T. P. (1997) Raptors in towns: towards an ecological model. *International Journal of Osteoarchaeology* 7, 440–9.

O'Connor, T. P. (1988) *Bones from the General Accident site, York. The Archaeology of York 15/2.* London, Council for British Archaeology.

Sheikh, N. and Thomas, J. (1994) Factors affecting food choice among ethnic minority adolescents. *Nutrition and Food Science* 94(4), 18–22.

Wikkramatileke, R. and Singh, K. (1970) Tradition and change in an Indian diary community in Singapore. *Annals of the Association of American Geographers.* 60(4), 717.

Wilson, B. (1996) *Spatial Patterning Among Animal Bones in Settlement Archaeology.* Oxford, Tempus Reparatum, British Archaeological Reports British Series 251.

Wyke, S. and Landman, J. (1997) Healthy eating? Diet and cuisine amongst Scottish Asian people. *British Food Journal* 99(1), 27–34.

Chapter 2

Medieval Bone Flutes in England

Helen Leaf

Bone flutes have been made and played in Europe since the Palaeolithic (Megaw 1960), but it is from medieval times that we have the greatest number of examples; current research in England yields a list of 116 medieval flutes, both complete and fragmentary. As a body of evidence, this is far more informative than the few well-known flutes that are commonly referred to, made popular in the 1960s by Megaw (1960, 1961 and 1968). It is also in significant contrast to supporting evidence from contemporary iconography and manuscripts, where bone flutes seem both silent and invisible. This lack of representation may infer that they were not used in religious contexts, or may suggest that bone flutes were not viewed as important instruments. Given the examples now available for study, a tentative and provisional typology can be offered. This chapter presents the information at its simplest; a broad overview of the variety of types of flutes as I see it, with additional comments relating to the animals or birds whose bones were used. The variables considered when suggesting types of flutes are the species of bird or animal, the skeletal element, and the number of toneholes.

The flutes have a broad date range, with the earliest being from 450–550 AD, and with a peak of occurrence in the 12th century (fig. 2.1). The dates used for this representation are taken as an average from a flute's given date range. Flutes that are dated with general dates such as 'medieval' or 'Saxon' are shown in separate columns. The bones used to make the flutes tend to be the ulna of birds (goose or swan) and the tibia or metatarsal of mammals (sheep or deer). These particular bones may have been selected over others due to their form, being suitably proportioned tubes ideal for making wind instruments. In the case of bird ulnae, this tube is long and slender, with a thin wall that is easy to cut and pierce with a knife. Figures 2.2 and 2.3 show these bones clearly.

Bird bone flutes are predominantly made from the ulnae of geese, a common domestic bird throughout the time period. They are also made from the bones of swans and cranes (fig. 2.4). Some flutes are made from bones that are only identified as 'bird', yet even these flutes add to the body of available information. Similarly, even fragments of flutes can yield useful information, such as the number and placement of toneholes, bone used, and tool marks from the manufacturing process.

The goose bone flute is simple in form, having a D-shaped window (sound hole) at

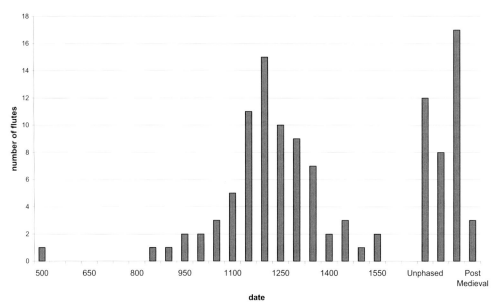

Fig. 2.1. Distribution of flutes over time.

the proximal end, and three toneholes (fingerholes) at the distal end (fig. 2.5). Typical examples of this type are those from Thetford (Lawson 1993, 163), Southampton (Megaw 1975, 252–253) and London (Egan 1998, 288). Other goose bone flutes are made with the same D-shaped window, but with no toneholes (fig. 2.5). These may represent unfinished flutes, or flutes that have no holes by design. Such flutes can produce more than one note, either by overblowing or by alternately covering and uncovering the open end (as produced by experimental reconstructions). Examples of these have been found at Westbury-by-Shenley (Riddler 1995, 392), and London (Egan 1998, 288). Some goose bone flute finds are fragments, consisting of just the proximal end with the D-shaped window. They may have been part of either of the above two types. Almost a third

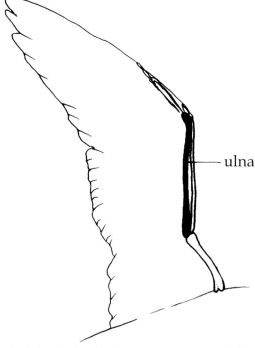

Fig. 2.2. Typical bird wing showing ulna (after Buisson 1990).

of all flutes found are made from goose bones, with a typical date in the 11th to the 14th centuries.

To a lesser extent the ulna of swans, a semi-domesticated species (Ticehurst 1957) was also used to make bone flutes. The window is D-shaped, and there are four toneholes at the distal end of the instrument (fig. 2.6). Many are fragmentary, but excellent examples are known from Norwich (Lawson and Margeson 1993, 211–3) and Old Sarum (MacGregor 2001, 21). One complete example from Waterford in Ireland has three toneholes (Hurley *et al.* 1997, 669). These date from the 10th to the 13th century.

There are few examples of crane bone flutes, with the only two complete examples coming from Thetford (Lawson 1984, 183) and Canterbury (Frere *et al.* 1987, 186). These too have a D-shaped window and three toneholes, though they are made from the tarsometatarsus, and not from the ulna (fig. 2.6). The two above examples differ in date, being from the 9th century (Thetford) and the 12th or 13th centuries (Canterbury) respectively. Other crane bone flutes may exist that were made from the ulna, but may be in the category of 'unidentified bird', or may have been identified as swan (the ulnae of swans and cranes are extremely similar). The crane was a seasonal

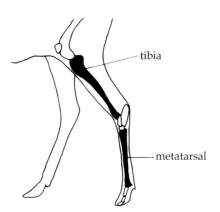

Fig. 2.3. *Rear mammal leg showing tibia and metatarsal (after O'Connor 2000).*

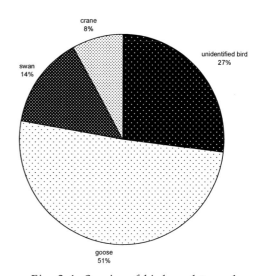

Fig. 2.4. *Species of bird used to make bone flutes.*

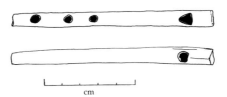

Fig. 2.5. *Goose bone flutes from London (top) and Westbury-by-Shenley (bottom).*

cm

Fig. 2.6. Swan bone flute from Norwich (top) and crane bone flute from Canterbury (bottom).

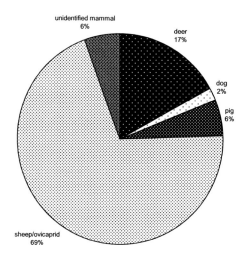

Fig. 2.7. Species of mammal used to make bone flutes.

yet breeding visitor (Boisseau and Yalden 1998) and in medieval times was hunted by noblemen using trained falcons (Cummins 1988). As such, it was not easily available to the majority of people.

Mammal bone flutes are most commonly made from the bones of sheep (or 'ovicaprid', a term that can mean either sheep or goat), but are also made from the bones of deer, pig and even (with one possible example) dog (fig. 2.7). They are made from the bones of the back leg of the animal; mainly the tibia but also the metatarsal (fig. 2.3).

Sheep bone flutes have a wide date range in England, occurring from the 9th through to the 16th century. Sheep were a common domestic animal in that time period, kept primarily for their wool. The flutes vary in form; smaller ones such as those from Exeter (Megaw 1984, 350) and Old Sarum (MacGregor 2001, 21) have three toneholes whereas larger sheep bone flutes (in this case made from the tibia) may vary in the number of toneholes, and may also have one or more thumbholes. An example from London (Egan 1998, 288) has four toneholes and one thumbhole, one from Irthling-borough (Chapman *et al.* 2003, 97) has two toneholes at its distal end but no thumbhole, and one from Castle Acre (Lawson 1982, 252) has two toneholes at its distal end and three thumbholes. They all still have the same D-shaped window (fig. 2.8).

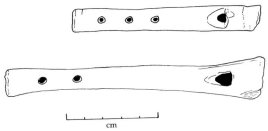

Fig. 2.8. Sheep bone flutes from Exeter (top) and Irthlingborough (bottom).

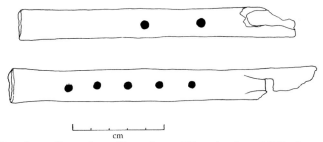

Fig. 2.9. Deer bone flutes from Keynsham Abbey (top) and Winchester (bottom).

Deer bone flutes are made from the metatarsal, a bone with an internal profile more square than round, and an exterior that requires much work to remove its characteristic ridges. Deer tibiae appear not to have been used. The flutes date from the 12th to the 14th century, and within the few examples are two potential 'types'. One type has five toneholes, one or more thumbholes, and a neat rectangular window (fig. 2.9). Two fine examples come from White Castle (Megaw 1961, 176–180) and Keynsham Abbey (Barrett 1969, 47–50).

Another type has two toneholes, centrally placed along the instrument's length (fig. 2.9), with two examples found in Winchester dating to the 13th century, one from a deer metatarsal and the other from a sheep metatarsal (Megaw 1990, 722–3). Bone flutes in general could be seen as the possible antecedents of more modern instruments such as the tabor pipe, recorder and penny whistle; however this particular type of bone flute appears to have no known descendent. There are flutes similar in form from medieval Europe (Brade 1975, Reimers and Vogel 1989, 28), though interestingly, supporting iconography may be found more locally. A 13th century misericord from Exeter depicts a man playing a pipe and tabor, clearly holding the short squat pipe in the centre, rather than at the distal end.

Deer were managed and hunted at this time according to Norman forest laws, which restricted access to venison to the nobility. Following the ritual of 'unmaking' the deer's body after the kill (see both Sykes and Thomas, this volume), the haunches (from which the flutes were made) were taken by the lord. It is interesting to note that almost all deer bone flutes are from high status sites, or from towns with castles in them. The exception is a 12th to 13th century deer bone flute that was found at the deserted medieval village of West Cotton (Windell *et al.* 1990, 39), a site where the faunal remains suggest a flouting or ignoring of forest laws (Chapman forthcoming).

A point to note is that all deer bone flutes are made from the metatarsal, with none seeming to have been made from the tibia. This choice of skeletal element is interesting, given that within the range of sheep bone flutes, 76% are made from tibiae and only 24% are made from metatarsals. Prompted by the content of the abovementioned papers in this volume, a re-assessment of species identification of sheep tibia flutes appears to be needed, specifically with some of the larger sheep tibia flutes that have been found at high status sites. Given that the identifying protuberances of bone may have been removed during the fabrication of the flute, the possibility should be considered that they may actually have been made from deer tibia rather than the previously suggested sheep tibia.

The craftsmanship involved in making bone flutes can vary from crude through to sophisticated and (very occasionally) highly decorated, and it is clear that a wide variety of levels of skill were employed. For the most part, bone flutes can be made with just a knife, though knowing a certain 'knack' for forming the window and the inserted block (the 'plug' of wood or wax) in the proximal end can make the difference between a successful and an unsuccessful instrument. The forming of a D-shaped window can be made by making two cuts into the naturally curved surface of the bone, and is easily made in a thin walled bird bone. The toneholes are also easily made, but by using the point of the knife like a drill. In the thicker walled sheep bone flutes, the same D-shaped window is seen, even when a flatter surface of the bone is used. In the experimental making of replicas it was found to be easy to 'drill' the start of the window with the point of a knife, and then to use the blade edge of the knife to scrape round to form the usual D-shape. The rectangular windows of the deer bone flutes show a high degree of skill in manufacture, producing a feature more commonly associated with later wooden instruments.

In summary it can be seen that medieval English bone flutes, in addition to being more commonplace than perhaps previously thought, can occur in a broad range of forms. Before addressing further avenues of investigation such as looking at what music they may have played, and how they compare to continental examples, it is considered to be important to make a basic yet thorough assessment of the flutes found thus far. Current research is being undertaken to collate the flutes together and to assess their physical, archaeological and cultural aspects. Clearly, medieval bone flutes are far from invisible and silent, and the development of this wealth of material will help bring these fascinating instruments to life.

Bibliography

Barrett, J. H. (1969) A Fipple Flute or Pipe from the site of Keynsham Abbey. *Galpin Society Journal* 22, 47–50.
Boisseau, S. and Yalden, D. W. (1998) The former status of the crane *Grus Grus* in Britain. *Ibis* 140, 482–500.

Brade, C. (1975) *Die mittelalterlichen Kernspaltflöten Mittel-und Nordeuropas*. Karl Wachholtz Verlag, Neumünster.

Buisson, D. (1990) Les Flutes Paleolithiques d'Isturitz (Pyrenees Atlantiques). *La Pluridisciplinarite en Archeolodie Musical*, 259–275.

Chapman, A. (forthcoming) *West Cotton, Raunds. A Study of Medieval Settlement Dynamics*. English Heritage Monograph.

Chapman, A., Atkins, R., and Lloyd, R. (2003) A medieval manorial farm at Lime Street Irthlingborough, Northamptonshire. *Northamptonshire Archaeology* 31, 71–103.

Cummins, J. (1988) *The Hound and the Hawk. The Art of Medieval Hunting*. London, Phoenix Press.

Egan, G. (1998) *The Medieval Household. Daily Living c.1150 – c.1450 Medieval Finds from Excavations in London*. London, Museum of London, The Stationery Office.

Frere, S. S., Bennet, P., Rady, J., and Stow, S. (1987) *Canterbury Excavations Intra- and Extra- Mural Sites 1949–55 and 1980–84. The Archaeology of Canterbury, Volume VIII*. Maidstone, Kent Archaeological Society for Canterbury Archaeological Trust.

Hurley, M. F., Scully, O. M. B. and McCutcheon, S. W. J. (1997) *Late Viking Age and Medieval Waterford. Excavations 1986–1992*. Waterford, Waterford Corporation.

Lawson, G. (1984) Flutes. In A. Rogerson, and C. Dallas (eds.) *Excavations in Thetford 1948–59 and 1973 80*, 182 3. East Anglican Archaeology Report No. 22, The Norfolk Archaeological Unit, Norfolk Museums Service.

Lawson, G. (1993) Note on bone flutes. In C. Dallas *Excavations in Thetford by B. K. Davison between 1964 and 1970*, 159–160. East Anglian Archaeology Report, No. 62, Norfolk Museums Service, Field Archaeology Division.

Lawson, G. and Margeson, S. (1993) Musical instruments. In S. Margeson *Norwich households. Medieval and Post-Medieval Finds from Norwich Survey Excavations 1971–78*, 211–3. East Anglian Archaeology Report No. 58.

MacGregor, A. (2001) Objects of bone, antler and ivory. In P. Saunders (ed.) *Salisbury Museum Medieval Catalogue Part 3*, 18–21. Salisbury, Salisbury and South Wiltshire Museum.

Megaw, J. V. S. (1960) Penny whistles and Prehistory. *Antiquity* 34, 6–13.

Megaw, J. V. S. (1961) An end blown flute or flageolet from White Castle. *Medieval Archaeology* 5, 176–180.

Megaw, J. V. S. (1968) An end blown flute from medieval Canterbury. *Medieval Archaeology* 12, 149–150.

Megaw, J. V. S. (1975) The bone pipe. In C. Platt and R. Coleman-Smith *Excavations in Medieval Southampton Volume 2*, 252–253. Leicester, Leicester University Press.

Megaw, J. V. S. (1984) Bone musical instruments from medieval Exeter. In J. P. Allan *Medieval and Post-Medieval Finds from Exeter, 1971–1980. Exeter Archaeological Reports: Volume 3*, 349–351. Exeter, Exeter City Council and the University of Exeter.

O'Connor, T. (2000) *The Archaeology of Animal Bones*. Stroud, Sutton.

Reimers, C and Vogel, V. (1989) Knochenpfeifen und Knochenflöten aus Schleswig. In *Ausgrabungen in Schleswig Berichte und Studien 7* Das archäeologische Fundmaterial I.

Riddler, I. (1995). In R. Ivens, P. Busby and N. Shepherd *Tattenhoe and Westbury. Two Deserted Medieval Settlements in Milton Keynes*. Buckinghamshire Archaeological Society Monograph Series No.8, 392.

Ticehurst, N. F. (1957) *The Mute Swan in England*. London, Cleaver-Hume Press Ltd.

Windell, D., Chapman, A. and Woodiwiss, J., (1990) *From Barrows to Bypass. Excavations at West Cotton, Raunds, Northamptonshire, 1985–1989*. Northampton, Northamptonshire County Council, 39.

Chapter 3

The Middle Ages on the Block: Animals, Guilds and Meat in the Medieval Period

Krish Seetah

Animals: their place in the medieval period

Understanding the place of butchery in the medieval period requires a more in depth appraisal of the place of animals in medieval English culture. Fortunately, this period is perhaps one of the most interesting in terms of the lines of information available for this assessment. The rich historical evidence has led to research detailing the manufacture and uses of tools (Cowgill *et al.* 2000); the animals acquired and eaten in a number of different social contexts (Woolgar 1999, 112; Lehman 2003) and accounts relating to the organisation of butchery (Rixson 2000, 91–151).

From artistic sources it would appear that animals played an integral part in medieval society with fauna portrayed in an array of genres (Benton 1992, 13). This ranges from depictions of animals within everyday settings, in some instances showing slaughter and processing of common domestic species (fig. 3.1), to the more fantastical. What is perhaps most remarkable is the sheer magnitude of illustrations and illuminations that have some faunal component included, many of which depict imaginary creatures or composites (see Wells this volume).

During the medieval period images of animals as part of the 'bestiary' became increasing popular with a vast array of mythical as well as more common species included in this inventory (Baxter 1998; Hassig 1995). There is also the extensive use of animals in medieval heraldry from the 12th century (Pastoureau 1997). While both of these were context specific and portrayed highly stylised representations of animals, their impact as a form of visual display reinforcing human-animal interactions must have been a strong one. Representations of fauna as beings with mythical powers may indicate that on a cultural level some animals were imbued with a sense of the numinous. The most important symbolic role of animals was within the Christian paradigm – animals could be used to represent a force of good (e.g. a saint or Christ) or evil (e.g. the Devil), and sometimes both forces could act through animals in the real world.

While this period is clearly one of great artistic expression, with animals seemingly an intrinsic part of the fabric of medieval visual culture, what is also clear is that animals were extremely important within the economic structure of medieval England. However, on the level of trade, animals [and their parts] are expressed in a very

Fig. 3.1. Taken from the Golf Book of Hours, c. 1500. By permission of The British Library (Add. 24098).

different manner; depictions of animals revert to a more commonplace re-enactment of everyday activity. Figure 3.2 illustrates a 12th century portrayal of a man warming his boots in February; above him is a side of bacon and stuffed intestines which are being preserved following the November kill. The image depicts tasks that were carried out on a seasonal basis; the 'labours of the month' cycle was a common motif in medieval art across Europe. Figure 3.3, shows another facet of these yearly cycles, this time the autumn kill of a pig (see also Rixson 2000, 96, 98). This image, from the early-14th century, highlights that these activities were embedded in society and perpetuated for a considerable period of time.

The seemingly mundane artistic imagery contrasts strongly with the actual economic significance of domesticates and may be an indication of the overall dichotomous view of animals. On the one hand they are seen as creatures of myth (with associated significance); on the other they are beasts under human dominion, merely an economic commodity to be exploited. By the Middle Ages the notion of animals as belonging to humans was well established, both in the sense of animals as food, and animals for functional activities. Through the act of domestication animals were altered to become property by changing their morphology and/or behaviour (Salisbury 1994, 13–43).

Fig. 3.2. Warming by the fire in February, English late-thirteenth century. By permission of Corpus Christi College (MS Corpus Christi College 285).

The emerging middle classes and extensive economic development (Carlin and Rosenthal 1998, 119), coupled with the establishment of the guilds and widespread national and international market growth meant that animals took on an increasingly significant role in the economic framework of medieval life. Evidently, this had a profound impact on the way animals were conceptualised and treated, not least because it was animal products that formed a crucial aspect of this development (Astill 1998, 168; Thomas 1983).

To understand what this 'broad view of animals' during the medieval period potentially signifies to butchery requires a number of further considerations. Key to this is the evidence that exists regarding butchers and the butchery trade and what

Fig. 3.3. Slaughtering and butchering pigs in December, Queen Mary Psalter. By permission of the British Library (BL MS Royal 2B VII, f. 82v).

Fig. 3.4. Photograph of the earliest Apprentice Indenture held at Butchers Hall, taken by the author with the kind permission of former Master Fred Mallion.

this can inform us about the way individuals involved in this particular trade (and therefore linked to the broader view of animals) were perceived.

The guilds

The Guild of Butchers was established in the 1300's although earlier historical references indicate that 'in the Ward of Farringdon Without there are divers slaughterhouses and a Butchers' Hall where the craftsmen meet' in 975 (Hammett and Nevell 1949, 11). It received a royal charter and officially became a Company in 1605 following James I granting the guild the 'Incorporation of the Company' (Pearce 1929, 7). The Butchers' Guild, as with all guilds of the day, was established for three main reasons. Primarily there was a need to provide an educational standard and it was common practice for an apprentice butcher to remain at this stage for seven years before being granted 'Freedom' following an 'Apprentices Indenture' (fig. 3.4).

The Butchers Guild also established codes of good practice and incidences are recorded where butchers accused and found guilty of selling inferior meat were placed in the stocks. The rotten meat they had sold was then burned under their noses; this punishment was dealt out to one Nicolas Schyngel, who had falsely accused another butcher of trading in putrid meat, but who was discovered to have committed the offence himself (Pearce 1929, 19). Most important of the Guild's roles was that of industry regulator and overall controlling body. This was accomplished by setting controls on weights and measures, providing a standard for cutting practice and generally forging a level of organisation that permitted a certain degree of political influence, even though the guilds themselves did not have any legal power or affiliation (Mallion, pers. comm.). This point having been made, it would be naïve to think that the economic development of the guilds can be removed from a political context; the guilds, after all, were effectively 'governing bodies' for some of the biggest industrial ventures in England at that time. Interestingly, the perception of animals as coming under 'human dominion' seems well established within the Butchers' Guild itself. The Arms of the Company was granted in 1540 at which time the 'Worshipful Company of Butchers' chose as its motto (Corsair and Fitzell 1975):

'Omnia Subjecisti Sub Pedibus, Oves et Boves'

> Thou hast put all things in subjection under His feet:
> all Sheep and Oxen, yea, and beasts of the field
> (from Psalms 8: 6–7)

In researching the guilds and general economic trends of the medieval period, an interesting factor is evident. While the economy of Britain at the time clearly owed a great deal to animals and animal products in general, what seems to be apparent is a greater emphasis on the subsequent products rather than on *meat* itself. The production and subsequent sale of hide, horn and bone was clearly a very important economic activity (Yeomans, this volume). However, the trade that provided the raw materials for all these subsequent activities is rarely found in literature relating to the guilds, or indeed medieval trade and finance. This point does not necessarily reflect an overall view that butchers and the butchers' trade was not an important one in a socio-cultural sense. Nor should it be used to indicate that butchers themselves were of lower social status than a tanner for example; what might be concluded from a lack of reporting on the affairs of the butchery trade relates to economic factors. Despite the advances made in preserving meat, and the fact that meat could be and was transported within a day from England to mainland Europe (Woolgar 1999, 113, Rixson 2000, 91–102) and around Britain itself along extensive networks, it cannot be considered as 'transportable' as cured hides, wool or horn. From a purely economic standpoint, wool and hides would invariably command a greater price per unit compared to meat simply because of the extra preparation that went into producing these commodities. Furthermore, once meat is sold it has basically reached the last stage at which monetary value can be added (with obvious exceptions such as curing or if the meat is cooked and re-sold). However, wool for example will be spun, turning it into thread, then woven, turning it into cloth, then used to create a broad array of garments; at each stage the potential for additional income is realised and value is added incrementally to the basic commodity.

This is obviously a very simplistic view, but it highlights why the butchery trade may not have gained the same level of precedence that other trades dealing with animal products were able to achieve. This is despite the fact that strong economic links must have existed between these industries as the wool and tanning trades depended on butchers (and farmers) for their raw materials.

The role of the butcher and meat in medieval England

The medieval period is one of complex human and animal interaction and evidently this carried over into the trade that had the most immediate links to the processing of animals. Individuals were becoming wealthy from trading meat; however, local levels of wealth, status and perceptions of the 'flesh hewers' would have been linked to the broader perceptions of animals and these are difficult to ascertain with the evidence available. What must also be remembered is that while it is crucial to integrate historical and archaeological information in order to draw a picture of how butchers and butchery functioned on both a social and economic level, certain *caveats* need to be addressed. Foremost of these is that the historical records present a certain perspective, which although highly relevant, can distort the overall view of the butcher and the level of trade. Much of the historical literature deals with either manors or urbanised enclaves, resulting in reports that focus on a certain echelon of society. This is not the level of society that a butcher, for example, is likely to have heralded from and accordingly is unlikely to have been influential in what was and was not recorded for posterity. While the butcher is generally seen solely as a purveyor of meat in the modern setting, within the medieval period, the butcher was fundamentally a slaughterman (Rixson 2000, 96). The butcher was no doubt appreciated however, as it was not uncommon for wealthy households to have their own (Woolgar 1999, 114). Indeed, what is clear from the historical records is that butchers were important to the nobility and generally maintained links and associations with royalty. Around 1369 a royal order granted butchers who provided offal for the bears of King Edward III a piece of land on which entrails could be washed (Hammett and Nevell 1949, 13). Playfote in 1545 was a Flesh Purveyor to the Royal Household, despite the fact that he was reported to the Court of Aldermen for slaughtering animals during Lent (Jones 1976, 124). Evidently his royal connections shielded him from serious punishment as the title of Senior Warden of the Butchers was conferred on him in 1546.

The historical evidence relating to manorial provisioning not only highlights the importance of meat, but also provides data on aspects of butchery practice. Woolgar, in his accounts of Goodrich Castle, highlighted what the underlying butchery technique (directed towards preservation and conservation of meat for middle-long term provisioning) involved (Woolgar 1999, 116). However, this type of synthesis is the exception rather than the rule and details of actual cutting practice are rarely recorded, illustrating how valuable zooarchaeological evidence can be.

This last point becomes more relevant when one looks at hunting strategies within the medieval period. Hunting was a very prominent pastime for the gentry and nobility of medieval Britain; it was highly ritualised and an important vehicle for expressing social status (Thomas 2001). Zooarchaeological studies have indicated a specific pattern of carcass sharing based on the specific role individuals undertook within the hunt. The 'unmaking' of deer developed in 12th century England within the context of the seigneurial hunt as part of the exclusive rituals surrounding this type of activity (Sykes, this volume). Most hunting in England was conducted by retinues rather than individual aristocrats (Birrell, 1992). It is possible that similar cultural attitudes to carcass portioning influenced the pattern of butchery practiced on domesticates.

The feast was an integral part of medieval social occasions and meat, from both 'bird and beast', formed the key component of this activity. Within these events, and in particular for the larger wedding banquets and aristocratic feasts, vast quantities of meat were prepared and consumed. Mead (1931, 33) highlights the feast held for the installation of Archbishop Neville at York in 1467; the meat component alone consisted of 104 oxen, 6 wild bulls, 1000 sheep, 304 calves, 304 'porkes', 400 swans, 2000 geese, 1000 capons, 2000 pigs, 104 peacocks and an additional 13,500 birds of various species and over 500 deer. The manner in which the particular animal was cooked was of great importance, as was the display and arrangement of the various courses (Pluskowski, this volume) and the organisation of the menu (Lehman 2003). Birds in particular were presented in a life-like manner as a centre piece for the course (van Winter 2003). Often social hierarchies were reinforced at these occasions, for example, at the wedding banquet of the Earl of Devon, 1431, only the high table was served with crane, swan and peacock (Lehman 2003).

The importance of animals as items of food, as well as the broader socially held ideals regarding what constituted key species to include in the feast, can both be appreciated. However, this only partly expresses the role *meat* played at these occasions, and within society as a whole. While certain animals, in particular species that were 'hunted' as opposed to those that were 'raised', seem to have commanded a more significant place within the feast (Albarella and Thomas 2002, Thomas 1999), meat *per se* might well have been seen and used as an indicator of social status and standing. Thus, the significance of different species on the one hand becomes more important as these are maintained as the 'essential dishes' for a feast situation (in particular by those able to afford to hunt), while at the same time, meat as a commodity becomes increasingly more important if it can confer a sense of social elevation. Why this should be more important in the medieval period as opposed to any preceding era relates to the burgeoning diversity within social hierarchies and the use of food as a form of visual display to distinguish rank.

Evidently, there was an increase in the numbers of people becoming wealthy from their endeavours within trade and finance; but the wealth attained is unlikely to have been sufficient to counter a lack of status as a result of unfavourable 'birthright'. In other words, money may not have been enough to make up for a lack of noble blood. However, what money could provide is the means to emulate the gentry and nobility, and one less expensive way of doing this (as opposed to building a castle for example) is through food and cuisine. Thus, the 'trickle down' effect allowed those with money to join those with noble blood (perceptually, if not literally) through their common affinity for 'luxury foods' (van der Veen 2003).

Class distinction was an integral part of medieval society, with vast differences in the standard of living between those with wealth and those without. The overwhelming majority of people were of the peasant classes and meat was very much a rarity (Carlin and Rosenthall 1998, 41). This point is made to illustrate just how important meat was to all factions of society; the social elite are documented to have eaten meat in quantities that would be surprising even by contemporary standards. Furthermore, quantity was not the only criteria by which the value of meat was judged; quality and importantly, variety were also crucial. Conversely, at the other end of the scale, meat was a scarce commodity that was rarely eaten (*ibid*); for the peasant classes financial restrictions proved the limiting factor. However, money was not the only restriction; meat was clearly identified as being the penchant of a certain echelon of society, and if distance was required from this group then abstinence was practiced, as was seen with monastic communities up to around the 11th century (Bond 2001, 77). While abstinence was called for as a factor of religious doctrine during Lent and on Fridays, meat asceticism was practiced outside of these requisite periods to distance those interested in piety from the gluttony of the social elite (Elias 2000, 118).

Thus, it can be seen that the role of meat within medieval England was a complex one; for the elite it helped maintain social standing and position by functioning as an item of luxury. The poor majority evidently saw meat as a luxury too, but one that was a rare treat, purchased only occasionally, or obtained illicitly by resorting to poaching / rustling; conversely the ascetics sought to reduce their intake of meat because it was so enjoyed by the elite. One group, emerging in the 14th century, is likely to have viewed meat with a certain degree of expectation of what it could provide for them. The middle classes and wealthy merchants could afford meat and probably used it as a means of attaining, at least perceptually, greater social status.

Integrating history and archaeology – knives and the slaughterman

The historical data outlined above provides a very useful account of the manner in which medieval populations used and viewed animals. However, there is the potential to understand and gain a clearer picture of both perceptual and economic attitudes by incorporating archaeological research. Aside from the actual cut marks that are observed on animal bones following archaeological excavation, the butchery implements found from this period are of considerable importance. Both of these are highly relevant to understanding and interpreting attitudes towards the 'breaking and shaping' of animal bodies.

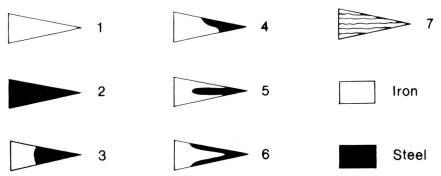

Fig. 3.5. *Combinations of iron and steel to control areas of hardness along the cutting edge of knives (aft. Cowgill et al 2000,10).*

Fig. 3.6. Medieval cleaver taken from the Luttrell Psalter. By permission of The British Library (Add. 42130 f.173)

By the medieval period, the manufacture and development of specific knives had become advanced and a great deal of experimentation with type and metallurgic techniques was taking place. Evidence for this comes from the variety of the implements excavated, as well as technical components such as the way carbon steel and iron were combined to create tools with specific regions of hardness (fig. 3.5). Interestingly, from London for example, there is no current archaeological data that indicates actual manufacture of tools; interpretations regarding how tools were made has mostly been derived from the tools themselves (Cowgill *et al.* 2000, 8). As with the butchery trade, there is archaeological evidence for blacksmiths enjoying something of a renaissance in terms of development and appreciation, as well as pride, in their burgeoning profession. This is seen in the finer indicators of individuality, such as the 'makers' marks' which clearly identify the particular tools' manufacturer; these are quite distinct from the patterning and artistic decorations that adorn some artefacts.

The techniques used for the creation of metal tools are complex and resulted in implements of considerable durability. Iconographic representations of cleavers, for example, illustrate large blades with riveted handles (fig. 3.6 – taken from the Luttrell Psalter). Having a riveted handle increased durability of the tool as a whole; combining steel into the cutting portion of the blade, results in a longer-lasting and easier to maintain cutting edge.

Evidence relating to the way these tools may have been used comes from the cut

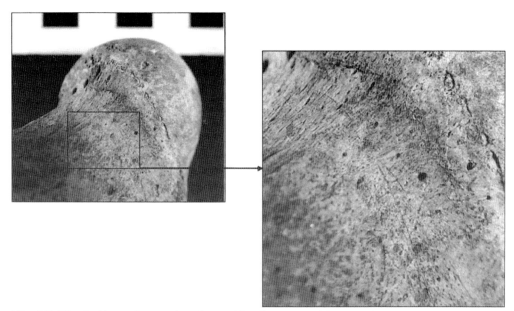

Fig. 3.7. Fine knife marks noted on femoral head – material from medieval York. Photographed by author.

marks found on archaeological bone. Previous periods, such as the Romano-British, have demonstrated a great deal of uniformity on urban and military sites, indicating a systematic method of butchery (Maltby 1989, 75; 1994, 89). This was achieved through creativity in tool technologies, a factor repeated in the medieval period; although there were fundamental differences between Romano-British and medieval implements. The most obvious difference was the inclusion of steel into the cutting edge of medieval tools, a feature unseen previously. The actual cutting practices seem to indicate a different *style* of butchery and the tools themselves demonstrate a greater level of individuality and functionality. For example the cut marks highlighted on Figure 3.7, found on the inferior surface of the femoral head, indicate a tool was used with a relatively thin, and sharp, cutting edge. This contrasts with the evidence found on urban and military Romano-British sites at which femoral heads are invariable chopped off with a cleaver at the same point. Clearly the medieval butchers had cleavers; these are not only illustrated in numerous artistic depictions, but also evident from the cut marks on the bones. Figure 3.8, showing a chopped vertebra, illustrates how effective the medieval cleaver was. The trabecular bone of the vertebra, which is less dense than the surrounding cancellous bone, is easily crushed during butchery. In this case the trabecular bone has maintained much of its integrity, indicting that the cleaver must have had a sharp cutting edge.

Synthesising these two strands of archaeological evidence, namely the butchery and tools used for carcass processing, leads to a number of conclusions. There is evidently a considerable development in the metallurgic techniques used to create the

Krish Seetah

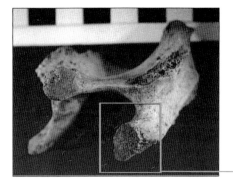
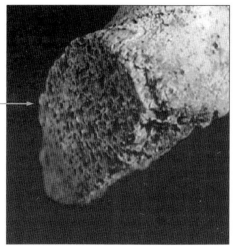

Fig. 3.8. Cleaver butchery of vertebra – material from medieval York. Photographed by author.

tools, and this is coupled with the creation of very specific tools during the Middle Ages, and indeed prior to this period. Blacksmiths in the Romano-British period appear to have created tools specifically for animal butchery (Seetah 2006), and this trend is continued in the medieval period. However, the level of complexity involved is far greater; tools are being created with specific regions of hardness so as to minimise cost (by using less steel), while at the same time maximising tool durability (less sharpening of the cutting edge means the tool will have a longer life) and functionality (a sharper edge makes for better and easier cutting). This is likely to have been instigated by members of the butchery trade; the cut marks seem to indicate a more *refined* style of butchery with less use of the cleaver for disarticulation (if compared to the Romano-British period) and a greater reliance on knives. The defining characteristic of these knives is that they were sharp edged and likely to have been made in much the same way as the cleavers, i.e. with a steel edge to maintain sharpness. Although tools are important to the butchery process, they are not the only factor that dictates the butchery methodology employed. Cleaver butchery dominates in the Romano-British period; knife butchery is prominent in both the medieval and Iron Age. Although there are clear distinctions between the Romano-British and Iron Age/medieval techniques, the fact that knives are favoured in the Iron Age and medieval does not mean they follow the same pattern, or are indicative of the same overriding principles.

Conclusion

Animals held a very important position within medieval society; they were employed in highly visual expressions of cultural perceptions and attitudes regarding the natural world and the place of human and beast with this paradigm. Artistic depictions portrayed animals in a wide variety of contexts, from the fantastical to the mundane, with the hunt often an important theme. Death and slaughter are commonly illustrated and while many animals seem to have been conferred mythical powers, much of the mythology details how animals can be captured and killed; beasts such as the unicorn, which no one could possibly have seen, could be slaughtered if lulled by a virgin (Barber 1999, 36; see Wells this volume). Many depictions demonstrate scenes of butchery following the hunt (such as the butchery of deer in *The Master of the Game*; see Baillie-Grohman 1909), indicating that the act of carcass processing was an important event. Butchers' premises and slaughter houses clearly illustrate the processing of various species and evidently the general population had far greater exposure, from both iconographic and actual observations of everyday butchery, to this type of activity.

However, we gain an arguably more realistic perspective from the remains of the animals themselves, and from the way their bodies have been disarticulated. From these lines of evidence it would seem that carcass dismemberment was dichotomous within this period; on the one hand there is the 'unmaking' practice that occurs after a hunt, and on the other there is regimented trade 'butchery'. The hunt, as one might expect, favours more ritualised activities although it is difficult to estimate how often this type of butchery took place if most hunting was through 'bow and stable' (the use of horsemen to drive game towards archers; see Cummins 2001) and conducted by retinues to obtain deer *en masse*, especially with the proliferation of parks in the high medieval period (Thomas 2001). Archaeological and historical evidence seems to suggest, at least on some occasions, a set pattern of processing (Sykes, this volume).

Trade butchery would likely follow the methods set out by the Butchers' Guild, at least by the members of the guild who had undergone its apprenticeship. In turn these would have been influenced by the particular culinary requirements of the general population, as well as the social elite for festive occasions (Mead 1931, 78–86). Much of the provisioning and preparation was dependent on the skills of the butcher in making sure the meat was processed in a certain manner and it is not surprising that a major concern of the Guild of Butchers was to provide a provision for the education of young apprentice butchers. This not only established but also maintained a certain standard with regard to cuts of meat and the methods of preparation, a situation that has been perpetuated to the present day in Britain.

We should also recognise the increased commercialism, as well as the socially dictated norms, surrounding meat consumption. The medieval period witnessed a level of commerce unseen in previous epochs and in particular this burgeoning monetary development centred to a large extent on animals, in particular domesticates. The dismemberment and processing of these animals obviously depended heavily on the butchery trade and it is likely that with profit and monetary gain in mind, it would have been commercial attitudes more than cultural ones, that dictated the styles of butchery used (although both are linked and of importance to the overall practice).

Although the material culture of the medieval period, as expressed in artistic representations, shows animals in a diverse range of cultural contexts, we should not fail to recognise that medieval populations saw animals as commodities (Salisbury 1994, 13–43). While there may well have been a more ritualistic treatment of an animal's body within a hunting context, attitudes towards consumption and trade indicate a far more exploitative perspective. This point having been made, it was not uncommon for the actual cutting of the body to result in a more poignant expression of faunal importance. While the act of separation and disarticulation of the carcass, for instance following a hunt, was designed to reinforce social inequalities and hierarchy; so too did culinary preparation have its meaning. The animal did not always lose all identify, in fact maintaining the integrity of the beast or bird was often crucial in relaying the socially loaded message of the animal's presence at the table. There would be no point in having a swan served at a banquet if no one could distinguish it from the rest of the dishes.

What is clear is that all facets of carcass dismemberment were important in medieval society. It was depicted in art; it formed an integral element of one of the favoured pastimes of the social elite; it provided an increasingly lucrative economic opportunity for those involved in the trade and it was pivotal to the social vying of those in, and those aspiring to, the upper echelons of medieval society. Butchery had its role to play in all these instances and it was essential to the pragmatic as well as societal norms that dictated how an animal's body was used and treated. In much the same way that animals form a crucial component of the medieval cultural tapestry, so too, did butchery.

Bibliography

Albarella, U. and Thomas, R. (2002) They dined on crane: bird consumption, wild fowling and status in medieval England. *Acta Zoological Cracoviensia* 45, 23–38.

Astill, G. (1998) Medieval and later: composing an agenda. In, J. Bayley, (ed.) *Science in Archaeology: an Agenda for the Future*, 168–79. London, English Heritage.

Baillie-Grohman, W. A and F (1909) (eds.) *The Master of Game / by Edward, 2nd Duke of York: The Oldest English Book of Hunting*. London, Chatto and Windus.

Barber, R. (1999) *Bestiary*. Woodbridge, Boydell.

Baxter, R. (1998) *Bestiaries and their Users in the Middle Ages*. Gloucestershire, Sutton Publishing.

Benton, J. R. (1992) *The Medieval Menagerie*. New York, Abbeville Press.

Birrell, J. (1992) Deer and deer farming in medieval England. *Agricultural History Review* 40, 12–126.

Bond, J. (2001) Production and consumption of food and drink in the medieval monastery. In, Keevill, G., Aston, M. and Hall, T. (eds.) *Monastic Archaeology*, 54–87. Oxford, Oxbow.

Carlin, M. and Rosenthall, J. T. (1998) *Food and Eating in Medieval Europe*. London, The Hambledon Press.

Corsair, B. A., and Fitzell, W. L. (1975) *The York Butchers Gild*. York, The Company of Butchers of York.

Cowgill, J., De Neergaard, M. and Griffiths, N. (2000) *Knives and Scabbards*. London, Museum of London.

Cummins, J. (2001) *The Hound and the Hawk. The Art of Medieval Hunting*. London, Weidenfeld and Nicholson.

Elias, F. (2000) *The Civilising Process*. London, Blackwell Publishing.

Jones, P. E. (1976) *The Butchers of London*. London, Secker and Warburg.

Hammett, R. C. and Nevell, W. H. (1949) *A Handbook on Meat*. London, The Meat Trades Journal Co.

Hassig, D. (1995) *Medieval Bestiaries*. Cambridge, Cambridge University Press.

Lehman, G. (2003) The late-medieval menu in England – a reappraisal. *Food and History* 1 (1), 49–83.

Maltby, M. (1989) Urban-rural variations in the butchering of cattle in Romano-British Hampshire. In D. Serjeantson and T. Waldron, (eds.) *Diets and Crafts in Towns*, 75–106. British Archaeological Reports British Series 199, Oxford, Archeopress.

Maltby, M. (1994) The meat supply in Roman Dorchester and Winchester. In A. R. Hall and H. K. Kenward, (eds.) *Urban-Rural Connexions: Perspectives from Environmental Archaeology*, 85–102. Oxford, Oxbow.

Mead, W. E. (1931) *The Medieval Feast*. London, George Allen and Unwin Ltd.

Pastoureau, M. (1997) *Heraldry: its Origins and Meaning*. London, Thames and Hudson.

Pearce, A. (1929) *The History of the Butchers' Company*. London, The Meat Trades Journal Co.

Rixson, D. (2000) *The History of Meat Trading*. Nottingham, Nottingham University Press.

Salisbury, J. E. (1994) *The Beast Within*. New York, Routledge.

Seetah, K. (2006) Multidisciplinary approach to Romano-British cattle butchery. In M. Maltby (ed.) *Integrating Zooarchaeology*. Oxford, Oxbow.

Thomas, K. (1983) *Man and the Natural World: Changing Attitudes in England 1500–1800*. London, Allen Lane.

Thomas, R. (1999) Feasting at Worcester Cathedral in the 17th century: A zooarchaeological and historical investigation. *Archaeological Journal* 156, 342–358.

Thomas, R. (2001) The medieval management of fallow deer: A pathological line of enquiry. In, M. La Verghetta and L. Capasso, (eds), *Proceedings of the XIIIth European Meeting of the Palaeopathology Association Cheiti*, (S.P.A. Teramo, Italy, 2001), 287–293.

Van der Veen, M. (2003) When is food a luxury? *World Archaeology* 34 (3), 405–27.

Van Winter, J. M. (2003) Festive meals in the late Middle Ages: an essay on dining as a means of communication. *Food and History* 1 (1), 95–102.

Woolgar, C. M. (1999) *The Great Household in Late Medieval England*. London, Yale University Press.

Chapter 4

Communicating Through Skin and Bone: Appropriating Animal Bodies in Medieval Western European Seigneurial Culture

Aleksander Pluskowski

Introduction

In the course of the second half of the first millennium AD, following the disintegration of the Roman Empire, the landed élites in Western Europe reformed into a new aristocratic class. By the beginning of the second millennium they had developed a common 'seigneurial' identity, expressed in part through distinct codes of behaviour, kinship affiliations, and types of material culture (Duggan 2000, 3). Alongside the organisation of space, distinctive speech, sumptuary codes and heraldry developing in the 12th century (Reuter 2000, 92–3), élites expressed their distinctive status through the appropriation of indigenous and exotic animal species, particularly by incorporating them into visual display – in a society where images functioned as a social language (Camille 1987, 33). But 'visual display' was not simply restricted to heraldic devices or casket decoration – indeed it permeated the fabric of daily life and included visible access to certain species of animals, ownership of their products and the consumption of their meat. In this respect, animals – particularly wild terrestrial mammals, were employed as key elements in the medieval semiotics of power, the symbolic system that communicated the separation of the seigneurial class from the other 'orders' in society (Ervynck 2004). This paper surveys the diversity of animal body parts employed in constructing, consolidating and communicating seigneurial identity from the 12th century, exploring firstly the acquisition of indigenous and exotic animals, followed by their use on the person and within seigneurial spaces, and finally how this use changed in the 16th century. The data set is fragmentary and eclectic, and encompasses animal products recovered from excavations, as well as those extant in private collections having never been discarded or buried, described in literary and documentary sources and represented in a range of public and private art. With a broad temporal and spatial span, its aims are twofold: to outline an inter-disciplinary framework of medieval seigneurial animal exploitation that can subsequently be criticised and problematised by specialists, particularly from an inter-regional perspective, and to demonstrate how animal bodies could be transformed into socially distinct material culture.

The acquisition of animal bodies

Central to medieval seigneurial appropriations of animal bodies was hunting (Cummins 1988; Thomas, Sykes, Salvadori, this volume). The praxis of hunting varied across Europe throughout the Middle Ages reflecting variable social and ecological contexts. In regions such as England from the late-11th century, south-east Scotland from the 12th century and Denmark from the 13th century, legitimate access to game animals and their habitats was controlled by the crown (Sykes 2001; Gilbert 1979; Andrén 1997), and, particularly in French provinces such as Anjou and Champagne following the disintegration of the Carolingian Empire, by the greater nobility (de Gislain 1980, 42). This is reflected in the archaeological distribution of game species, of which the highest numbers and diversity are found at seigneurial sites such as castles. This is unlikely to reflect distinctive disposal practices at seigneurial sites but rather access to game, coinciding initially with the emergence of new European aristocracies in the latter half of the first millennium (Pluskowski forthcoming), and subsequently most distinctly with the development of Norman aristocratic hunting culture in England in the late-11th century (Sykes 2001). From the 12th century, the association between aristocracy and hunting had become effectively codified, expressed as an essential skill and activity for the courtly gentleman in English, French and German literature (Rösener 1997, 147). By this time it was as a recognisable motif in religious art and secular ornament (Camille 1998, 8, 95–102) as well as in the organisation of hunts themselves. Indeed, the hunting landscape with its population of quarry species was increasingly sculpted to seigneurial preferences, culminating in the late medieval park (Cummins 2002, 46–7). Although a range of species was pursued, aristocratic hunters across Western Europe all exalted deer as the ultimate prey; both red (*Cervus elaphus*) and roe deer (*Capreolus capreolus*). This is reflected in all types of primary evidence: faunal remains, representations in artistic and literary sources and documentary records. Fallow deer (*Dama dama*) were introduced to England in the late-11th century and subsequently other regions of Western Europe, and were perhaps better-suited to enclosure in royal and seigneurial parks than native species (Birrel 1992, 123; Sykes 2001, 190–199). Thus the increase in emparkment in England after the 14th century has been linked to the growing representation of fallow deer at the expense of red, and particularly roe deer in faunal assemblages from high-status sites across England (Thomas 2002). There is regional variation; a similar decline in the representation of roe deer is evident in late medieval assemblages in northern France (Clavel 2001, 113–4). The pursuit of the hart 'by strength of hounds' or *par force*, where an individual animal was identified and pursued by a pack of running hounds followed by mounted hunters, came to exemplify the ultimate seigneurial hunt. But although certain lords (and even ladies) were noted for their enthusiasm for the activity, seigneurial inclination or perhaps opportunity to hunt appears to have been limited (Almond 2003, 39; Thomas and Sykes this volume). Legitimate hunting was more socially inclusive, and carried out far more frequently by aristocratic retinues, effectively providing venison on demand and following general patterns of household provisioning (Birrell 1992, 113; Woolgar 1999, 114–6).

The hunting and trapping of furbearers, particularly squirrels, was also typically carried out by individuals from lower social backgrounds, although in some regions seigneurial groups reserved the hunting of particular species for themselves (Delort, 1978, 181). With exceptions such as rabbits, there is no evidence for the breeding of fur-bearers; furriers and tailors were almost entirely reliant on animals caught in the wild. Furs were available locally across Europe and traded on a regional level, even recycled (Veale 1966, 13), however the growing demand for luxury furs relied upon regular suppliers, in turn linked to local ecological, economic and political conditions. Because many fur-bearers were small mammals such as squirrels, their fragile remains are rarely recovered from archaeological contexts. Written sources on the other hand indicate that those regions with abundant wild fur-bearer populations, i.e. the Scandinavian Peninsula until the 14th century, the Baltic and Russia, were major exporters of fur (fig. 4.1). They were consistently sustained by the political leadership of the region, facilitated by mercantile networks and supplied by the combined efforts of peasants and specialist hunters (Delort 1987, 198, 240–276; Martin 1986, 168). The relative representation of fur-bearers within faunal assemblages may complement written sources to pinpoint centres of production; international centres such as early medieval Birka (Wigh 2001, 122–3) and late medieval Novgorod (Brisbane and Maltby 2002, 109) are well known, but regional differences between urban and rural sites remain to be explored in depth (Albarella 1996, 14).

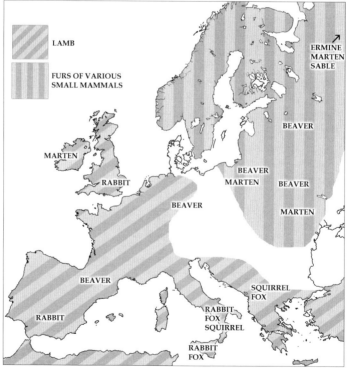

Fig. 4.1. Major sources of fur in late-medieval Europe (aft. Delort 1978).

The wearing and display of furs was almost certainly more important than their acquisition in the medieval semiotics of power, and this is also true for imported exotics, valued for their rarity, their aesthetic appeal and, in some instances, their perceived zoological identity (Pluskowski 2005). Commerce was only one of the ways in which exotica changed hands in medieval Europe – live animals as primary or secondary acquisitions were frequently presented as gifts, and artefacts including components derived from exotica were sometimes included in marriage settlements and frequently donated to church treasuries. However, a significant proportion of exotica moving around Europe can be associated with mercantile activity; demand for raw materials such as ivory was relatively frequent and these were shipped to centres of production with concentrations of specialist craftsmen, such as Paris from the late-13th to early-15th century. Demand for live animals, more expensive and difficult to acquire and transport, was far less frequent and these were moved along established trade routes to centres of wealth where sales were guaranteed (Spufford 2002, 106–139).

Thus the visible acquisition of animals was of variable importance in medieval seigneurial culture. On the Continent, the deer or boar hunt *par force* became an iconic representation of aristocratic control of hunting space and game (fig. 4.2), and remained a popular arena for the theatrical display of wealth and physical prowess into the 16th century. However, game animals were usually acquired by retinues, easily facilitated by emparking deer or employing the bow-and-stable technique of hunting, whilst furs and exotica were provided by regular suppliers. The subsequent use of animal bodies became as important as the act of hunting for defining seigneurial identity.

Fig. 4.2. The deer hunt par force, *part of a frieze on the west front of Santa Maria Matricolare, 12th century, Verona, photographed by author.*

Animal bodies and the semiotics of power

Animals proliferated in medieval Western European visual and oral culture. In seigneurial contexts, they were employed as fundamental elements in the vocabulary of power relations; in art and literature, predominantly associated with heraldry, hunting and love (Camille 1998, 96–107), but also as products derived from real animals, acquired in the various ways described above and transformed into a distinct form of material culture. These were incorporated into vignettes of visual display – on the person, within the house and outside following a seigneurial hunt; categories explored in more detail below.

1. Display on the person

Personal attire was a fundamental means of social communication in medieval Europe. Alongside the selective use of colour, the skins of different animals were used to communicate social distinctions. Leather, with the exception of chamois hide obtained from populations in the Alps, Pyrenees, Carpathians, Balkans or perhaps even Asia Minor, was available to everyone in varying quantity and quality. Fur, more difficult to acquire and therefore expensive became a key indicator of personal status – perhaps more so in Western Europe that in colder regions such as northern Scandinavia with abundant fur-bearer populations (Piponnier and Mane 1997, 45). Fur was most frequently used to line woollen garments, and was generally hidden, only discreetly visible at the edges – indeed almost any item of clothing could be fur-lined, including horse furniture in the 15th century. Coats made entirely from fur, which we are very familiar with today, whether through fashion advertising or animal welfare campaigns, were very unusual in the Middle Ages (*ibid*, 23, 74). Our understanding of the social significance of fur-wearing in early medieval Europe is, at present, limited (Cameron 1998), but during the 12th century, the three most expensive furs – ermine, vair and miniver – were established enough as expressions of aristocratic status to be incorporated into heraldry (Pastoureau 1993, 103–4). By the 14th century enough merchants and craftsmen had invested in luxury furs that social distinctions embodied in clothing began to blur, prompting the introduction of sumptuary legislation in many regions of Western Europe (Martin 1986, 64). In England for example, the sumptuary laws of the reign of Edward III used £200 as a threshold for knights; those possessing annual incomes below this amount were forbidden from wearing mantles or gowns furred with miniver, whilst those on or above this threshold were permitted to use miniver, and both groups were forbidden ermine (Baldwin 1926, 49). The introduction of such legislation was an important final step in the construction of a complex social hierarchy, now, in the minds of legislators, expressed through visual display, although the inefficiency of Edward III's sumptuary laws is evident from widespread criticism of the luxury extravagance of dress during the subsequent reign of Richard II (Lachaud 2002, 119).

Fashions of course changed and fur-wearing peaked at the end of the 14th century after which it slowly declined, accompanied by a change in male preference from pale to dark furs – women continued to favour miniver, ermine and white Russian weasel

(Piponnier and Mane 1997, 79). The combination of cost and legislation restricted ermine, vair and sable for the upper eschelons of the aristocracy, fox, wild cat, lamb and rabbit were found amongst affluent merchants and artisans, whilst peasants were generally limited to rabbit or kid (*ibid*, 24). Aside from lining garments, fox tails hung from hats are noted in 13th century Austria, and in 14th century England and possibly France, and they could be worn suspended at the back of women's skirts (Jones 2002, 57). The pelts of exotic animals, particularly leopards (fig. 4.3), were also incorporated into garments, and although they did not sit comfortably in the indigenous fur hierarchy in Western Europe, as rare and expensive items they were found in the possession of royalty and affluent aristocrats, particularly favoured by the Teutonic Order (Delort 1978, 422).

In addition to furs, feathers were used in headgear, particularly during the 15th century and obtained from birds associated with the aristocratic sphere, namely peacocks and ostriches. In waterlogged deposits, delicate fragments have been recovered, such as the peacock feather dating to the late-14th century from the Thames Waterfront (Egan 1998, 12, plate 1a), but as in the case of furs, our information on the use of feathers is largely based on artistic and written sources. The comparison of a knight to a bird of prey was a common motif in medieval poetry, echoed by the popularity of the eagle in personal heraldry (Cummins 1988, 233), and the swan was employed as a badge by those who sought association with Christian militarism (Hinton 2005, 220). Heraldic animals, as highly stylised and instantly recognisable emblems of personal or, from the 14th century, group identity, were incorporated into a variety of personal effects from garments through to jewellery, and, in the context of jousting, helmet crests. In some cases the association between heraldic animal and personal identity was taken one step further; preserved bird skins appear to have been used as heraldic decoration on armour and weaponry, and Frederick II's mid-13th century *De arte venandi cum avibus* hints at how these may have been preserved; wings were rubbed on the inside with ash and hung until the moisture had completely evaporated (Schulze-Hagen *et al,* 2003, 470–1).

Clothing transformed the seigneurial household into a distinct community identifiable on sight, but courtly households also maintained an internal hierarchy, marked by liveries – the issue and distribution of clothing identifying rank, function and affiliation. As a means of social display these became increasingly important outside the seigneurial household during the 14th century when emblematic devices were adopted (Vale 2001, 93–99). The seasonal distribution of liveries included a hierarchy of furs, complementing the deployment of animal bodies in and around the house.

2. Display in the house

The buildings and spaces of the household were the stage for pageantry and drama, equally intended to increase the standing of the head of the house. Like personal attire, the arrangement and display of furnishings and artefacts was used for social communication, and the restrictive use of expensive furs on the person was echoed in the visible ownership and consumption of certain animal products. Whilst a diverse

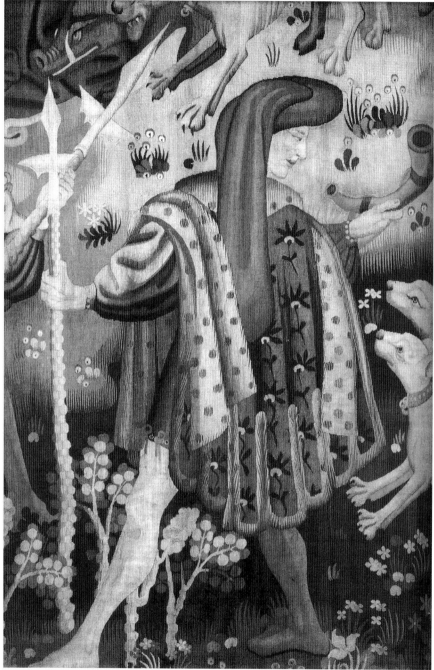

Fig. 4.3. Man wearing a garment lined with leopard skin from 'The Boar and Bear Hunt' of the Devonshire Hunting Tapestries, 1425–1450, Victoria and Albert Museum. By permission of the Victoria and Albert Museum.

range of animal remains, bone and leather objects have been recovered from medieval sites of varying character across Western Europe, certain types of animal products tend to be found, at least in higher quantities, only on seigneurial sites. The use of these products in social communication centred on the major focus of display in the seigneurial household – the hall (Bumke 2000, 114). Here, exclusive foods would be consumed and seen to be consumed, distinctive artefacts constructed from exotic animals could be presented alongside other treasures on display, complemented by hangings, tapestries and wallpaintings from the 14th through to 16th century (Woolgar 1999, 147; Crossley-Holland 1996, 172). Objects at the table particularly connected with ceremonial and magnificence were distinguished by sumptuous programmes of decoration based on episodes of aristocratic life, religious scenes and heraldry, particularly emphasising family connections. A recurring motif decorating artefacts and hangings was hunting, often loaded with multiple meanings but persistently reinforcing its association with seigneurial culture and identity (Woolley 2002, 40). The lesser nobility, aspiring to emulate their social betters, invested in this identity; the 15th century inventories and notes from Caister Castle indicate that Sir John Fastolf had two tapestries – of hunting and hawking – hung in a chamber above the Nether Hall on the southwest side of the castle (Woolgar 1999, table 5).

Before room functions became increasingly fixed in the 14th and 15th centuries, these decorative elements were brought together for impressive social occasions such as banquets, and would be moved from one residence to another. The most spectacular aristocratic feasts involved the elaborate and skilful preparation of animal bodies for visual display first, and consumption second. The diversity and quantity of birds, especially wildfowl, recovered from seigneurial sites is much higher than from any other type of site, a trend that increases in England and northern France in the 14th and 15th centuries (Albarella and Thomas 2002; Clavel 2001, 120–121). The few archaeological examples of bird preparation for display and consumption are supported by more detailed insights in written sources. The rituals of vowing at courtly feasts occasionally included the use of birds; the choice of species was invested with multiple levels of meaning and carefully related to the occasion (Vale 2001, 214–20). Preparing birds with elaborate plumage such as peacocks involved careful flaying followed by preserving their skin and feathers with cumin and spices, re-positioning their bones and re-feathering their bodies after roasting to present them as if 'living' – but other examples of preparation simply involved plucking the body bare save for the heads and tails (Cosman 1976, 24, 65). In 1368, the chef Taillevent, in the service of the French King Charles V, served roast swan and peacock that had been re-dressed after cooking in their entire plumage, with gilded bills and set in a natural miniaturised landscape sculpted from sugar (Schulze-Hagen *et al.* 2003, 470).

In addition to the aristocratic monopoly on the consumption of wildfowl, a consistent preference for pork and varying species of game is a typical faunal signature for seigneurial sites in England (Thomas 2002), northern France (Clavel 2001), Belgium (Ervynck 2004, 216), the Netherlands (Groenman-van Waateringe and van Wijn-gaarden-Bakker 1990, 289–290, 294) and Germany (Meyer 1997). Although appearing in higher quantities in seigneurial sites than in other types of site, game species usually make up a fraction of the total assemblage, and this suggests the consumption of hunted animals was an infrequent and special event. Therefore the impression that medieval aristocrats were obsessed with hunting on the basis of its popularity in literature and art may be misleading in this respect, but it is clear that prey animals occupied a significant place within the semiotics of power.

3. Breaking and displaying the hunted animal

It is often assumed that animal carcasses would only be revealed as finished set-pieces, but even if we accept that much park and even forest hunting was conducted by retinues, it is clear that seigneurial hunting expeditions were opportunities for impressive visual display. The presentation of the hunt and the kill were clearly important, but the treatment of the animal body was more controllable. The bounty of the hunt would be brought back to the hunting lodge, palace or house and formally presented, perhaps eviscerated if the unmaking – the ritualistic dismemberment of the animal introduced into England after the Norman Conquest and to France and Germany in the 13th century (Sykes 2001, 203) – had not been carried out earlier, hung, and then prepared and consumed at a feast (Thomas, Sykes this volume). What happened to the body then? As noted above, physical remains of game animals are found predominantly at seigneurial sites, where their discard is typically related to the butchery and culinary process.

A more unusual example of the treatment of a slain quarry comes from the vicinity of the Bishop's Palace at Sonning (Berkshire), belonging to the Bishops of Salisbury from the 13th–15th centuries. Here, a large quantity of pottery and five bones of fallow deer including a complete antler were found in a 12th/early-13th century pit (no. 142). This antler had been obtained from a killed buck rather collected after being shed and included part of the cranium (fig. 4.4). The frontal and parietal had been chopped in a manner used in recent specimens to create a trophy – angled cuts better facilitate the hanging of the antler pair against the wall – and the antlered part of the skull may have been removed to enable the head meat and brain to be used (Hamilton-Dyer 2003, 85), perhaps for medicinal purposes – *The Master of Game* states that 'the head of the hart beareth medicine against the hardness of the sinews and is good to take away all aches, especially when these come from cold; and so is the marrow" (Baillie-Grohman and Baillie-Grohman 1909, 34). If we accept this interpretation, this fragment may represent a rare if not unique example of a medieval hunting trophy. The display of trophies would have been one way of distinguishing personal hunting from hunting by proxy, which accounted for the majority of venison acquired. But why was it discarded? The 'life-span' of a trophy may have been relatively short; with the death of the hunter who acquired it, or a change in the ownership of the property, the trophy was no longer meaningful and there is no evidence such objects were kept as heirlooms before the 16th century. Or perhaps it was only used during the temporary theatrical display following a hunt. Literary and artistic evidence suggests that the display of animal heads was a recognised element of the performance which followed some seigneurial hunts, in England and other parts of the Continent.

For example, the map of Bernwood Forest from the Boarstall cartulary (1444–46) shows the forester-in-fee displaying a bleeding boar head on a sword to Edward the

Fig. 4.4. Fallow deer antler and cranium recovered from 12th/early 13th century contexts in pil no. 142, St. Andrews Church Vicarage, Sonning. Copyright Reading Museum Service (Reading Borough Council). All rights reserved.

Confessor; in *Sir Gawain and the Green Knight* the boar hunt concludes with the severing of the boar's head which was 'hoisted on high' and then borne before the baron on the return journey to the castle before being presented to Gawain (lines 1607–1657; Stone, 1964, 88). Hunting scenes in Middle English and in Continental contemporary literature include the severing of the deer's head as part of the *curée* – the ritual rewarding of the hounds – and its presentation to the lymer, after which it might be paraded at the front of the procession bearing the venison home to the accompaniment of horns (fig. 4.5) (Cummins 1988, 44–5). In the context of the seigneurial hunt, the presentation of trophies may have been a short-lived event confined to the hunt and feast, which is perhaps why none appear as decorative features of halls in contemporary illustrations. Interestingly, the *Ménagier de Paris*, a 14th century text on culinary preparation and household skills, states that the head and foot of venison are to be presented to the lord not for eating but for inspection, after which worthy cuts are to be offered (Crossley-Holland 1996, 122). Inedible quarry may have been displayed in this way before being passed onto skinners and tawyers; a passage in the 14th century *Le Livre de Seyntz Medicines* refers to fox skins hanging on the wall of the hall (Arnould 1940, 115).

Whilst fox remains are rarely encountered in medieval archaeological contexts, cranial fragments of deer are found at both high-status and urban manufacturing sites (Thomas this volume), suggesting that certain parts of the head were used following the hunt and other parts moved down-the-line (Sykes this volume). Taking the example of London, fragments of antler-working – whether cut from carcasses or collected when shed – are sparse, a trend found across England from the late-11th century (MacGregor 1989, 113–4); the fragments from St. John Clerkenwell represent an unusual concentration, possibly supplied by the local meat market at Smithfield (Egan and

Fig. 4.5. A marginalia illustration condensing aspects of the unmaking of a stag, performed here, unusually, by four women. From the Taymouth Hours, *English, 1325–40 (BL Yates Thompson MS. 13. f. 84). By permission of the British Library.*

Shepherd 2004, 359). Indeed, a unique example comes from the Moor House site, just outside the medieval city walls, where 81 roe deer antlers were recovered from a large tanning pit and a smaller ditch dating from 1180–1300 (Armitage and Butler 2005). All the antlers had been obtained from hunted animals and mostly from mature individuals aged three or over. The deer had been skinned and their antlers left on to enable leatherworkers to readily separate older from younger skins. After sorting the antlers were disposed of – there was no evidence the antlers were subsequently used in the manufacture of objects (Yeomans this volume). Even impressive animals worthy of the seigneurial hunt and prime candidates for trophies ultimately found their way to the manufacturing sphere: antlers attached to red deer skulls found at Lincoln as manufacturing waste included a six-year-old ten-pointer (O'Connor 1982, 40). So whilst the seigneurial association with hunting was perpetually present for others to see – from idealised representations of hunting on artefacts or wallpaintings, to the ownership of stables, kennels and mews, to the herd of deer enclosed within a park attached to the manorial site – the appropriation of the hunted animal body, extending from the park to the banquet table, was a relatively infrequent, brief, violent and spectacular event. As a semiotic tool in the arena of visual display it was arguably even more effective than exotic fauna.

The role of exotic animals

Our understanding of the roles of non-indigenous animals in medieval European society is far from complete, and many have stressed the novelty value of imported species and their role in seigneurial culture. However, whereas the physical exploitation of deer and wild boar and the use of raptors, horses and hounds were supported by a robust cultural framework developed and perpetuated by the aristocracy, only a few exotic species could be employed effectively beyond their basic role as rare and expensive possessions. This is where a holistic and inter-regional understanding of seigneurial contexts is essential. Predatory animals dominated medieval heraldry, and, as personal emblems, they supported the conceptualisation of the aristocracy as a class of predators, dominating both human and animal realms (Pluskowski forthcoming). The lion was the most popular heraldic animal, and live individuals were increasingly imported and housed in royal and subsequently lesser seigneurial and civic premises during the Middle Ages (Loisel 1912; O'Regan *et al.* 2005); there is only one documented example of imported lion pelts (Delort 1978, 170). Indeed, its proliferation in art led Pastoureau (1999, 23) to label it 'indigenous' to medieval Europe. Certainly, along with the imported fallow deer and rabbit it had become established, or even re-established, in seigneurial semiotics during the course of the 12th century. Few other exotics became so popular or so familiar.

The zoological identity of certain animals was actively constructed in order to make them culturally relevant – this is a plausible explanation for the transformation of narwhal tusks into unicorn horns and bison or ibex horns into griffin claws (Pluskowski 2005). Such artefacts, readily suited for visual display, only became popular additions to seigneurial inventories from the 15th century, foreshadowing the interest in 'cabinets of curiosity'. These were very rare in aristocratic households before the 16th century, a notable exception is one set up by Jean, Duc de Berry (1340–1416), which included dried fish, polar bear skins and ostrich eggs (Schulze-Hagen *et al.* 2003, 462). This is perhaps how walrus skulls may have been displayed – a number of examples, whole and fragmentary, some decorated, have been found in Trondheim, Bergen, Oslo, Uppsala, Sigtuna, Lund, Schleswig, as well as Dublin and Novgorod; written sources attest to their use as prestigious gifts (Roesdahl 2003, 150). This treatment of exotic animal bodies is unusual; a leopard cranium recovered from a 14th century pit in Segesd-Pékóföld, Hungary (fig. 4.6), may have been a decorative addition of a pelt used as a rug, and is to date unique (Bartosiewicz 2001), and whereas bed coverlets lined with, or made from ermine and miniver are documented in aristocratic inventories, a rare example of a leopard skin coverlet was owned by a London merchant – one of the 'new lords' (Veale 1966, 15). More commonly artefacts constructed from exotic animal body parts were designed as ornaments or tableware. A number of these artefacts were donated to various religious institutions after varying periods of seigneurial ownership and so have survived in church treasuries across Europe. One such artefact type was the oliphant or a carved ivory horn made from elephant tusk. Of the 75 or so that have survived, many are decorated with hunting scenes, wild or fantastic animals. Most were probably made in southern Italy and commissioned by Norman noblemen, and in the crusading climate of the late-

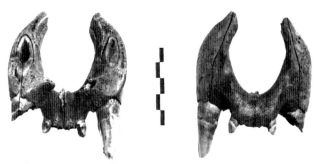

Fig. 4.6. Fragment of a leopard maxilla recovered from a 14th century pit in Segesd-Pékóföld, Hungary (photograph by Laszlo Bartosiewicz and reproduced with his permission).

11th–13th century may have been regarded as an attribute of a valiant knight, modelled on heroic figures such as Charlemagne, Roland and El Cid (Shalem 1998, 107, 110).

Exotic animals represent complex examples of material culture: some, such as lions, were long-established in the semiotics of power and commonly understood. Others, such as walrus, were less common and less useful. Others still, such as narwhals, were assigned new identities and elemental status. As the source for artefacts and raw materials they were not solely used in the context of power relations, but also in religious devotion, increasingly in the late medieval period and through to the 16th century.

Der Trophäenkult: changing material culture in the 16th century

The changing use of animal bodies during the course of the 16th century is not a complete break with previous centuries, but a continuation and development of existing trends within the sphere of seigneurial visual display. What did change was a new valuation of curiosity which drove collection, consumerism and scientific inquiry (Smith and Findlen 2002, 18–19). The emergence of avian and mammalian taxidermy for scientific purposes in Europe was enabled by an increasingly sophisticated market of natural history goods (Schulze-Hagen *et al.* 2003, 462, 466), facilitated in turn by a virtually continuous supply of New World and African exotica (Meadow 2002; Lloyd 1971). Both merchants and taxidermists supplied aristocratic cabinets of curiosities, and the importation of live tigers and rhinoceros reflected the diversification of existing 'menageries' (Guggisberg 1975, 181). Hunting remained central to the expression of seigneurial status and a source of social tension; weapons, techniques and the presentation of the chase were slowly changing with the adoption of guns alongside crossbows in the 16th century. The temporary use of animal bodies within the ceremonial setting of the hunt, which characterised medieval seigneurial culture was increasingly complemented by their preservation as trophies (fig. 4.7). These start to appear in castle inventories from 1500 as visible testaments to physical

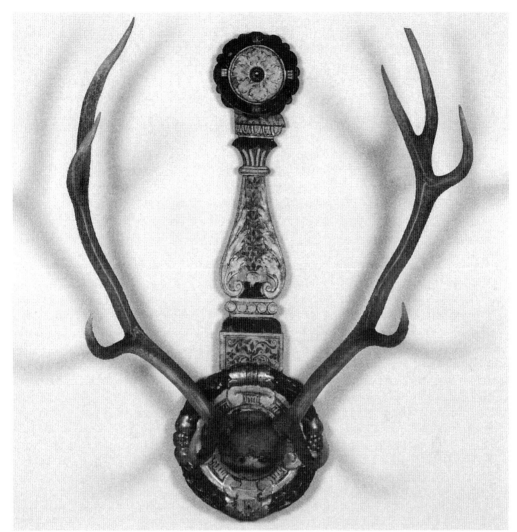

Fig. 4.7. Red deer trophy of Duke Ferdinand II, Tyrol, 1585. By permission of the Kunsthistorisches Museum Wien.

prowess, marking the start of *der trophäenkult* – a proliferation of interest in preserving the memory of the hunt as well as the amuletic use of wild animal body parts (Graf 1998; Rauch 2004, 49).

This trend is detectable in the archaeological record. At Castle Rising Castle, 12 antlers butchered in the manner used for trophies occur in the 16th century/post-medieval contexts contrasting with earlier treatments of deer remains (Jones, Reilly and Pipe 1997, 128). The infrequency of hunting at the site at this time (in possession of the duchy of Cornwall) suggested by other evidence corresponds to the keeping of skulls as personal trophies and their discard may be related to the abandonment of seigneurial hunting at the site in the 17th century. Excavated examples of trophies are significantly outnumbered by objects extant in private collections, most recently documented at an exhibition in Schloss Ambross in the Tyroll (Seipel 2004). By the late-16th century, the *trophäenkult* was established amongst Central and Western European aristocracies, reflected in the proliferation of cervine material culture and the continued celebration of hunting. Noel du Fail's imaginary description of a gentleman's *salle* in his *Contes et Discours d'Eutrapel* published in 1585, included:

> "A stag's antler, tipped with iron and fastened to the ceiling from which hung bonnets, hats, collars, couplings and leads for dogs, and a big rosary for communal prayers." (Girouard 2000, 98–9)

The display of stag heads was matched by their lifelike representation in three-dimensions, as on the decorated chimney-piece at the chateau de Filain, a frieze in the 'Salle des Cerfs' at the chateau de Louye and the great hall at Meillant (*ibid*, 14–15). The display of antlers in aristocratic households was emulated by lower social groups; in late 16th century Prague, tapestries and antlers were the most common wall furnishing in the multi-functional *svietnice* (living areas where guests would be invited) of burgher households, reflecting the diffusion of courtly lifestyles (Palmitessa 1997, 155).

The exalted status of the deer, particularly the hart, in medieval seigneurial culture was underlined by late medieval aristocratic interest in the cult of St. Hubert (Salter 2001, 57). Centred on the Abbey of St. Hubert in the Ardennes which contained the saint's relics, the cult adopted the cruciferous stag from the vision of St. Eustace as a recognisable attribute in the 15th century (Dupont 1991, 28). Devotion to St. Eustace, predominantly within the knightly classes of northern France, peaked in the 12th and 13th centuries (Bugslag 2003) but he remained a popular patron of hunters in regions such as the Tyrol into the 16th century (Sandbichler 2004, 162). Both Eustace and Hubert, although not exclusively seigneurial saints, particularly in the case of the latter, were frequently represented in late medieval religious art as aristocrats (Sternelle 1963, 16, 28); amongst the unusual artefacts associated with the cult of St. Hubert in the 16th through to 18th centuries is what can best be described as a devotional trophy (Grinder-Hansen 2002, 129) (fig. 4.8). This novel expression of aristocratic material culture and the amuletic use of animal bodies can be situated within the *trophäenkult* which would peak in the 19th and early-20th century during the era of big game hunters, epitomised by Archduke Franz Ferdinand's collection of some 3000 trophies at Konopište Castle (now in the Czech Republic).

Conclusion: a framework for future research

This paper has considered the major trends in seigneurial appropriation of animal bodies in Western Europe from the 12th through to 16th century. In it, I have argued that seigneurial groups used animal bodies in similar ways within a common semiotic system – a visual language expressing and negotiating power relations which became

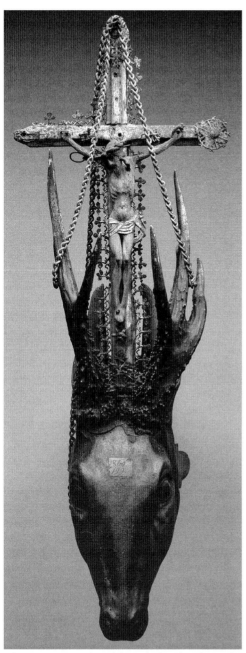

Fig. 4.8. Devotional 'trophy' related to the cult of St. Hubert, Copenhagen, dated by an inscription to the 16th century. By permission of The National Museum of Denmark.

increasingly elaborate from the 14th century. This agrees with Salisbury's (1994, 10) observation in her study of medieval human-animal relations that 'it is possible to speak of a Western European culture'. However, the recommended direction for future research is a return to detailed case studies, in order to comprehensively test the hypothesis that animals were used by Western European aristocracies to bridge the gaps between cultural, geographic, dynastic and political differences. A number of papers in this volume provide focused insights into the seigneurial appropriation of animals (*e.g.* Thomas, Sykes, Valenti and Salvadori, Bejenaru and Tarcan). Our understanding of human-animal relations during the Middle Ages can never be removed from broader cultural and ecological contexts, and having isolated categories of animal material culture for the sake of analytical clarity, it is all too easy to overplay the significance of animal bodies in the construction and negotiation of élite identity.

Faunal assemblages consistently indicate the overwhelming dominance of domesticates in seigneurial diets and lifestyle, with evidence for regional variation (*e.g.* Clavel 2001; Groenman-van Waateringe 1994). Much personal display revolved around precious metals and delicate textiles whilst household display was focused on structural elements such as portals, towers, as well as furnishings such as hangings, tapestries and precious artefacts (Hinton 2005). Even the heraldic lion was outnumbered by more abstract designs such as chevrons on medieval coats of arms (Pastoureau 1993, 122–3). Furthermore, the seigneurial class referred to in this paper included a range of different groups: royalty, greater and lesser nobility and less affluent landowners – knights. The precise nature of these sub-groups varied from region to region, as well as over time. It encompassed upwardly mobile individuals as well as members of the ecclesiastical hierarchy; cardinals, bishops and abbots could wield immense temporal power, emulate the behaviour and trappings of the secular aristocracy and indeed come from aristocratic backgrounds themselves. All of these groups participated in comparable appropriations of animals to varying degrees: wearing fur, eating venison, employing animal emblems, hunting, owning dogs, horses, raptors, exotic pets, parks stocked with deer and moats with swans and fish. But even at the highest levels of seigneurial society there were differences between individuals, split along the lines of gender, taste, wealth, opportunity – after all, not everyone hunted, and not everyone owned a garment lined with leopard fur. Moreover, some privileges such as access to venison and fur garments could be granted to members of seigneurial retinues, or they could be sold or even breached. Here again, a return to detailed case studies from multi- and inter-disciplinary perspectives is essential to test the flexibility of what appears to be a common semiotic system.

Acknowledgements

I would like to thank all my colleagues for their suggestions and support, and in particular Dr Katharina Seidl, Dr Christoph Gasser, Krish Seetah, Prof. Sheila Hamilton-Dyer, Dr Richard Thomas, Dr Chris Woolgar and Dr Philippa Patrick. I would also like to thank Dr Laszlo Bartosiewicz, The British Library, The Victoria and Albert Museum, Reading Museum Service, Kunsthistorisches Museum Wien and The National Museum of Denmark for their permission to reproduce the relevant images in this paper.

Bibliography

Albarella, U. (1996) The animal economy of rural settlements: a zooarchaeological case study from Northamptonshire. *Annual Report of the Medieval Settlement Research Group* 11, 16–18.

Albarella, U. and Thomas, R. (2002) They dined on crane: bird consumption, wild fowling and status in medieval England. *Acta zoological cracoviensia* 45, 23–38.

Almond, R. (2003) *Medieval Hunting*. Stroud, Sutton.

Andrén, A. (1997) Paradise lost. Looking for deer parks in medieval Denmark and Sweden. In H. Andersson, P. Carelli and L. Ersgård (eds.) *Visions of the Past. Trends and Traditions in Swedish Medieval Archaeology*, 469–490. Stockholm, Central Board of National Antiquities.

Arnould, E. J. (ed.) (1940) *Le Livre de Seyntz Medicines: the Unpublished Devotional Treatise of Henry of Lancaster*. Oxford, Blackwell.

Armitage, P. L. and Butler, J. (2005) Medieval deerskin processing waste at the Moor House site, London EC2. *London Archaeologist* Spring 2005, 323–327.

Baillie-Grohman, Wm.A. and Baillie-Grohman, F. (eds.) (1909) *The Master of Game*. London, Chatto and Windus.

Baldwin, F. E. (1926). *Sumptuary Legislation and Personal Regulation in England*. Baltimore, The Johns Hopkins Press.

Bartosiewicz, L. (2001) A leopard (*Pathera Pardus L.* 1758) find from the Late Middle Ages in

Hungary. In H. Buitenhuis and W. Prummel (eds.) *Animals and Man in the Past*, 151–160. Groningen, Rijksuniversiteit.

Birrel, J. (1992) Deer and deer farming in medieval England. *Agricultural History Review* 40, 112–126.

Brisbane, M. and Maltby, M. (2002) Love letters to bare bones: a comparison of two types of evidence for the use of animals in medieval Novgorod. *Archaeological Review from Cambridge* 18, 99–119.

Bugslag, J. (2003) St Eustace and St. George: Crusading saints in the sculpture and stained glass of Chartres Cathedral. *Zeitschrift für Kunstgeschichte* 66, 441–64.

Bumke, J. (2000) *Courtly Culture: Literature and Society in the High Middle Ages*. Woodstock, Overlook Press.

Burnley, D. (1998) *Courtliness and Literature in Medieval England*. New York, Longman.

Cameron, E. (ed.) (1998) *Leather and Fur: Aspects of Early Medieval Trade and Technology*. London, Archetype for the Archaeological Leather Group.

Camille, M. (1987) The language of images in medieval England, 1200–1400. In J. Alexander and P. Binski (eds.) *Age of Chivalry: Art in Plantagenet England, 1200–1400*, 33–40. London, Weidenfeld and Nicolson.

Camille, M. (1998). *The Medieval Art of Love: Objects and Subjects of Desire*. New York, Abrams.

Clavel, B. (2001) *L'animal dans l'alimentation mediévale et moderne en France du nord (XIIe – XVIIe si'ecles)*. Picardie, Revue Archaelogique de Picardie.

Cosman, M. P. (1976) *Fabulous Feasts: Medieval Cookery and Ceremony*. New York, George Braziller.

Crossley-Holland, N. (1996) *Living and Dining in Medieval Paris: The Household of a Fourteenth Century Knight*. Cardiff, University of Wales Press.

Cummins, J. (2002) *Veneurs s'en vont en Paradis*: Medieval hunting and the 'natural' landscape. In J. Howe and M. Wolfe (eds.) *Inventing Medieval Landscapes: Senses of Place in Western Europe*, 33–56. Gainesville: University Press of Florida

Cummins, J. (1988) *The Hound and the Hawk: the Art of Medieval Hunting*. London, Weidenfeld and Nicolson.

Delort, R. (1978) *Le commerce des fourrures en occident á la fin du Moyen âge: (vers 1300 – vers 1450)*. Rome, École Française de Rome.

Duggan, A. J. (2000) Introduction. In A. J. Duggan (ed.) *Nobles and Nobility in Medieval Europe*, 1–14. Woodbridge, Boydell.

Dupont, C. A. (1991) Aux origines de deux aspects particuliers du culte de saint Hubert: Hubert guérisseur de la rage et patron des chasseurs. In A. Dierkens and J-M. Duvosquel (eds.) *Le culte de Saint Hubert au pays de Liège*, 19–30. Liège, Crédit Communal.

Egan, G. (1998) *The Medieval Household: Daily Living c. 1150–c. 1450*. London, HMSO.

Egan, G. and Sheppherd, J. (2004) The non-ceramic finds. In B. Sloane and G. Malcolm (eds.) *Excavations at the Priory of the Order of the Hospital of St John of Jerusalem, Clerkenwell, London*, 355–367. London, Museum of London.

Ervynck, A. (2004) *Orant, pugnant, laborant*. The diet of the three orders in the feudal society of medieval north-western Europe. In S. J. O'Day, W. Van Neer and A. Ervynck (eds.) *Behaviour Behind Bones: The Zooarchaeology of Ritual, Religion, Status and Identity*, 215–223. Oxford, Oxbow.

Gilbert, J. M. (1979) *Hunting and Hunting Reserves in Medieval Scotland*. Edinburgh, Donald.

Girouard, M. (2000) *Life in the French Country House*. London, Cassell and Co.

Gislain, de. G. (1980) L'évolution du droit de garenne au Moyen Age. In La Centre d'Etudes Médiévales de Nice (eds.) *La Chasse au Moyen Age*, 37–58. Paris, les Belles lettres.

Graf, K. (1998) Fürstliche Erinnerungskultur. Eine Skizze zum neuen Modell des Gedenkens in Deutschland im 15. und 16. Jahrhundert. In C. Grell, W. Paravicini and J. Voss (eds.) *Les princes et l'histoire du XIVe au XVIIIe siècle*, 1–11. Bonn, Bouvier.

Grinder-Hansen, P. (2002) *Danish Middle Ages and Renaissance*. Copenhagen, Nationalmuseet.

Groenman-van Waateringe, W. (1994) The menu of different classes in Dutch medieval society. In A. R. Hall and H. K. Kenward (eds.) *Urban-Rural Connexions: Perspectives from Environmental Archaeology*, 147–169. Oxford, Oxbow.

Groenman-van Waateringe, W. and van Wijngaarden-Bakker, I. H. (1990) Medieval archaeology and environmental research in the Netherlands. In J. C. Besteman, J. M. Bos and H. A. Heidinga (eds.) *Medieval Archaeology in the Netherlands*, 283–297. Assen, Van Gorcum.

Gugissberg, C. A. W. (1975) *Wild Cats of the World*. Newton Abbot, David and Charles.

Hinton, D. A. (2005) *Gold and Gilt, Pots and Pins: Possessions and People in Medieval Britain*. Oxford, Oxford University Press.

Jones, M. (2002) *The Secret Middle Ages: Discovering the Real Medieval World*. Stroud, Sutton.

Jones, R. T. Reilly, K. and Pipe, A. R. (1997) The animal bones. In B. Morely and D. Gurney (eds.) *Castle Rising Castle, Norfolk*. East Anglian Archaeology Report No. 81, 123–131. Norfolk, Field Archaeology Division, Norfolk Museums Service.

Hamilton-Dyer, S. (2003) The animal bone. In G. Hull and M. Hall (eds.) Excavation of medieval features at St. Andrews Church vicarage, Sonning, Berkshire, *Berkshire Archaeological Journal* 76, 73–93 (85–87).

Lachaud, F. (2002). Dress and social status in England before the sumptuary laws. In P. Coss and M. Keen (eds.) *Heraldry, Pageantry and Social Display in Medieval England*, 105–123. Woodbridge, Boydell.

Lloyd, J. B. (1971) *African Animals in Renaissance Literature and Art*. Oxford, Clarendon Press.

Loisel, G. (1912) *Histoire des Ménageries de l'antiquité a nos jours, Volume 1: Antiquité, Moyen Age, Renaissance*. Paris.

MacGregor, A. (1989) Bone, antler and horn industries in the urban context. In D. Serjeantson and T. Waldron (eds.) *Diet and Crafts in Towns: The Evidence of Animal Remains from the Roman to the Post-Medieval Periods*, 107–128. British Archaeological Reports British Series 199. Oxford, Archaeopress.

Martin, J. (1986) *Treasure of the Land of Darkness: the Fur Trade and its Significance for Medieval Russia*. Cambridge, Cambridge University Press.

Meadow, M. A. (2002) Merchants and marvels – Hans Jacob Fugger and the origins of the Wunderkammer. In P. H. Smith and P. Findlen (eds.) *Merchants and Marvels: Commerce, Science and Art in Early Modern Europe*, 182–200. New York, Routledge.

Meyer, W. (1997) Jagd und Fischfang aus der Sicht der Burgenarchäologie. In W. Rösener (ed.) *Jagd und höfische Kultur im Mittelalter*, 462–491. Göttingen, Vandenhoeck and Ruprecht.

O'Connor, T. (1982) *Animal Bones from Flaxengate, Lincoln, c. 870–1500*. London, CBA.

Palmitessa, J. R. (1997) *Material Culture and Daily Life in the New City of Prague in the Age of Rudolf II*. Krems, Medium Aevum Quotidianum.

Pastoureau, M. (1993) *Traité d'Héraldique*. Paris, Picard.

Pastoureau, M. (1999) L'animal et l'historien du Moyen Âge. In J. Berlioz and M. A. P. de Beaulieu (eds.) *L'animal Exemplaire au Moyen Âge (V^e–X^{ve} siècles)*, 13–26. Rennes, Presses Universitaires de Rennes.

Piponnier, F and Mane, P. (1997) *Dress in the Middle Ages*. New Haven, Yale University Press.

Pluskowski, A. G. (2005) Narwhals or unicorns? Exotic animals as material culture in medieval Europe. *European Journal of Archaeology* 7(3), 291–313.

Pluskowski, A. G. (forthcoming) Holy and exalted prey: eco-cosmological relationships between hunters and deer in medieval seigneurial culture. In I. Siderra (ed.) *La Chasse Pratiques, Sociales et Symboliques, Colloque de la Maison René Ginouvès, Archéologie et Ethnologie*, Paris.

Pluskowski A. G. (in preparation) The status of exotic animals in medieval Europe: an interdisciplinary review.

Rauch, M. (2004) Trophäen und Mirabilien. In W. Seipel (ed.) *Herrlich Wild: Höfische Jagd in Tirol*, 48–80. Vienna, Kunsthistorisches Museum Wien.

Reuter, T. (2000) Nobles and others: the social and cultural expressions of power relations in the Middle Ages. In A. J. Duggan (ed.) *Nobles and Nobility in Medieval Europe*, 85–98. Woodbridge, Boydell.

Roesdahl, E. (2003) Walrus ivory and other northern luxuries: their importance for Norse voyages and settlements in Greenland and America. In S. Lewis-Simpson (ed.) *Vínland Revisited: the Norse World at the Turn of the First Millennium*, 145–152. St. John's, NL: Historic Sites Association of Newfoundland and Labrador.

Rösener, W. (1997) Jagd, Rittertum und Fürstenhof in Hochmittelalter. In W. Rösener (ed.) *Jagd und höfische Kultur im Mittelalter*, 123–147. Göttingen, Vandenhoeck and Ruprecht.

Salisbury, J. E. (1994) *The Beast Within: Animals in the Middle Ages*. London, Routledge.

Salter, D. (2001) *Holy and Noble Beasts: Encounters with Animals in Medieval Literature*. Woodbridge, Boydell and Brewer.

Sandbichler, V. (2004) Jagdmythen, -feste und -legenden. In W. Seipel (ed.) *Herrlich Wild: Höfische Jagd in Tirol*, 160–184. Vienna, Kunsthistorisches Museum Wien.

Seipel, W. (ed.) (2004) *Herrlich Wild: Höfische Jagd in Tirol*. Vienna, Kunsthistorisches Museum Wien.

Shalem, A. (1998) *Islam Christianized: Islamic Portable Objects in the Medieval Church Treasuries of the Latin West*. Frankfurt am Main, Peter Lang.

Schulze-Hagen, K. Steinheimer, F. Kinzelbach, R. and Gasser, C. (2003) Avian taxidermy in Europe from the Middle Ages to the Renaissance. *Journal of Ornithology* 144, 459–478.

Smith, P. H. and Findlen, P. (2002) Commerce and the representation of nature in art and science. In P. H. Smith and P. Findlen (eds.) *Merchants and Marvels: Commerce, Science and Art in Early Modern Europe*, 1–25. New York, Routledge.

Spufford, P. (2002) *Power and Profit: the Merchant in Medieval Europe*. London, Thames and Hudson.

Sternelle, K. (1963) *Lucas Cranach d.Ä.* Hamburg, P. Parey.

Stone, B. (trans.) (1964) *Sir Gawain and the Green Knight*. Harmondsworth, Penguin.

Sykes, N. J. (2001) *The Norman Conquest: A Zooarchaeological Perspective*. Unpublished Ph.D. dissertation, Department of Archaeology, University of Southampton.

Thomas, R. (2002) Animals, economy and status: the integration of historical and zoo-archaeological evidence in the study of a medieval castle. Unpublished Ph.D. dissertation, Department of Ancient History and Archaeology, University of Birmingham (published by Archaeopress as British Archaeological Reports 392, 2005).

Vale, M. (2001) *The Princely Court: Medieval Courts and Culture in North-West Europe*. Oxford, Oxford University Press.

Veale, E. M. (1966) *The English Fur Trade in the Later Middle Ages*. Oxford, Clarendon.

Wigh, B. (2001) *Animal Husbandry in the Viking Age Town of Birka and its Hinterland: Excavations in the Black Earth, 1990–95*. Stockholm, Birka Project Riksantikvarieambetet

Woolgar, C. M. (1999) *The Great Household in Late Medieval England*. London, Yale University Press.

Woolley, L. (2002) *Medieval Life and Leisure in the Devonshire Hunting Tapesteries*. London, V&A.

Chapter 5

Taphonomy or Transfiguration: Do We Need to Change the Subject?

Sue Stallibrass

Introduction

Archaeozoologists have two main areas of interest. They are interested in animals (the 'zoo' part of the term) and in people in the past (the 'archaeologist' part). But having two subjects of interest can lead to one of them taking priority to the detriment of the other.

Many taphonomic models concentrate on the animals whose taphonomy is being investigated rather than on people. In these models, animals or animal remains form the focus for attention. Human activities tend to be considered in relation to the zoological remains rather than *vice versa*. Three well-known examples are presented here as very brief and very over-simplified illustrations. Please note that these are selective and chosen simply to make a point. They are not intended as balanced critiques. In each case, it is the summary diagram or illustration that is being criticised not the total discourse.

Hesse and Wapnish (1985, fig. 5.9) used a palaeontological system (and concomitant jargon) to describe a series of processes that an animal assemblage can pass through. Many of these processes involve human activities, but the overall impression of the model is that an assemblage is gradually reduced by various things happening to it. The main question can be summarised as: "Is the assemblage that is being investigated by a zooarchaeologist in the present a representative sample of the original assemblage in the past?" In the 1980s, statistics and scientific rigour were paramount in many archaeozoologists' minds, and this is reflected by this model's preoccupations.

Reitz and Wing's (1999) model is more preoccupied with ecology and how animals interacted with their natural environment. The main question is "What has happened to the animals?" and it may be significant that their pictorial representation of taphonomic processes does not include any human figures at all (Reitz and Wing, 1999, fig. 5.1) although human activities are considered at many stages.

Davis' (1987) model, like its near contemporary (Hesse and Wapnish, 1985) has a reductionist basis that emphasises the small and biased quantity of animal remains surviving into the analytical stages and published records. Davis (1987, fig. 1.1) gives much more emphasis to the roles of people but his main question is still focused on "What factors have impacted upon the animal remains that we have recovered?"

The Whodunit Model

Question	Murder Mystery	Archaeolog. Taphonomy	Do we Ask??
Event	WHAT?	WHAT?	√
Means	HOW?	HOW?	√
Opportunity	WHERE? WHEN?	WHERE? WHEN?	√ √
Suspect	WHO?	WHO?	?.....
Motive	WHY?	WHY?	X

Fig. 5.1. A Whodunit model for archaeozoologists

The taphonomic models briefly described above are mostly interested in (a) how representative the bones are that we work with and (b) what has happened to the bones since the animals were alive.

The Whodunit model

I shall now introduce a more people-orientated model based on formulaic detective novels of the early- to mid-20th century (often referred to as 'Whodunits'). Figure 5.1 is a table listing the main aspects of a Whodunit: the Event (what happened– usually a murder), the Means (how was the murder committed?), the Opportunity (when and where did the event take place?), the Suspect (who is thought to have perpetrated the deed?) and the Motive (why did the suspect commit the deed?). Classic detective novels have all of these main ingredients and I would claim that archaeological taphonomy has them too. However, as Figure 5.1 suggests, we are better at asking some of the questions than others. We are very good, using taphonomic methodology, at investigating the Event (*e.g.* the slaughter or butchery of an animal), the Means (how it was killed and butchered) and the Opportunity (when it was killed or butchered and where). We are far more reticent when it comes to asking 'WHO killed or butchered an animal in the past?' and 'WHY did they do it or do it that way?'. When we do consider the people involved in any such activities, we tend to be preoccupied with classification systems: does the method of butchery or the choice of species suggest a particular ethnic group, for instance (such as Anglo-Saxon immigrants), or a particular class of people (*e.g.* joints of venison at a castle interpreted as food for high status aristocrats). Although these interpretations do include people, the people are considered as 'types' or 'classes' not as actual people i.e. individuals with at least a degree of free choice.

A case study: Chevington medieval chapel

Background to the site

In 1997 the site of a demolished medieval (mainly 13th/14th century) Christian chapel at Chevington, Northumberland, England was excavated by the Archaeological Practice of Newcastle University. The excavation was undertaken as part of planning permission conditions prior to total destruction of the area by an opencast coal mine. During routine post-excavation assessment it became clear that some of the animal bones recovered from the site were unusual, both in terms of their depositional context and the ways in which they had been modified by people in the past.

The site of Chevington Chapel lies five kilometres from the coast of the North Sea near the Scottish/English border at National Grid Reference NZ 241981. The local area is not good arable land: it is low-lying on heavy clay and is prone to waterlogging and flooding. But it is quite productive as cattle pasture (sheep are less productive as they are more prone to foot rot and liver fluke in damp ground). Apart from cattle husbandry and coal mining, the other main natural resource is fish in the North Sea. The offshore waters are good habitats for herring *Clupea harengus* and for various members of the cod family (Gadidae) such as cod *Gadus morhua*, ling *Molva molva* and whiting *Merlangius merlangus*. Whilst trying to avoid environmental determinism, it is true that these factors are inherent in the landscape and are likely to have been as relevant in the past as they are in the present.

The site itself was a small, simple chapel consisting of a rectangular nave connected to a smaller rectangular chancel at its eastern end (see Stallibrass 2005 for a site plan). The wall foundations were constructed of stone rubble but the walls themselves had been robbed or raised to the ground sometime in the past four hundred years. Within the nave towards its western end was a rectangular rubble platform, presumably to support a baptismal font (as is the case in most Christian chapels and churches). Two other areas of stone rubble lay up against the inner face of the east wall of the nave, on either side of the gap through to the chancel. Using further analogies with extant structures, these areas of rubble have been interpreted as the bases for altars. Near these ?altar bases and against the inner face of the south wall of the chancel were a few isolated small pits or post-holes, initially interpreted as pits to take scaffolding posts during the construction of the chapel.

The animal bones from the chapel

The finds from the small pits or post-holes within the chapel include some animal bones. All of them derive either from cattle or from fish. Not only are they restricted in species but they are also very selective in terms of skeletal element and almost every bone has been modified and made into an artefact. The only exception is a bone that could be used without modification. Figure 5.2 is a photograph of three groups of bones. Each group forms the entire collection of bones recovered by hand during excavation of a single archaeological deposit. Some items may have been missed due to their small size and their method of excavation. The smallest group was recovered from a disturbed context (a modern land drain had cut through an earlier feature beside an ?altar base) and may be particularly incomplete in terms of numbers of bones originally deposited in the feature. The numbers of fish vertebrae in each context ranged from four in the disturbed context to over 100 in one of the pits against the south chancel wall.

In each case, the group consists of several fish vertebrae together with a single modified fragment taken from a roundish articular end of a cattle long bone. Two of the cattle bone fragments derive from the caputs (heads) of femurs, the third is from the trochlea at the distal end of a cattle humerus. Each of the cattle bones has been cut from the main shaft with a heavy metal blade and has then been perforated through its centre, perpendicular to the cut base. In the case of the two cattle femur heads, these artefacts resemble spindle whorls, but the humerus trochlea, despite trimming, is not symmetrical and definitely would not perform adequately as a spindle whorl.

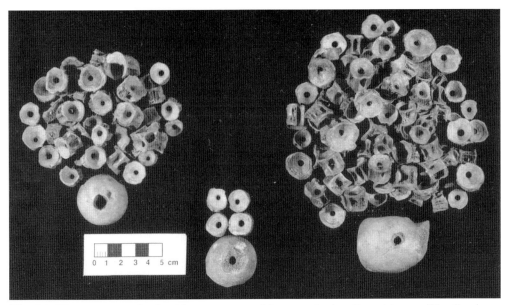

Fig. 5.2. Three groups of animal bones recovered from contexts adjacent to possible altar bases in the nave of Chevington Chapel and adjacent to the south wall of the chancel

The fish vertebrae have been treated in a similar manner: all projecting spines have been trimmed off each bone, leaving the more-or-less symmetrical centrum of the vertebra which has then been perforated through the centre. There are no signs of toolmarks in the perforations; the internal edges have all been worn smooth, as though something like a cord had been drawn through them and polished the edges. Similarly, although uneven in shape, the outside surfaces of the vertebrae are also polished as though rubbed by something (cloth? people's hands?). The only unmodified bone is a vertebra from an elasmobranch (fish of the shark family) which naturally has no spines and is naturally centrally perforated. The other fish vertebrae all derive from gadids. Those that could be identified to species (many thanks to Alison Locker for these identifications) are from ling (*Molva molva*). Not only are the fish bones all vertebrae, but they are all from the upper and middle sections of the spine. These are traditionally the bones that are filleted out of fish when they are split before being preserved by drying, smoking or salting. The sizes of the vertebrae are larger than those from the skeleton of a modern ling that was one metre in length.

In summary: there are groups of bones from small cut features near the chancel wall and the ?altar bases inside the chapel; each group consists of one perforated cattle bone fragment in association with several perforated and trimmed fish vertebrae; the fish vertebrae are all from parts of the spine that are normally discarded during fish processing and the species represented are nearly all from the cod family (mostly ling), and from fish that were over one metre in length.

Initial interpretation

The modified animal bones all have the appearance of beads, with their central perforations and smoothed appearance. Beads on cords or threads are used by many people and are associated in Christianity with the telling of prayers: either Paternosters (Our Fathers) or Ave Marias (Hail Maries). The latter are associated with rosaries, in which the beads are threaded ten at a time, usually separated by a knot in the thread or a different type of bead. Some, but not all rosaries and paternosters have a single large bead that holds the ends of the thread together and acts as a weight as the item is held and used for counting prayers. Rosaries are associated with the Catholic sect of Christianity, which was the dominant form of the religion in medieval England until the reformation in the 16th century. Paternosters are used in all types of Christianity.

The most likely explanation of how the cattle and fish bones came to be found in small pits or post-holes within the chapel appears to be that they had been fashioned into paternosters or rosaries and deposited deliberately in purpose-dug cut features in sacred parts of the sacred site i.e.: next to the side altars in the nave or in the chancel where the main religious ceremonies were conducted.

Supporting circumstantial evidence comes from two sources. Firstly, the use of fish bones as raw materials should not be surprising since rosary beads were made from a very wide range of natural and artificial materials including wood, bone, shell, stone and glass (Winston-Allen 1997). There is even a picture of a rosary or paternoster made of fish vertebrae in a famous piece of medieval Christian iconography. The St

Vincent polyptych by the Portuguese painter Nuno Gonçalves (active AD 1450–1467) clearly shows a fisherman holding a rosary made of fish vertebrae, in this instance almost certainly those of elasmobranchs (Royal College of Art 1955). Secondly, the concept of burying something at a sacred site is familiar from many cultures and periods in archaeology (c.f. structured deposits in the Iron Age: Hill 1996). More pertinently, there is another example at the chapel itself: beneath the stone foundation for the baptismal font, the excavators found an earlier font buried *in situ*. Stocker (1997) has surveyed this practice in an area of medieval Lincolnshire and suggests that the practice was due to the sacred nature of the fonts: having been blessed, it was forbidden to dispose of a font in non-consecrated ground. Modern rosaries are also blessed by priests, and there is a similar prohibition on their disposal in profane contexts.

Why might rosaries or paternosters be deposited in a Christian chapel? Like many religions, Catholic Christianity encourages or permits the donation of special items in devotional activities. Rosaries can be given to Mary the mother of Jesus (the son of the Christian god) as thanks for good fortune or for bad fortune averted, or as a request for the same. Paternosters are more likely to be offered to God himself. When giving something to God, Jesus or Mary, the item could be placed on an icon or statue or on (or beneath) an altar. This appears to be what has happened at Chevington.

The choice of cattle and fish bones appears to be serendipitous: they were available as waste from normal economic activities of cattle husbandry and deep sea fishing and processing. The choice of elements was similarly affected by logistical and practical considerations: only the upper and middle vertebrae of the fish would have been filleted out, the tail vertebrae being left in the cured fish during storage or transport for sale or exchange elsewhere. The vertebrae only needed minor modifications to turn them into beads, and anybody could have perforated the centra using a simple awl and then trimmed off the spines. The cattle bones selected were also the most suitable for modification into more-or-less symmetrical perforated beads or weights.

From an economic perspective, the bones imply that cattle husbandry was practised locally and that deep sea fish provided food and a potentially marketable product.

From an ecological perspective, the sizes of the bones support evidence from many sites in Britain that caught marine fish used to be larger (i.e. older) than those available today, modern fish stocks having been severely reduced by over-fishing in the 20th century (Barrett *et al.* 2004).

Re-interpreting the material using explicit taphonomic and Whodunit models

Taphonomic model

Figure 5.3 presents a taphonomic interpretation of how the fish bones came to be deposited in small pits or post-holes within a medieval chapel in Northumberland. At the start of the sequence, some fish are caught (in Fig. 5.3 only one fish is shown for

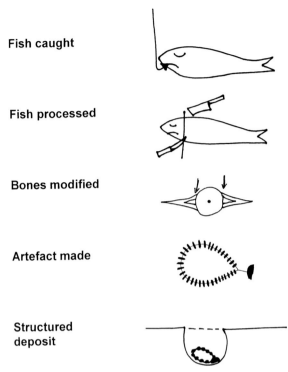

Fish caught

Fish processed

Bones modified

Artefact made

**Structured
deposit**

Fig. 5.3. A classic taphonomic interpretation of the fish bones from Chevington Chapel.

clarity). These are then processed by filleting. The discarded vertebrae are modified, then made into an artefact by being strung onto thread. The whole item is then placed in a pit. This provides an entire sequence from live fish to structured deposit, with the fish bones as the centre of attention. Figure 5.3 contains no representations of people. This *châine opératoire* gives the impression that the linearity of the sequence is inevitable, and that the final deposition is the end of the sequence until an archaeologist excavates the site.

Whodunit model

Figure 5.4 provides a sketch view of some of the activities that people might have been involved in during the medieval period at Chevington. Some of these might have related to the fish and cattle bones during their taphonomic histories. A checklist of the key aspects of a whodunit (Event, Means, Opportunity, Suspect and Motive) is placed at the side of the picture. The sketch reminds us of several factors: people act and react in conjunction with other people, people die, they worship gods and may have special structures where this occurs, they throw things away and things decompose, people go fishing and look after animals.

   If we take a people-centred approach to the taphonomy of the fish bones, it becomes

Event

Means

Opportunity

Suspect

Motive

Fig. 5.4. A Whodunit interpretation of the fish bones from Chevington Chapel

clear that the linearity of the *châine opératoire* is not so inevitable after all. The deceptively simple statement at the start of the taphonomic chain of events: the capture and killing of the fish is, in fact, the climax of a complex sequence of activities and co-operations rather than a starting point. Gadid fish live in deep water and are unlikely to have been caught regularly by someone standing onshore. Their capture presupposes the use of a sea-worthy boat. Who built the boat? Where did the timber for it come from and how was it grown? Who paid for and owned the boat – one person, a family, a village community? Resources would have been needed to maintain the boat as well: sails, nets and lines tear and break, and boats get damaged and need repair. Successful fishing also requires much skill, experience and local knowledge: where are the best places to go, and at what time of year? Do you use lines rather than nets and, if so, what is the best bait and how many lines do you need? There are also, of course, the skills required to navigate and to sail the boat in various weather conditions, regardless of whether or not you have fishing skills.

Given all these preparatory requirements of skill, experience and capital investment quite apart from the need to rely on other people in a team and to risk one's own health and safety in a dangerous activity: what motives might people have had to go sea fishing? Several are possible, and none of them are mutually exclusive. They include: immediate food requirements, long term food requirements (i.e. if processed and stored for later use) and a marketable commodity to trade either locally or long distance. These are all utilitarian or economic considerations, but the relative attractiveness of marine fishing was also affected by politics, society and religion.

Medieval Catholic Christian religious dogma forbad the consumption of flesh from mammals (and sometimes from birds) on many days of the year (Woolgar, 2000), raising the value of fish as an important permitted source of protein. Fishing was also a means of increasing and maintaining stocks of sea-worthy vessels and skilled sailors: resources that were often called upon during medieval wars between England and other countries. By the Tudor period, these resources were being actively developed and encouraged by national rulers and governments (Jackson, 2000).

The bald statement 'fish caught' and accompanying picture of a fish with a hook in its mouth in the taphonomic model seems very inadequate when compared with this more realistic scenario of what might have happened in the past. Similarly, the processing of the fish is likely to have been a very sociable affair (fishwives being notable in post-medieval and recent history for their vocal skills!). Gutting and filleting fish produces much offal that would have built up rich organic deposits and attracted many scavengers. Where did this take place? Whoever modified the bones into beads probably had easy access to the refuse from fish filleting, even if he or she did not do the filleting themselves. Similarly, the cattle bones may derive from animals slaughtered and consumed by the person who made them into artefacts, or could have been obtained from a communal midden.

When the bones were modified to form beads and strung together into paternosters or rosaries, it is very probable that other raw materials could have been used: wood, bone, shell and clay are likely to have been available, as well as artificial materials such as potsherds. Glass might have been rather expensive compared to these naturally-occurring local resources. Is it just chance, therefore, that these artefacts were made out of bone refuse, or was there an underlying significance for the person or people making them i.e.: did people who worked with fish during the day deliberately choose to use remains of fish to construct artefacts that became their religious talismans and links with their divine protectors?

If these rosaries or paternosters were intended as offerings, their deposition may have been accompanied by prayers for the safe return of family members out at sea on fishing trips (either as propitiations or as thanks for a safe return). If so, it would be fitting that the offered artefacts were made from materials won (during an earlier fishing activity) from the same sea that continued to endanger people.

Unlike the taphonomic model, in which the sequence of taphonomic events halts with the deposition of the rosary or paternoster, the Whodunit model suggests that the 'active life' of the deposited artefact continued for a very long time after the deposition event. There are three main prerequisites for this type of structured deposition in a Catholic context, and these are likely to be common to many religious and belief systems: (1) there is a belief system and a faith (2) there are emotional bonds between individual people, and (3) there is an awareness of time past (tradition) and time in the future. In this instance, the belief system is that of Christianity and there is faith that divine characters (Mary, Jesus or God) will protect and take care of believers who pray to them. Christian prayers can be offered on behalf of oneself but are frequently offered on behalf of other people. In medieval Europe, the Order of the Rose was a cost-free society to which anyone could belong (even women). Within the order, an individual could offer prayers on behalf of all of the other people in the order. All of the prayers offered by all of the other people in the order on a person's behalf earned that person a specific amount of redeemed time from their expected stay in Purgatory (a place between life and death) (Winston-Allen 1997). Prayers, therefore, were a social and religious tie, and were usually offered using a rosary or paternoster as an instrument. There was a tradition of offering rosaries to Mary, giving a time depth into the past for the practice. Since prayers are often offered for protection for a length of time (often an infinite length of time *e.g.* 'for now and ever more') there is also the expectation that the prophylactic qualities of the structured deposit will last into the infinite future (or until a particular person's death, at the very least).

Comparing the efficacy of the taphonomic and Whodunit models

A set of questions was provided by Aleks Pluskowski in the conference synopsis where this paper was first presented. Some of them are considered here to illustrate more succinctly the differences in productivity and relevance of these two models.

1: What was the 'lifespan' of animal bodies and how often were they reused or modified?
For the second part of this question, the two approaches have identical results and applicability. Figure 5.3 (the Taphonomic model illustration) demonstrates the series of events during which the animal remains were reused and modified.

The first part of the question, however, has very different results using the two models. The taphonomic model has a very clear start and a very clear end: Start = fish caught; End = deposition of rosary or paternoster. The people-orientated Whodunit model, however, permits the concept that the knowledge of the fish existed prior to their capture and slaughter. More importantly, it expects the significance of the structured deposit to continue into the future, perhaps the indefinite future.

2: Was the breaking and shaping of animals' body parts guided by social as well as practical concerns?
The taphonomic model has problems addressing this question. The economic interpretation suggests that the raw materials were simply to hand through normal 'economic' activities. That is, the 'breaking' was a process required to render animal carcases into food and marketable commodities. But this does not help any consideration of why they were 'shaped', apart from the fact that fish vertebrae are easy to convert into rough beads if beads are a desired product.

The Whodunit model emphasises various social aspects including the likelihood that fish processing was undertaken as a communal activity, which might affect where refuse from this activity might be located (although refuse location is also likely to have been affected by practical considerations such as quantities of noxious waste), and who might have access to it. The decision to 'shape' the bones, however, is very much guided by social and religious concerns and is completely unnecessary in practical terms of fish processing and waste disposal.

3: To what extent was the animal physically or conceptually visible in the finished product and does this reflect a transformation in identity?
Again, the taphonomic model has nothing to contribute to this debate apart from the fact that fish vertebrae are highly distinctive. Even with their spines trimmed off, the centra of fish vertebrae are instantly recognisable to anyone who has eaten fish, even if they have never prepared a carcase. The trimmed cattle bones are less distinctive and may have been reduced to 'lumps of bone' rather than 'pieces of cattle bone' in people's perceptions.

In the people-orientated model, the presence of fish bones in the finished artefacts of religious devotion was probably more important conceptually than physically. Fishing in the North Sea has always been a dangerous and risky activity. The products or inhabitants of that sea may have been considered to be particularly potent and efficacious raw materials for talismans intended to protect someone from its inherent dangers. After all, a fish is at home in the sea, so a talisman made from a fish might confer the fish's skills to the wearer and make him or her able to swim and survive like a fish in the water.

In both models, the fish bones would have been physically visible in the finished products but, in the Whodunit model it becomes clear that the concept of the original animals was equally visible and potentially highly significant, providing a form of transfiguration (see Fig. 5.5).

Discussion and conclusions

The data from Chevington Chapel and their interpretations are presented here as a case study to test two models of site formation and interpretation. The basic interpretation of these modified fish and cattle bones as rosaries or paternosters may be flawed, but the main aim of this paper has been to demonstrate how much more information can be obtained from archaeozoological analyses if the focus of attention is shifted from the animal bones themselves to the people who were active at the sites being investigated. Both subject areas: people and animals, need to be investigated.

Taphonomic models can be used to give the impression that structured deposits are an end in themselves, as though people followed a routine procedure from start to finish, with the finish being the deposition event itself. But a Whodunit model is people-centred not bone-centred. Besides investigating the event, i.e. what happened, how it happened, and when and where it happened, the Whodunit model seeks to consider WHY it happened, and WHO was involved in it happening. Taphonomic models tend to take linear views of sequences of events: (i) animals killed, (ii) animal carcases butchered, (iii) waste skeletal elements modified into artefacts, (iv) artefacts utilised and (v) artefacts deposited. The linearity can instigate a sense of inevitability. In contrast, a people-orientated model clarifies these stages as separate events, each surrounded by multiple opportunities and choices, and each affected by the people involved. The questions 'Why?' and 'By whom?' add much-needed social context to the simple observation that 'fish were caught'. It also helps to elucidate some of the connections between various different aspects of people's lives. Archaeologists still tend to split their investigations between specialists without any subsequent re-

Fig. 5.5. A schematic representation of how the fish bones found at Chevington Chapel might have been perceived by the people who were involved in their taphonomic history

integration. It is possible to consider the economy of a site, as evidenced by its biological plant and animal remains, as a separate aspect from artefact typologies and site stratigraphy. In reality, of course, when a site was in use and deposits being formed, most if not all aspects interacted with each other, and people were a major agent in many site formation processes.

Rosaries and paternosters were intermediaries between individual people and their deities, facilitating direct communication between mortals and their gods. The reality of people's lives is that they lived in a community with family, friends, neighbours, relatives and strangers. No one single person was involved in the taphonomic processes even of a single rosary or paternoster. Even if someone caught and filleted the fish, slaughtered and butchered a cow, obtained and modified several bones from the fish and cattle butchery waste, created a rosary or paternoster, used it to help themselves say their prayers, and then dug a small pit inside the chapel and buried their rosary or paternoster in it, almost all of these activities would have been undertaken in collaboration with other people: obtaining/building/maintaining the boat, going out on a fishing expedition, catching the fish, filleting them, attending religious services in the chapel etc. Similarly, the presence of the buried rosaries or paternosters within the chapel was probably common knowledge amongst the congregation and community, providing reassurance both in terms of past tradition and in terms of future protection provided by the divinities.

Rigorous scientific techniques and methodology have to be applied to taphonomic concerns such as: 'Have we recovered all of the bones that were in the deposit?' or 'Have the bones undergone any gnawing or sub-aerial weathering?' etc. But we should not become so pre-occupied with investigations of how representative the sample is that we forget that the real reason for investigating any animal bones recovered from an archaeological site is that we are interested in archaeological sites as evidence of people's past lives. Hopefully, the adoption of a Whodunit-style model will keep us thinking not only about What, How, When and Where but the real crux of the mystery: Who and Why?

Acknowledgements

I should like to thank Alison Locker for identifying the fish bones and discussing their significance with me, Alan Williams of the Archaeological Practice for providing information about the site, Lindsay Allason-Jones of the Hancock Museum, University of Newcastle for research and discussion on rosaries, and Omri Lernau for introducing me to the St Vincent polyptych. Ian Qualtrough of the Department of Geography, University of Liverpool took the photograph of the modified bones. The other 'artwork' and all mistakes are my own.

Bibliography

Barrett, J. H., Locker, A. M. and Roberts, C. M. (2004) The origins of fishing in medieval Europe: the English evidence. *Proceedings of the Royal Society of London* B 271, 2417–2421

Davis, S. J. M. (1988) *The Archaeology of Animals*. London, Batsford.

Hesse, B. and Wapnish, P. (1985) *Animal Bone Archaeology. From Objectives to Analysis*. Washington, D. C. Taraxacum

Hill, J. D. (1996) *Ritual and Rubbish in the Iron Age of Wessex: a Study on the Formation of a Specific Archaeological Record*. British Archaeological Reports 242, Oxford, Tempus Reparatum.

Jackson, G. (2000) State concern for the fisheries, 1485–1815. In D. J. Starkey, C. Reid, and N. Ashcroft, (eds.) *England's Sea Fisheries. The Commercial Sea Fisheries of England and Wales since 1300*, 46–53. London, Chatham Publishing.

Reitz, E. J. and Wing, E. S. (1999) *Zooarchaeology*. Cambridge, Cambridge University Press.

Royal Academy of Arts (1955) *A Thousand Years of Portuguese Art, Portuguese Art 800–1800*, London, Exhibition Catalogue 1955–56.

Stocker, D. (1997) *Fons et origo*. The symbolic death, burial and resurrection of English font stones. *Church Archaeology* 1, 17–25

Winston-Allen, A. (1997) *Stories of the Rose. The Making of the Rosary in the Middle Ages*. Pennsylvania, Pennsylvanian State University Press.

Woolgar, C. M. (2000) 'Take this penance now, and afterwards the fare will improve': seafood and late medieval diet. In D. J. Starkey, C. Reid, and N. Ashcroft, (eds.) *England's Sea Fisheries. The Commercial Sea Fisheries of England and Wales since 1300*, 36–44. London, Chatham Publishing.

Chapter 6

Seeing is Believing: Animal Material Culture in Medieval England

Sarah Wells

Introduction

A wide range of realistic, stylistic, heraldic and symbolic depictions of animals can be found within the material culture of the Middle Ages. This chapter aims to focus upon one type of medium, the representations of creatures within misericord wood carvings. Many of the choir stalls across Europe have a wooden bracket and ledge underneath them that can be used as a seat. This ledge is frequently carved, and the resultant carving or misericord is found as a seat ledge, within the choir stall assemble. The style of the choir stall and bracket, ledge or hinged seat, can be quite different between choir stalls in chapels, churches, and cathedrals of various dates (refer to fig. 6.1). Animals can be most easily identified in English misericordia between the 14th to 17th centuries. The extant creatures range from realistic land animals to creatures of the sea, air and mind (composite creatures, mythological and fabulous animals); and of these, over a hundred different creatures can be identified within the published catalogues and surveys of misericords (refer to Phipson 1896; Bond 1910; Remnant, 1969, 1998; Laird 1986; Tracy 1987, 1990; Grössinger 1997; Wood and Curry 1999; and Wells 2005a, 2005b).

Why represent animals in misericords?

There are a wide range of animals that were known to the people of the Middle Ages, either from life and flesh or from voice, texts and pictures. It is clear that some animals appear as visual depictions with greater frequency than others, so understanding precisely why one animal was chosen above another is an interesting challenge to attempt to investigate. Whilst certain creatures may have been highly valued for their visual appearance and character (refer to Gunnthorsdottir 2001); the majority of those depicted in misericords were popular because they carried with them, or were associated with particular meanings or values. These may have had their origin in cultural folklore (refer to Handoo 1990; Jones 1991, 2002); or more significantly magical, moralized, religious, allegorical or other symbolism that was communicated as guiding principles and appropriate conduct for life at that time

Fig. 6.1. Choir Stall Misericord from York, England, UK (Photograph: Sarah Wells 2004).

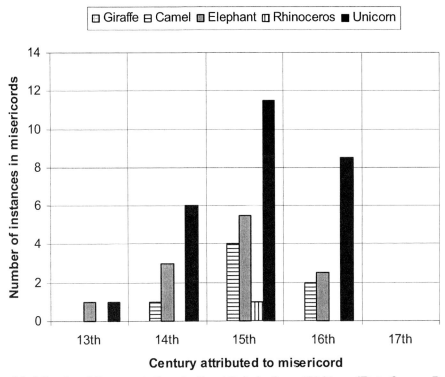

Fig. 6.2. Misericord Representations in Great Britain Over 400 Years (Data Source: Remnant 1969).

(refer to Evans 1896; Wildridge 1989 and Collins 1913; Derrick 1935; Cirlot 1962; Anderson 1969; Henderson 1982; Jones 1991; Fontana 1993; Cohen 1994; Telesko 2001; Werness 2004; Mellinkoff 2004 for further discussion). Those creatures selected for investigation and discussion in this chapter are the representation of the Giraffe, Camel, Elephant, Rhinoceros and Unicorn (refer to fig. 6.2). The meanings discussed here are not the only ones attributed to these animals, only a selection of those that might have influenced the motifs carved.

Medieval sources of animals

It is beyond the scope of this chapter to detail all the parallels between the misericords and possible sources of animal images, so only an outline will be provided. Animals could have been observed from life, such as a real sighting following the receipt of a gift or souvenir from foreign trade and exploration (refer to Buczacki 2002); or perhaps from a visit to a travelling animal show, ménagerie or zoo (refer to Baratay and Hardouin-Fugier 2002; and Hahn 2003). The specific details of a creature to be carved could also be obtained through descriptions passed on by word of mouth, recounted from the viewing of other drawings and model books (refer to Scheller 1995), from animals seen in work of tapestry, textiles, pottery, glass, stone and metalwork; from animals illustrated within maps, manuscripts and their accompanying illuminations (refer to McCulloch 1962, Gotfredsen 1999, and Bovey 2002), consultation of animal histories (*e.g.* Topsell, refer to South 1981), to knowledge of stories found within the romances, pilgrim and travellers tales such as those of Sir John Mandeville and Marco Polo. Other works would also have been influential such as readings of the Bible, the *Septuagint*, the *Physiologus,* or the Bestiaries (*e.g.* White 1984; Mermier 1992; Barber 1993); as well as consultation of the traditional classical sources such as Aristotle (refer to Peck 1965, 1970; Balme 1991; Lennox 2001) and Claudius Aelianus 'Aelain' (refer to Scholfield 1972a, 1972b); amongst others *e.g.* Cosmas; Ctesias; Honorius; Isadore; Solinus; Tertullian and Pliny.

Medieval perception of animals

There are a variety of modern works which provide us with images of different types of creatures found in a variety of media, from the medieval and post medieval period (*e.g.* Klingender 1971; Clark 1975; Benton 1992; Hicks 1993; Salisbury 1994; and Gravestock 1999). Any of these creatures could have been regarded as unusual or exotic depending on its physical appearance (colouring, shape and size), geographical origin (native creature or one from another country) natural habitat, diet, behaviour, or other attributes. Indeed, there are many creatures that could be considered to be unusual, out of the ordinary, striking, interesting, bizarre, mysterious, glamorous, colourful, outlandish, rare, alien, that were native species (in addition to those from a strange or distant land). However, the country of origin does not necessarily mean a creature would be considered to be unusual or exotic or have exotic associations; a non-native creature could be well known or common to the inhabitants of another land *e.g.* the lion was a non-native species of England, yet one of the most common creatures represented overall in its misericords. The frequency of trade in verbal or visual information, or through the exchange of animal products, animal parts or in the movement of animals themselves, both dead and alive, was also an important factor in the shaping of attitudes and attributed values toward animals. This is further discussed with reference to the unicorn later on in the chapter.

The representation of the giraffe

The giraffe was chosen as a creature to investigate, because it has an extremely unusual appearance, on account of its exceptionally long neck and glamorously patterned skin, and since being the tallest living terrestrial animal. Ancient writers in the time of the Romans, describe the giraffe as a creature rather like a camel, apart from the fact that its legs were not equal in length; and also as a creature like a leopard on account of the spot like pattern and colouring of its skin (Toynbee 1996, 141–142). Although it has been suggested that the giraffe remained unknown in most parts of Europe for about a thousand years after the fall of the Roman Empire, medieval travellers such as Marco Polo and Sir John Mandeville, clearly saw the creature to enable the few images of the animal to have been made and survived in circulation as woodcuts across Europe (Laufer 1928). However, it appears the giraffe was relatively unknown in medieval England compared with other exotic creatures, and there were no representations that could be found in the catalogued misericords. Unfortunately, the creature is not easily found with the English bestiary either, and perhaps its exclusion is significant on account of its lack of moral, religious, allegorical or other symbolic meaning, and therefore is one reason why we don't find the giraffe carved. Although it was as an exotic animal, it was one with no other obvious story to tell (Werness 2004, 196), and this might indicate that visual appearance and exotic charisma alone, were generally not the motivating factors behind the patronage and carving of misericords in medieval England.

The representation of the camel

Camels can be regarded as strange and exotic creatures, chiefly on account of their unique appearance, either of their smaller single hump (the camel native to Africa and Arabia) or with double storage humps (found in the old world type of Bactrian camel from Asia). Archaeologically we have traces of camels, their activities and uses (refer to Ripinsky 1975; Masry 1978; Zarins 1978; Muñiz 1995; Bartosiewicz 1996; and Telesko 2001, 56), including presentation as a curiosity in public shows. Around 1392, a camel was given as a gift to King Richard by the people of London (Hahn 2002, 48), and in 1623, five camels arrived with an elephant as a gift for King James from the King of Spain. The camel has been depicted on coins, statuettes and lamps in the Hellenistic and Roman periods (Toynbee 1996, 137–140); in manuscripts and in maps in the medieval period *e.g.* M.S. Bodley 764; and the Hereford World Map (refer to Collins 1913, 34); and on tombs bosses, choir stalls, benches and bench ends *e.g.* at Sefton and Stowlangtoft (refer to Anderson 1938, 79–80). However, there are only six misericord carvings of the camel that are recorded, dating between the 14th and 16th century (Remnant 1969/1998). The camels represented on the misericords are shown crouching, kneeling and standing, or depicted alone and with other animals such as the ape, elephant, hound, lion, stag, wodehouse, wyvern, and human riders. Two thirds of these carvings are distributed in the North of England, with one each found in Boston, Old Malton, Beverley and Manchester, and the remaining two are to be found in the South of England with one camel in Faversham and one found in Stratford-upon-Avon. The number of camel representations found in the UK is much greater than the combined number of those found in France (refer to Block 2003), and from the Iberian Peninsula, where only one camel was represented, displaying a single hump and shown with a collar and reins (refer to Block 2004).

The bestiaries can provide us with clues as to what associations people might have attributed with this creature and why it could have been chosen to be carved in a religious context. The bestiaries became common in England during the 12th and 13th centuries and offered illustrations, a description of the animals' physique, as well as explanative stories linked to their behaviours, which were useful in educating illiterate audiences (for further discussion of the content and function of bestiaries refer to Cronin 1941; Clark and McMunn 1989; George and Yapp 1991; Baxter 1998; Hassig 1999; and Brown 2000). Payne suggests that "to the medieval mind the camel might symbolize a number of things: temperance, because it could survive without liquid; prudence, because of its careful storage of water against future need; lust, because of a reputedly prodigious sexual appetite" (1990, 54); and that foremost "it stood for humility, because the camel was willing to kneel submissively to receive heavy loads". Anderson says the camel "typified Christ, who took upon Him the sins of the world. The humility of Christ in taking on himself the burden of man's sinfulness was implicit" (1938, 31). In the New Testament, Matthew comments that "It is easier for a camel to go through the eye of a needle, than for a rich man to enter the kingdom of God" (Matthew 19, 24), thus offering a lesson in how difficult it is for people to give up the excess of a materialistic life and convert to Christ. Therefore the representation of the camel might have been carved to demonstrate good qualities and godly attributes; since these were suitable themes to represent within an ecclesiastical context. However, because of its multifaceted symbolism, I expected to see more camels on the misericords and supporters than there were. So, were other animals just more popular or were the associations of other animals more socially popular as models for living life?

The representation of the elephant

The elephant is a very charismatic creature, predominantly on account of its size, ears and characteristic trunk. As an exotic creature, the elephant was the most common animal to be identified in the misericords out of all of those real creatures discussed here. The elephant is known from the earliest times from its offering as a gift presented to Charlemagne in 801 (by Haran al-Rashid); and four centuries later, it was still regarded as unusual and exotic enough to be given as a gift in 1255 to King Henry III of England by Louis IX of France (Hahn, 2003). From then on the elephant became more widely known as small herds reached Europe by the 15th and 16th centuries (Clarke 1986, 16). If elephants were being given as gifts might we might expect to see representations of them closer to the location where these gifts resided. However, of the twelve carvings of the elephant distributed throughout the UK (dating from the 13th to 16th centuries) half come from the North of England, with one each found in Carlisle, Cartmel, Beverley, Manchester, Garstang, and the others from the South of England, two from Windsor and one each in Gloucester, London and Exeter (the oldest dated misericord). Again this is a much greater number than those found in Iberia (where only two elephants are recorded, one saddled and one with a castle); and only three in France (all depicted with castles), refer to Block 2003, 2004. Collins (1913, 38), states that in the bestiaries the elephant is said to be "so strong that it can carry a tower full of armed men on its back, and therefore it is of great service in battle". Payne (1990, 31) suggests this was "the most popular bestiary illustration for this animal and became a familiar subject in ecclesiastical carving and heraldry" (refer also to Druce 1919). There are many depictions of the elephant with a tower on its back ('elephant and castle'), at least eight of the misericords (the larger majority) depict the elephants in this manner, thus it seems a message of strength was popular. The image of the elephant and castle is one that relates to the *'Howdah'* (the strong wooden towers) used in India and Persia, and used for war. Other misericords depict the elephant alone, or in one case, the elephant fighting with a dragon which was considered the elephant's mortal enemy, and likened to the devil and sin (Payne 1990, 82). Collins (1913, 41–42) also suggests that the male elephant had to protect its young from dragons who seek to devour newborn elephants – thus the elephant protects its offspring by giving birth in a pool (like Eve who conceived Cain in the waters of tribulation). The elephant was also thought to go to paradise to eat mandragora or mandrake (a plant shaped like a human being and luminous at night), so that the female elephant could give it to the passionless male to get him 'in the mood' as the plant was considered an aphrodisiac (thus a little like Adam and Eve who eat the forbidden fruit and share the same evil enemy in the dragon), refer to Anderson (1938, 34). Anderson further suggests elephants were thought to have no joints in their legs so slept leaning up against a tree, thus a young elephant (representing Christ) could then help the older elephant (fallen one) to get up with his trunk. However, no images were found that showed elephants eating plants or depicted scenes with baby elephants or in fact multiple elephants to support the depiction of bestiary knowledge. Another reason why the elephant might have been represented was that it was thought to live to 300 after breeding only once in life and therefore perhaps was associated with longevity, eternity and the afterlife, according to the 12th century bestiaries (refer to Anderson 1938; White 1984).

The representation of the rhinoceros

The rhinoceros is a striking creature mainly on account of its bulky size and shape, horn, and 3 toed foot with hooves. Those frequently illustrated in visual art, show the Asian or Indian rhinoceros famously presented by Dürer (refer to Dodgson 1938, 45–56; Bartrum 2003; Salley 2003). The creature is characterised with its single horn on its snout and its characteristic armour plated appearance on account of its deep skin folds with plates and rivets or lumps (tubercles) on its skin, bulky frame and thick legs (Burnie 2001). There is a selection of visual media which depict the rhinoceros from periods pre-dating the medieval period such as Roman coins, cameos and mosaics, though many of these would have been unknown during the medieval period until more recent excavation occurred, and therefore knowledge of their circulation is likely to have been unknown. Images of the rhinoceros appear visually in individual format as sketches and woodcuts, to illustrations with other animals (in particular the elephant), and in a number of scenes depicting subjects ranging from natural history to mythology and scenes from animal parks and those from the old testament such as the creation of 'Adam and Eve' or 'Noah and the Ark' (see Clarke 1986, 31; and refer also to Clarke 1973, 1974, 1976; Gowers 1950, 1952, and Rookmaaker 1973, 1983; Toynbee 1996). It was surprising to find that there are so few depictions to be found of the rhinoceros in misericords. There was only one surviving misericord of a rhinoceros from Windsor (and the identification of that is not clear cut). Anderson is doubtful about this identification, and thinks this is a hippopotamus (1938, 39). The horn of the creature looks as if it is located above the eye and there does appear to be a hairy mane – more in keeping with a monoceros or unicorn than a hippopotamus or rhino; so perhaps there are no representations of the rhinoceros in the misericords at all? Certainly there are none surviving from Iberia or France (Block 2003, 2004). However, what goes in favour of this misericord possibly being a rhinoceros, are that the toes are more rhino like, along with the squat body shape – as opposed to the more equine or gracile physique frequently associated with the unicorn or monoceros. The representation of anatomically and accurately carved native and non-native fauna is not always consistent in the miseriords, as some animals look more realistic than others. This may be due to the quality and accuracy of the information available to the carver and the interpretation of that information, since in most cases the carvers' skills were sufficiently good to render the correct and proportioned physical attributes had they intended so. The date of this misericord, if correct, also pre-dates some of the better circulated images of the rhino by Dürer, which would also make it particularly special if it were in fact a representation of the rhinoceros. If the misericord was intended to portray a rhinoceros, it might be depicted because it has long been associated with virility. However, the appearance of the rhinoceros in Europe was relatively rare during the medieval and post-medieval period (compared with other creatures such as the elephant) and this made its arrival and display always a newsworthy event (Clarke 1986, 70). This might reflect one reason why this animal is only represented by a single misericord, as a commemoration. There are also early literary references to the creature such as that presented by the classical author 'Pliny', whose account emphasised animosity between the elephant and the rhinoceros (refer to Clarke 1983, 19 and 1986, 158–159; Werness 2004, 348) although this is not reflected in the surviving single misericord scene, or in fact any of those containing elephants.

The representation of the unicorn

The unicorn (or perhaps its relation the monoceros) was the most popular creature to be represented in misericords of the creatures discussed in this chapter. There are over twenty five representations of this creature in the UK, twelve are found in the North of England from the counties of Cumbria, Durham, Lancashire, Cheshire, Yorkshire and Lincolnshire, eleven are from the South of England from the counties of Berkshire, Cambridgeshire, Oxfordshire, Warwickshire, Nottinghamshire and London; and the remainder are split between Wales and Ireland. The unicorn is represented with a variety of animals including the ape, bull, camel, dog, deer, dragon, eagle, griffin, hart, lion, owl, wodehouse and wyvern. The total number of unicorns shown on misericords is greater than the total number of all representations of the real exotic creatures – the giraffe, camel, elephant and rhinoceros combined. This number of unicorns in the UK is also five times greater than those found within Iberia

Fig. 6.3. Unicorn on Misericord Seat Ledge, Durham, England, UK (Photograph: Sarah Wells 2004).

(refer to Block 2004), and more still compared with France from which only two survive (Block 2003). Lum (1952, 57) suggests "In appearance it is far more plausible than many another living creature and, except for one or two mediaeval fancies as to the means of its capture and the remarkable value of its horn, it has none of the supernatural qualities or the absurdities ascribed to other fabulous beasts." In some bestiaries the monoceros and unicorn were the same creature. In others, the monoceros is the fierce cousin of the unicorn with a much longer four foot horn, which makes it difficult to capture alive and was said a single monoceros had never ever been taken alive (Payne 1990, 41). The monoceros is described as having a terrible bellow, and just like the unicorn had the body of a horse, feet of an elephant, tail of a stag (Anderson 1938, 74; Collins 1913, 210). Collins 1913, 210 suggests that the unicorn was "at enmity with the elephant", whilst other authors discuss its relationship to other regal beasts such as the lion (Bunt 1930). The unicorn was also thought to fight elephants defeating them by spearing them in the belly. The unicorn depicted in Figure 6.3, was said by Anderson (1969) to be associated with the fall of man as it tramples a human headed serpent (refer also to Grundy 1997). This is a unique image of a unicorn for England, since most of the other misericords depict the unicorn in other scenes either alone, or with other creatures, being ridden on (similar to the manuscript illuminations, M.S. Douce 219, fol. 96 v and MS Douce 220, fol. 159 which show apes riding on the unicorn as an animal of chastity); fighting with dragons, in heraldic coats of arms, or with a maiden/virgin in scenes of its capture or the hunting of the unicorn – which account for at least six of all unicorn scenes in misericords. The unicorn was thought to be too quick for the fastest hunter, therefore invincible, and only able to be caught by the deception of a chaste virgin or maiden, sitting in a forest, where the unicorn would approach and lay its head in her lap, and then could be captured off guard by the hunter. The unicorn as a representation might have been so popular because it was believed to be the symbol of Christ. The unicorn was also thought to have been used as a symbol of female chastity, having been associated with virgins since the 6th century (Gotfredsen 1999, 45); and as Collins suggests "It is appropriate especially to the Blessed Virgin Mary and to St. Justina, the pure virgin martyr of Antioch (Collins 1913, 216). These are obvious virtues that a clerical audience would hopefully aspire to.

Animal material culture: a reflection of faith

Misericords can serve as a manifestation of medieval faith at a number of levels; since the representation of particular creatures demonstrates that there is a faith given in the existence of particular creatures – ones which people did not have the opportunity to see or have experience of in the flesh, and often ones that we know were not native species, or did not in fact exist. There were greater limits and restrictions on the opportunities to increase ones' life experience in the Middle Ages, so a greater reliance and trust was bestowed in other more learned authorities to impart accurate knowledge. Some of the descriptions and images of real creatures that reached medieval audiences would have been, just as shocking, outrageous and unbelievable as the non-real composite and mythological creatures that we are familiar with today. Certain creatures were chosen to be represented because they were popular, not because of physical appearance, or ease of carving, but perhaps on account of their associations, folklore, symbolic value and meanings or relationship with God. In the case of the unicorn, its popularity was long-lasting and its inclusion in religious texts gave it credence as a real creature. Collins (1913, 215) and Gotfredsen (1999, 34), both comment how the unicorn's horn was equated to the horn of faith, the horn of salvation; whilst others consider it an emblem of the sword of god (Cirlot 1962, 357). The horn itself was prized for its magical properties, these included the ability to purify poison, and therefore as an antidote to poisoning. As a result, drinking from a unicorn's horn or out of a cup made from the horn was regarded as a prized and valuable possession (Anderson 1938, 74; Lum 1952, 68).

We have records of unicorn horns being kept at St. Mark's (Venice), St. Denis (France), Milan Cathedral (Italy), St. Paul's Cathedral and Westminster Abbey (London), and some even believed it was "so potent that even the water in which it had been steeped would cure the sick"; whilst "one included in the inventory of the treasure of Charles I; and another, or perhaps the same, that was seen at Windsor

Castle by travellers to the court of Queen Elizabeth and valued at £100,000" (Lum 1952, 69). Other unicorn horns could be found listed in the inventories of various Dukes *e.g.* those of Mantua, Berry, Burgundy and the Medicis (refer to Gotfredsen 1999; Hahn 2003). The antidote value of the unicorn's horn was obviously an attractive and powerful lure, which might explain one reason why the horn became a valuable medieval commodity. The unicorn's horn became a form of material culture, and a trade for this sort of thing emerged, meaning similar or twisted looking horns began to be collected and passed off as coming from a unicorn (such as that of the narwhal, a small whale and sometimes called a sea unicorn, Lum 1952, 71). Faith in the unicorn's existence remained seriously unquestioned until the 16th century (Hahn 2002, 59), yet by 1652 this came to a head as scientific writings prevailed (Gotfredsen 1999), and empirical testing and experimentation began to gain momentum. That people had faith in the existence of certain creatures that they never saw, such as the unicorn, and that were imaginary, perhaps is more easily appreciated in a world, where seeing was not required for believing. In the Middle Ages people generally had faith, and were required to have faith, since the opportunity for personal experience, knowledge and growth was restricted and limited.

The benefits of misericords as a source of animal material culture

Misericords are a fruitful a source to investigate for animal material culture. An examination of misericord carvings reveals an extensive variety of human themes, including a large number of real and fantastic creatures that have been represented over the centuries. There are thousands of surviving misericords from the UK which are able to be viewed, and there are more that survive across Europe (refer to Block, 2003, 2004, Kraus and Kraus 1976), this has enabled investigation of misericords and their motifs to be analysed, not only at a regional, but at a national and European level by leading scholars in this field. Misericords studies can also provide an interesting benchmark for representational research in terms of how animals are depicted in specific contexts, chronologically and geographically, as compared with portable images from other surviving medieval media such as manuscript surveys of animals (*e.g.* Salisbury 1994, 1996).

The limitations of misericords as a source of animal material culture

The proportional representation of major creature subjects originally carved within the high Middle Ages might have been very different from those extant today. Unfortunately, a number of choirs or choir stalls with misericords have deteriorated, been removed, moved or in fact destroyed, and therefore not survived. Environmental deterioration such as dry rot, wood-boring insects, and disasters such as fires will also have caused the loss of misericords over the years. In addition to this, people's political and religious influences are responsible for the greater losses, some selective such as through the unroofing, pillaging, defacing, destruction, torching, and general desolation caused during the reformation, as well as by more recent iconoclasts who removed or censored some of the perhaps cruder and more objectionable misericords. The movement and destruction of misericord carvings clouds the distribution of misericords geographically and chronologically over time, which confuses any effort to trace the representation of ideas through the carvings of animals. There are also numerous problems with the accuracy of some of the data recorded in the published catalogues and survey records, and the method of dating the misericords themselves leads to difficulties in chronological definition and reliability (for further discussion on these points refer to Wells 2005a, 2005b).

Conclusion

Misericords are a unique form of animal material culture from the medieval period that can demonstrate the spiritual pre-occupations of their commissioners, carvers and perhaps intended audience across time and space. Their existence indicates the life of ideas that people had about particular creatures, and the popularity of the animal packaged messages people wanted to transmit and be associated with. Whilst misericords are not a form of material culture designed to impress an audience (in view of their rather concealed location), to the patron, sponsor or carver who chose the image – they had meaning and significance. People carved the creatures they did because they believed in those creatures, either that they believed they physically existed, but mainly that they had faith in what the animals they represented offered to them in terms of how to conduct their lives, be it aspirational. The study of misericords can therefore be used to provide clues as to the popularity of creatures as a unified form of communication and education. Unfortunately, the clarity and precision of the original meanings may be blurred over time and lost to us through changes in our cultural understanding; nevertheless whether creatures existed in the flesh or not, spiritually they were very much alive in peoples minds for a very long period of time. By examining the choice of animals chosen, we can explore the reflections of what was on people's minds in medieval England, and what they didn't want to advertise.

Bibliography

Aelian (Claudius Aelianus), *On The Characteristics of Animals* (seventeen books in three volumes, with an english translation by A F Scholfield, 1972a), Loeb Classical Library. William Heinemann Ltd, London.

Anderson, M. D. (1938) *Animal Carvings in British Churches*. London, Cambridge at the University Press.

Anderson, M. D. (1969) The iconography of British misericords. In G. L. Remnant (ed.) *A Catalogue of Misericords in Great Britain*, xxiii–xl. Oxford, Clarendon Press.

Balme, D. M. (1991) *Aristotle. History of Animals Books VII–X*. London, Harvard University Press.

Barber, R. (1993) *Bestiary.* Woodbridge, Boydell Press.

Baratay, E. and Hardouin-Fugier (2002) *Zoo: A History of Zoological Gardens in the West.* Reaktion Books.

Bartosiewicz, L. (1996) Camels in Antiquity: The Hungarian connection. *Antiquity* 70, 447–53.

Bartrum, G. (2002, 2003 Reprint) *Albrecht Durer and his Legacy. The Graphic Work of a Renaissance Artist.* The British Museum Press, London.

Baxter, R. (1998) *Bestiaries And Their Users in The Middle Ages.* Stroud, Sutton Publishing, in association with the Courtauld Institute.

Benton, J. R. (1992) *The Medieval Menagerie: Animals in the Art of the Middle Ages.* New York, Abbeville Press.

Block, E. C. (2003) *Corpus of Medieval Misericords in France XIII–XVI Century.* Turnhout, Brepolis.

Block, E. C. (2004) *Corpus of Medieval Misericords. Iberia (Portugal Spain) XIII–XVI Century.* Turnhout, Brepolis.

Bond, F. (1910) *Wood Carvings in English Churches. I – Misericords.* London, Henry Frowde.

Bovey, A. (2002) *Monsters and Grotesques in Medieval Manuscripts.* The British Library.

Brown, C. (2000) Bestiary lessons on pride and lust. In D. Hassig, (ed.) *The Mark of The Beast.* London, Routledge.

Bunt, C. G. E. (1930) The lion and the unicorn. *Antiquity* 4, 425–37.

Buczacki, S. (2002) *Fauna Britannica.* London, Hamlyn.

Burnie, D. (2001) *Animal.* London, Doring Kindersley.

Cirlot, J. E. (1962) *A Dictionary of Symbols,* Routledge and Kegan Paul, London.

Cohen, E. (1994) Animals in medieval perceptions. The image of the ubiquitous other. In, A. Manning and J. Serpell (eds.) *Animals and Human Society. Changing Perspectives,* 59–80. London, Routledge.

Clark, A. (1975) *Beasts and Bawdy.* London, J M Dent and Sons Ltd.

Clark, W. B. and McMunn, M. T. (1989) *Beasts and Birds of the Middle Ages: The Bestiary and Its Legacy.* University of Pennsylvania Press, Philadelphia.

Clarke, T. H. (1973) The iconography of the rhinoceros from Durer to Stubbs, part I: Durer's Ganda. *Connoisseur* 184 (739), 2–13.

Clarke, T. H. (1974) The iconography of the rhinoceros, part II: The Leyden Rhinoceros. *Connoisseur* 185 (744), 113–22.

Clarke, T. H. (1976) The rhinoceros in European ceramics. *Keramik-Freunde der Schweiz Mitteilungsblatt* 89 (November), 3–20.

Clarke, T. H. (1986) *Rhinoceros From Durer to Stubbs 1515–1799.* New York, Sothebys.

Collins, A. H. (1913) *Symbolism of Animals and Birds Represented in English Church Architecture.* London, Sir Isaac Pitman and Sons, Ltd.

Cronin, G. J. (1941) The bestiary and the medieval mind. *Modern Language Quarterly,* 191–98.

Derrick, F. (1935) *Tales Told in Church Stones. Symbolism and Legend in Medieval Architecture and Handicrafts.* London, The Lutterworth Press.

Dodgson, C. (1938) *The Story of Durers Ganda. The Romance of Fine Prints.* Kansas City, A. Fowler.

Druce, G. C. (1919) The elephant in medieval legend and art. *Archaeological Journal* 76, 1–73.

Evans, E. P. (1896) *Animal Symbolism in Ecclesiastical Architecture.* London, William Heinemann.

Fontana, D. (1993) *The Secret Language of Symbols. A Visual Key to Symbols and their Meaning.* Pavilion Books Limited, London.

George, W. and B. Yapp (1991) *The Naming of the Beasts: Natural History in the Medieval Bestiary.* London, Duckworth.

Gotfredsen, L. (1999) *The Unicorn.* The Harvill Press, London.

Gowers, W. S. (1950) The Classical rhinoceros. *Antiquity* XXIV, 61–71.

Gowers, W. S. (1952) Early rhinoceros in Europe. *Country Life* III (I February), 288–9.

Gravestock, P. (1999) Did imaginary animals exist? In D. Hassig (ed.) *The Mark of the Beast.* New York And London, Routledge.

Grössinger, C. (1997) *The World Upside Down: English Misericords.* London, Harvey Miller.

Grundy, T. (1997) *The Misericord Carvings in Durham Cathedral.* Carlisle, Cumbria, The Studio.

Gunnthorsdottir, A. (2001) Physical attractiveness of an animal species as a decision factor for its preservation. *Anthrozoos* 14, 204–215.

Handoo, J. (1990) Cultural attitudes to birds and animals in folklore. In R. Willis (ed.), *Signifying Animals: Human Meaning in the Natural World*, 37–41. London, Unwin Hyman.

Hahn, D. (2003) *The Tower Menagerie. Behind the Amazing True Story of the Royal Collection of Wild and Ferocious Beasts.* Simon and Schuster UK Ltd.

Hassig, D. (1999) Sex in the bestiaries. In D. Hassig (ed.) *The Mark of the Beast.* New York and London, Routledge.

Henderson, A. C. (1982) Medieval beasts and modern cages: the making of meaning in fables and bestiaries. *Publications of the Modern Language Association of America* 97, 40–49.

Hicks, C. (1993) *Animals in Early Medieval Art.* Edinburgh, Edinburgh University Press.

Jones, M (1991) Folklore motifs in late medieval art III: erotic animal imagery. *Folklore* 102, 2.

Jones, M. (2002) *The Secret Middle Ages. Discovering the Real Medieval World.* Stroud, Sutton Publishing.

Klingender, F. D. (1971) *Animals in Art and Thought to the End of the Middle Ages.* London, Routledge and Kegan Paul.

Kraus, D. and H. Kraus (1976) *The Hidden World Of Misericords.* London, Michael Joseph.

Laird, M. (1986) *English Misericords.* London, John Murray (Publishers) Ltd.

Laufer, B. (1928) *The Giraffe in History and Art. Field Museum of Natural History.* Chicago.

Lennox, J. G. (2001) *Aristotle. On the Parts of Animals I–IV.* Oxford, Clarendon Press.

Lum, P. (1952) *Fabulous Beasts.* Thames and Hudson. London.

Masry, A. H. (1978) Camels at Persepolis. *Antiquity* 52, 228–231.

McCulloch, F. (1962) *Medieval Latin and French Bestiaries.* University of North Carolina Press.

Mellinkof, R. (2004) *Averting Demons. The Protective Power of Medieval Visual Motifs and Themes.* Los Angeles, Ruth Mellinkof Publications.

Mermier, G. R., (ed, 1992) *A Medieval Book of Beasts Pierre de Beauvais' Bestiary.* Lewiston/ Queenston/Lampeter, The Edwin Mellen Press.

Muñiz, A. M., J. A. Riquelme, *et al.* (1995) Dromedaries in Antiquity: Iberia and beyond. *Antiquity* 69, 368–75.

Payne, A. (1990) *Medieval Beasts.* London, The British Library.

Peck, A. (1965) *Aristotle. History of Animals. Books I–III.* London, Harvard University Press.

Peck, A. (1970) *Aristotle. History of Animals. Books IV–VI.* London, Harvard University Press.

Phipson, E. (1896) *Choir Stalls and their Carvings.* London, Batsford.

Pliny, *Natural History.* (ten books in three volumes with an english translations by H. Rackham (I–V and X), W. H. S. Jones (VI–VIII), D. E. Eichholz (X). Loeb Classical Library. William Heinemann Ltd, London.

Remnant, G. L. (1969, Reprint 1998) *A Catalogue of Misericords in Great Britain.* Oxford, Clarendon Press.

Ripinsky, M. M. (1975) The camel in ancient Arabia. *Antiquity* 46, 295–8.

Rookmaaker, L. C. (1973). Captive rhinoceroses in Europe from 1500 until 1810. *Bijdragen tot de Dierkunde* 43(1), 39–63.

Rookmaaker, L. C. (1983) *Bibliography of the Rhinoceros: An analysis of the Literature on the*

Recent Rhinoceros in Culture, History and Biology. A A Balkema, Rotterdam.

Salisbury, J. E. (1994) *The Beast Within: Animals in the Middle Ages.* New York, Routledge.

Salisbury, J. E. (1996) Human animals of medieval fables. In N. C. Flores (ed.) *Animals in The Middle Ages*, 49–65. London, Routledge.

Salley, V. (2003) *Nature's Artist. Plants and Animals by Albrecht Dürer.* Prestel. London.

Scheller, R. W. (1995) *Exemplum. Model-Book Drawings and the Practice of Artistic Transmission in the Middle Ages (ca. 900–ca. 1470),* Amsterdam, Amsterdam University Press.

Scholfield, A. F., (ed, 1972b) *Aelian. On the Characteristics of Animals.* London, William Heinemann Ltd.

South, M. (ed, 1981) *Topsell's Histories of Beasts.* Chicago, Nelson-Hall.

Telesko, W. (2001) *The Wisdom of Nature. The Healing Powers and Symbolism of Plants and Animals in the Middle Ages.* London, Prestel.

Toynbee, J. M. C. (1996) *Animals in Roman Life and Art.* Baltimore and London, The John Hopkins University Press.

Tracy, C. (1987) *English Gothic Choir-Stalls, 1200–1400.* Woodbridge, Suffok, The Boydell Press.

Tracy, C. (1990) *English Gothic Choir-Stalls, 1400–1500.* Woodbridge, Suffolk, The Boydell Press.

Wells, S. J. F. S. (2005a, in press) Carved for consumption: birds in English medieval misericordia, In G. Grupe and J. Peters, (eds.) *Documenta Archaeobiologiae, Yearbook of the State Collection of Anthropology and Palaeoanatomy, München, Germany*; Rahden/Westf, Verlag Marie Leidorf.

Wells, S. J. F. S. (2005b, in press) Flying low down under: winged mammals, fowl and bird representations in medieval England. In *The Profane Arts of the Middle Ages,* Brepolis 9.

Werness, H. (2004) *The Continuum Encyclopedia of Animal Symbolism in Art.* London, Continuum International Publishing Group Ltd.

White, T. H. (1984) *The Book of Beasts.* New York, Dover.

Wildridge, T. T. (1898) *Animals of the Church. In Wood, Stone and Bronze.* Loughborough, Heart of Albion Press.

Wood, J. and C. Curry, A. (1999) *Wooden Images: Misericords and Medieval England.* London, Associated University Presses.

Zarins, J. (1978) The camel in ancient Arabia: a further note. *Antiquity* 52, 44–6.

Chapter 7

The Beast, the Book and the Belt: an Introduction to the Study of Girdle or Belt Books from the Medieval Period

Jim Bloxam

Introduction

The book is at the centre of this paper's title, and the study of the book as a physical object is, likewise, central throughout. This paper introduces the examination and documentation of girdle or belt books, from the medieval period. Such a study offers an opportunity to make a significant addition to the expanding field of the archaeology of the book, as previous studies of the girdle book are patchy and leave many questions unanswered. Indeed, the study of book structures is a relatively new science as, until comparatively recently, bookbinding studies have focused on the outward appearance of the book, concentrating on such elements as the decoration of the covers. These studies have attempted to identify where and by whom the bindings might have been made, but by ignoring the structural aspects of the book, an important source of potential provenance information has been missed. More recently, there has been a serious attempt to focus on the structural elements of the very few medieval bookbindings which survive, but this work has not yet been extended to girdle books. However, in his studies on the structure of early codex bookbindings, J. A. Szirmai has summarised and commented on the literature of earlier girdle book studies. (Szirmai 1999, 236–239). Moreover, Szirmai has published a specific study on the girdle book of the Museum Meermanno-Westreenianum (Szirmai 1988). In the aforementioned study Szirmai concludes his discussion with the following comment:

> … a thorough study summary [of girdle books] is still wanting, and apparently not even all the existing girdle books have been studied in sufficient detail or even recorded… (Szirmai 1988, 34)

The physical book is, of course, worthy of study for its own sake and yet it is part of a bigger historical picture which includes cultural, social and economic issues. Indeed, one historical approach is to start with the study of objects; to examine them, comprehend them and even reconstruct them. During such a process one may begin to enquire as to the maker's intention. One is attracted to Michael Baxandall's (1985) challenging intentionalist approach to art history; his preferred approach is to treat an object as a solution to a problem. What is the maker's charge and brief, his cultural circumstances and finally his solution?

One may begin to understand the physical construction of the book by conducting a rigorous study of the exploitation, by the medieval bookbinder, of both parchment and alum-tawed skin. Furthermore, this paper will focus on one specific book to illustrate what is essentially a report of research in progress. The book is Cambridge University Library, Additional Manuscript 2601, Terrarium Cantabrigiae, or Cambridge Terrier; dated at around 1360 (see fig. 7.1).

The Cambridge Terrier; its context and content

The Cambridge Terrier lists all the arable land in the Cambridge West Fields; field by field, furlong by furlong, giving the strips in sequence. Throughout it gives the tithe owner for each strip. The purpose of those who made the original survey may well have been mainly to record the tithing. The book, which would appear to have come into the possession of Corpus Christi College at about the end of the fourteenth-century, perhaps to replace documents destroyed in the Peasants Revolt of 1381, was certainly still with the college two centuries later. However, it appears on the open market in the nineteenth-century and Henry Bradshaw, the then

Fig. 7.1. The Cambridge Terrier, Cambridge University Library (CUL), Add 2601 – closed book, with tail uppermost.

Cambridge University Librarian, bought it in 1878. It is now part of the Additional Manuscript collection at Cambridge University Library (Hall and Ravensdale 1976, 6).

The Cambridge Terrier; its major components of parchment and alum-tawed skin

The Cambridge Terrier has a parchment text-block, probably sheepskin. Parchment, by the late medieval period, had become a well established medium prepared for use as a writing support. It covers all animal species but those most used were sheep, goat and calf, the latter being also known as vellum. The skin has three fundamental layers: the epidermis, the dermis and the hypodermis. During the parchment making process both the epidermis and the hypodermis are removed and only the dermis remains. The dermis is formed from two layers: the papillary layer and the reticular layer, or corium, which is composed of collagen fibres interwoven among themselves (Reed, 1972, 19–18). In the manufacture of parchment the skin is limed and unhaired by scraping the skin with a blunt knife. It is then dried under tension. Whilst the drying process is taking place more lime is applied to facilitate the removal of moisture and grease.

Finally the parchment is finished, whilst still in its taut condition: the surface is smoothed with a semi-circular or semi-lunar, knife and rubbed with pumice.

In order to understand the availability of animal skins in England for the secondary trade of parchment making, Hadgraft considers the nature of English farming from the twelfth-century to the fifteenth-century. He notes that as well as the fact that livestock were held in small numbers, which were largely the responsibility of the villein, their were also the huge flocks of sheep belonging to wealthy landlords such as the King, the Barons, Lords and others. The Monasteries also owned large estates: the Benedictines of Ely had 13,000 sheep in 1086, as recorded in the Domesday Book. By the twelfth-century there was an increase in the availability of animal skin as a result of the large and lucrative markets for English wool. The chief weaving towns of Lincoln, Beverley, Stamford, Northampton, Leicester, York, Oxford, Winchester and London demanded wool, as did the major continental centres in Flanders and Brabant (Hadgraft 1997, 117–118). Furthermore, the Cistercians developed their potential in the natural sheep pastures they acquired. For example, the white monks of Meaux had 11,000 sheep. However, Cistercian ascendancy did not last into the fourteenth-century: the Benedictines achieved such high numbers of sheep that by 1320, at Winchester Cathedral Priory the flock was in excess of 20,000 and at Christ Church, Canterbury, the flock there in the early fourteenth-century was around 14,000 (Butler 1987, 80–93).

Lander underlines the fact that the growth and development of the wool trade continued through the fourteenth-century and into the fifteenth-century. Wool prices remained high and landowners such as the Berkeley's, the Howards, the Hungerfords, the Stonors, Sir John Fastolf, and the Abbots of Gloucester, Dorchester, Oseney, Winchcombe and many others all departed from arable farming in favour of sheep farming (Lander 1974, 35–36). Butler notes that farm building increased dramatically in the medieval period: the great medieval barns would have played an important role in maintaining such large flocks (Butler 1987, 91).

Hadgraft concludes:

> An understanding of the scale of the wool trade allows us to appreciate a number of factors concerning the production and use of parchment in the Middle Ages. There were many fine young animal skins available throughout the medieval period especially during the latter part of the Middle Ages as flock sizes grew. Therefore, when the market for books increased exponentially, a large stock of skin from which to select raw material was available to the lay craftsman who had supplanted the monastic scribe. This enabled the craftsman more easily to offer grades of parchment related to the grade of manuscript – according to commission by patron, subject and so on. The lay craftsman had far less need to care about the quality of materials once a larger market gave rise to a far wider range of texts at differing levels of prestige. That is not to say that cheaper manuscripts were not produced earlier in a monastic setting, but it does suggest that the scale of production led to a far greater flexibility in the use of inferior skins (Hadgraft 1997, 120).

The identification of skin type is something one cannot always be sure of when employing simple visual techniques. Whilst it is usually possible to identify species type on a new skin, those that have survived over hundreds of years are less easy to decipher. However, it is possible to study some factors which aid the identification of animal species, such as the inclination of hairs in relation to skin surfaces and also the depth of the papillary layer in relation to the entire skin thickness. A microscopic examination of the revealed hair follicles can sometimes provide evidence of skin type, as sheep hair emerges at 90 degrees to the skin surface, whereas goat hair emerges at an angle to the skin surface of around 45 degrees. Furthermore, it is possible to pass cold light through the thickness of the skin and observe not only the hair follicle arrangement, or grain pattern, but also the differing types of patterns in different species. Once the hairs have been removed in the parchment making process the individual follicles have an appearance similar to that of empty cones. Goat, sheep, calf and pig all have very different appearances (Federici *et al.* 1996). However, whilst this technique may be helpful there remains the problem of the extent of stretching in the making of parchment, which may distort the direction and angle of hairs and follicles. An examination of the parchment of the Cambridge Terrier employing the afore-mentioned technique proved to be inconclusive.

The latest research into skin identification using DNA analysis is in its infancy. The research of Caroline Checkley-Scott utilising DNA testing is, as yet, unpublished. Spencer and Howe's published paper, recommending appropriate experimental designs for ancient-DNA studies, and a statistical analysis, highlights well the challenge of gaining a suitable sample size and the risk of contamination of individual samples (Spencer and Howe 2004).

It is not unreasonable to assert that the Cambridge Terrier is written on sheep skin rather than calf given that calf usually produced superior parchment for more prestigious manuscripts, such as Bibles and Antiphonals. Gullick has discovered in the Beaulieu Abbey Accounts of the mid-thirteenth-century that Grade 1 calf parchment cost 2s 6d per dozen and Grade 4 calf parchment cost 1s 4d, whereas Grade 1 sheep parchment was 1s per dozen and Grade 4 was 3d per dozen (Gullick 1991, 145–158). Furthermore, Hadgraft (1997, 130) records in his survey of fifteenth-century books that over 95% of secular manuscripts were written on sheepskin parchment. The Cambridge Terrier fits into this picture, where secular activities were judged worthy of only sheep parchment.

The Cambridge Terrier, when closed, is 204mm high, 143mm wide and 25mm thick. It has a primary cover of reversed alum-tawed skin and a secondary cover which extends a further 120mm, also made from alum-tawed skin, hairside out and possible goatskin (see fig. 7.2). Alum-tawed skin is well suited to the structural demands of bookbinding. It does not deteriorate as quickly as tanned skin and has survived acting as a sewing support and covering material on books for hundreds of years. It is usually much stronger than tanned skin. Tawing is an ancient process of treating skin with

Fig. 7.2. The Cambridge Terrier, CUL, Add 2601 – open book, showing parchment text block and extended secondary cover.

aluminum salts and usually other materials, such as egg yolk, flour and salt. A skin may be tawed by simply immersing it in an aqueous solution of potash alum at a temperature of between 20 to 30 degrees Celsius. After treatment the skin is usually air-dried (Roberts and Etherington 1982, 260–261). Alum-tawed skins were produced using sheep goat, calf and also pigskin. Furthermore, Christopher Clarkson suggests the possibility of the use of deer (Clarkson 1993, 194).

Hadgraft asserts that alum-tawed was almost certainly made in monasteries in the twelfth-century and earlier, as was parchment and that the use of tawed-skin declines significantly as the printed book gradually eroded the demand for parchment. However, he emphasises that there is no historical or archaeological evidence to prove that tawed skin was made by parchment makers (Hadgraft 1997, 232). Nevertheless, the fact that the use of tawed skin falls away in parallel with the decline in the use of parchment would seem to support the idea that the two materials were to some extent linked in production. Despite the decline in the use of both materials, both parchment and alum-tawed survived at a reduced level. However, Thomas records that tawyers certainly existed in their own right in the middle ages, appearing in books of trade (Thomas 1983, 1–8).

Identifying skin type is not always straightforward: whilst surviving in terms of strength it is inevitable that skin surfaces have become worn, damaged and dirty, thus preventing simple visual analysis. The outermost cover of the Cambridge Terrier would appear to be goat. However, Hall and Ravensdale suggest sheep (Hall and Ravensdale 1976, 6).

Parchment and alum-tawed skins are, of course, commonly used in book production in the medieval period. Furthermore, the addition of a secondary cover, or chemise, is not unusual in this period. However, the secondary cover of the Cambridge Terrier is considerably extended from the tail of the book. It is, therefore, not an unreasonable assertion, given the nature of its content, that this book is a girdle or belt book. To substantiate this claim one will elucidate the study of the Cambridge Terrier, beginning with the context of girdle books and the Medieval girdle book project.

Girdle books

The girdle or belt book is a particular form of late medieval bookbinding, apparently very popular given the hundreds of representations of such books in the visual arts (see figs. 7.3, 7.4 and 7.5). The term belt or girdle book describes a book, which has a cover that extends beyond the limits of the book itself, and could either be fixed to the girdle or held in the hand. Hanging upside down, the book could then be swung up and read without being detached from the belt or girdle. There are only twenty-three known or cited girdle books which survive. They have been identified and listed by Bruckner (Bruckner 1995). However, the Cambridge Terrier and another Cambridge manuscript from Jesus College, Cambridge, Jesus Ms Q. G. 30, both exhibit characteristics which suggest that they were meant to be carried in the aforementioned fashion. The Cambridge Terrier is the stronger candidate whilst Jesus Ms Q. G. 30 has considerable losses which pose more questions than give answers. Jesus Ms Q. G. 30 is

Fig. 7.4. Lucas van Leyden, Temptation of Saint Anthony, *circa 1509.*

Fig. 7.5. Lucas van Leyden, Temptation of Saint Anthony, *circa 1509 (detail – Saint Anthony reading from the girdle book whilst it is still attached to his belt).*

Fig. 7.3. *Martin Schonguar,* Saint Anthony, *circa 1470.*

a small devotional book (105mm × 85mm × 55mm) from the fifteenth-century: it contains prayers, and psalms. It was first examined by Dr. Nicholas Hadgraft in his PhD thesis 'English Fifteenth Century Book Structures' (Hadgraft 1997, 28–84), where he describes certain aspects of its structure. However, the possibility of it being a girdle book did not emerge until preparation for a summer school, by the author and Dr. Hadgraft. The course entitled 'Girdles, Books, and Prayers' formed part of the 'Montefiascone Conservation Project', 2003 (www.monteproject.com). The course tutors noted that it was clearly evident that the secondary cover had once been larger, before it had been crudely cut down, so that it could stand vertically on the bookshelf. The size of the little prayer book also recommended it as a candidate for portable use. Moreover, the clasping device would have held the secondary cover around the text-block thus ensuring a compact and secure entity, well protected whilst it was carried around on the belt. Jesus Ms Q. G. 30 is an example of what might be described as a 'possible girdle book': closer examination of this and other candidates is necessary.

Neither Jesus Ms Q. G. 30 or the Cambridge Terrier are in Bruckner's list of twenty-three. Most of 'Bruckner's' twenty-three girdle books contain religious texts, however four are legal texts. Eleven are parchment manuscripts, seven are paper manuscripts and five are printed works. Nineteen of the girdle books originate in the fifteenth-century and the remainder from the sixteenth-century.

The Medieval Girdle Book Project

The Medieval Girdle Book Project is a research project involving the author and Margit Smith, Head of Cataloguing and Preservation at Copley Library, University of San Diego. The aim of the research is to provide clear and full descriptions of the bindings of all twenty-three girdle books. The study will include the recording of bibliographical details, textual origins, place of writing or printing, place of binding and early provenance notes. The make-up of the text-block will be considered, concerning its material, size and collation. Details will be recorded regarding endleaf and endleaf construction.The study will examine the sewing of the text-block in terms of the supports, materials, lacing types and the layout and disposition of the sewing supports in relation to the text-block height. Thread will be examined in terms of material, colour, size and dimension. The treatment of the edges of the text-block will be considered in terms of decoration, colouring, polishing and titling. Examination of the spine and its treatment will reveal shape, lining and the use of adhesives. Consideration will be given to endband construction and its lacing. The study will look at the boards, types of covering skin and adhesives employed. Allied to the information on the primary covering methods are the considerations to the make up, if present, of the secondary cover or chemise. The study will also include an examination of the use of metal fittings, chains, clasps, catchpins, markers and registers. Finally any other characteristic of the binding, which is not covered by the above categories, will be recorded. In short, all aspects of the books' structure will be examined. Furthermore, there will be an attempt to consider the books in relation to one another and draw some conclusions. Diagrams and photographs will support the written descriptions. There are more potential girdle books to be discovered: the Cambridge Terrier and Jesus Ms Q. G. 30 bear witness to this assertion. The proposed documentation supported by sound argument and good illustrations will help and inspire others to look again at their collections and discover or rediscover more girdle books or potential girdle books, to enable more research into this field. However, even with the imposition of a rigorous methodology and a painstaking attempt to establish an empathetic relationship with the bookbinder one remains, at this stage, tentative and open to criticism. One may not yet be able to explain girdle books, rather one may make informed comments about girdle books.

The Cambridge Terrier – text-block, sewing and boards

Could the Cambridge Terrier be a girdle book? Hall and Ravensdale state that it was 'a document that was expected to be carried round and handled a good deal' (Hall and Ravensdale 1976, 6). Furthermore, Dr. Elizabeth Leedham-Green, the archivist at Corpus Christi College, Cambridge affirms that it was built for use in the field. However, the Cambridge Terrier probably remained unbound until almost a century after it was written. Indeed, at some point later in the middle ages, probably the mid to late fifteenth-century, two sets of endleaves were added to the front and back of the original text. These consist each of four parchment leaves approximately twice the size of the main text block leaves, trimmed and folded to make four bifolia for the endleaves. They come from a fifteenth century '*Leganda Sanctorum*' (see fig. 7.6). The reuse of manuscript material is extremely common in the medieval period and beyond: studies into the exploitation of such fragments include N. Ker's (1954) *Fragments of medieval manuscripts used as pastedowns in Oxford bindings with a survey of Oxford binding*

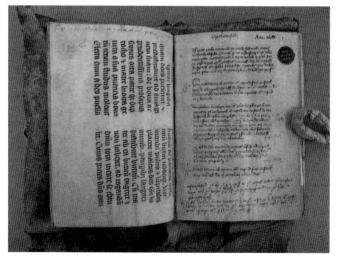

Fig. 7.6. The Cambridge Terrier, CUL, Add 2601 – endleaves and fol. 1.

　　　　　　　　　　　　　　　Jim Bloxam

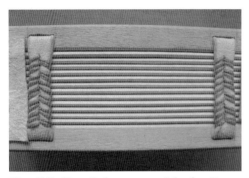

Fig. 7.7. Detail from a model of a Romanesque binding structure (constructed by the author), showing sewing through and around split-tawed thongs which enter square sectioned, tunneled boards.

Fig. 7.8. Detail from a model of a Romanesque binding structure (constructed by the author), showing the route of the laced-in support. Also visible is the endband which follows a similar route.

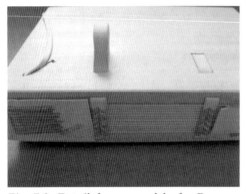

Fig. 7.9. Detail from a model of a Romanesque binding structure (constructed by the author), showing the route of the laced-in support at various stages, the endband and the tab liners.

c. 1515–1620. According to Hall and Ravensdale the notes written on the endleaves from the Cambridge Terrier are in hands dating from late fifteenth-century to mid sixteenth-century and that it was during this time that the text block was bound (Hall and Ravensdale 1976, 6).

The folios and the endleaves are sewn with linen thread onto four, evenly spaced, slit thongs of alum-tawed skin, which are laced into oak boards. This sewing material and indeed the technique are, by the fifteenth-century, well established: the earliest surviving significant group of bindings, from the twelfth-century, exhibits these sewing characteristics. The great Romanesque bindings of Bury, first examined by Graham Pollard (1962) are excellent examples of what might be argued as the most structurally sound bookbindings in the western tradition. Romanesque books have parchment leaves sewn onto two, sometimes three, slit alum-tawed supports which are attached to square sectioned oak boards by lacing through tunnels in the spine edge of the board. The boards have the effect of holding the parchment leaves firmly under light pressure (see figs. 7.7–7.9). However, by the fifteenth-century boards have become thinner, at least at the edge of the board. Boards were shaped to give a chamfered or cushioned appearance. Such a change in the appearance of book boards results from the necessity, in part, to cope with smaller text blocks sewn onto thinner supports (see fig. 7.11). Consequently the supports are laced

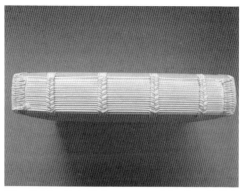

Fig. 7.10. Detail from a model of a Gothic binding structure (constructed by the author), sewn on four supports, which are thinner than in the Romanesque structure.

Fig. 7.11. Detail from a model of a Gothic binding structure (constructed by the author), the supports are laced-on in the 'over the board' style.

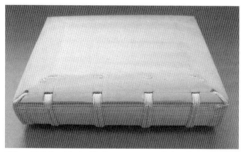

Fig. 7.12. Detail from a model of a Gothic binding structure (constructed by the author), detail shows the sewing supports and endbands laced into the boards. The boards are chamfered, in this case, from 10mm down to 4mm.

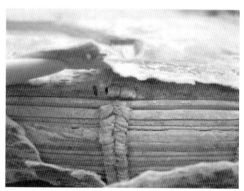

Fig. 7.13. Peterhouse Ms 144, a fifteenth-century binding with tunneled lacing (partially damaged).

over the board and not through tunnels, as were their Romanesque precursors. The Cambridge Terrier has its sewing supports laced on in this over-the-board style. This is typical of most fifteenth-century books: the text-block supports travel over the outer face of the board into a knifed or chiseled channel and into a drilled hole and continue on the inner surface of the board into another channeled recess and through a further hole where they finally pegged with either wood or alum-tawed stays (see figs. 7.11 and 7.12). However, the technique of tunneling was not completely discarded by the fifteenth-century, witness Peterhouse Ms 144 (see figs. 7.13–7.15). This manuscript appears to be from another era and those who have seen it are challenged by its existence as it refuses to fit into a seamless, linear approach to history. Nicholas Hadgraft records that:

Fig. 7.14. Peterhouse Ms 144, detail of a support emerging from the tunnel to the board surface.

Fig. 7.15. Peterhouse Ms 144, close-up detail of a support emerging from the tunnel to the board surface.

Peterhouse Ms 144 contains texts of the late fourteenth and early fifteenth centuries *(Ps. Chrysostomi opus imperfectum. Homiliae Chrystomi).* The book is sewn on six stations [supports], and the boards are quite steeply cushioned on all edges, although the shaping on the spine edge is somewhat less severe. The binding appears to be undisturbed and the primary cover, though a little damaged with a partially detached board, is original. The chemise [secondary cover], once present, has been lost. The upper board pastedown has been lifted and there can be no doubt about the nature of the lacing… The tawed slip [support] passes through a tunnel with a thin bridge in the edge of the board in a channel 30mm long on the outer board-face before passing back through the board and along an inner board-face channel which extends for 25mm before being terminated with a wedge of oak in the narrow oblong chiseled hole. The boards have a center calliper of 12mm and are cushioned to an edge of 4mm, and thus display the typical Gothic appearance… [This book] does not prove anything other than that the technique [of tunneled lacing] had not been forgotten (Hadgraft 1997b, 120–121).

The Cambridge Terrier – a companion volume

The Cambridge Terrier has what might be termed a companion. A similar volume for the East Fields of Cambridge (C.C.C. XVII–4), still in possession of Corpus Christi College, provides a useful example to compare and contrast with the Cambridge Terrier. Hall and Ravensdale note many textual similarities in the two volumes and indeed in a third volume, also concerning the East Fields, which has been sewn and is in oak boards but appears to have remained uncovered (C.C.C. XVII–5). The bound Eastfield Terrier has similar binding characteristics to the Cambridge Terrier: it is very close in size to the Cambridge Terrier and, whilst having no secondary cover, its primary cover is of reversed alum-tawed skin, a la the Cambridge Terrier. One can observe the structural elements showing through the skin like a skeleton: the four alum-tawed supports are evenly spread along the spine and have been laced over the board in the aforementioned style (see fig. 7.16). However, with the Eastfield Terrier

Fig. 7.16. The Eastfield Terrier, Corpus Christi College, Cambridge (C.C.C) XVIII–4. Sewn on four supports, clearly visible through the primary cover of alum-tawed skin.

Fig. 7.17. The Eastfield Terrier, C.C.C XVIII–4. detail showing the convergent lacing style, and the primary covering skin cut to allow for 'turn-in'.

the lacing path is convergent and not straight as it is in the Cambridge Terrier: there are four entry holes through which the alum-tawed supports are first laced and after they emerge on the inside surface of the board they sit into angled channels cut into the wood. The then paired supports converge to share an exit hole to the outer face of the board and they are finally secured with wooden pegs (see fig. 7.17).

The Cambridge Terrier – endbands, primary covering

One would agree with their assertion that the Cambridge Terrier was bound in the fifteenth-century but not with Hall and Ravensdale's later comments on the binding, when they propose that the book had a resewing in the eighteenth-century, a new endband, the secondary cover, alum-tawed strap, brass catch and pin (Hall and Ravensdale 1976, 6). Although the endleaves are indeed later than the text, there is no evidence to suggest that the sewing has been interfered with. Hall and Ravensdale have misunderstood a fascinating detail at the head and tail of the book, which they assign to the wrongly claimed resewing process. The primary covering skin has been cut at the head and tail, not to facilitate the sewing of an endband, as Hall and Ravensdale suggest, but to allow it to be turned in on the board side of the endband during the covering process. Such a technique is common and indeed necessary when endbands are laced into the boards, which they invariably were in this period. One need look no further than the aforementioned Eastfield Terrier for an example of this

Fig. 7.18. The Eastfield Terrier, C.C.C XVIII–4. detail of the secondary end-band.

Fig. 7.19. The Cambridge Terrier, CUL, Add 2601 – detail of the endband and the primary covering skin.

feature (see fig. 7.17). Furthermore, the binder would cut the covering skin at the head and tail, allowing it to fold over the endbands. Conventionally, a secondary endband would be sewn around the endband and through the covering skin to complete the covering process, witness again the Eastfield Terrier (see fig. 7.18). However, in the case of The Cambridge Terrier, the primary cover has been left unsewn (see fig. 7.19). Such an omission, if one may describe it as such, is not unique: the author has seen this feature on the girdle book from the Spencer Collection in the New York Public Library, Spencer Ms 39. In both the Cambridge Terrier and with Spencer Ms 39 such an approach leads one to conclude that the primary and secondary coverings were carried out by the same binder. Despite Szirmai's suggestion that the construction of Spencer Ms 39 may allow for the possibility that it received its secondary cover sometime after its original binding and thus became a girdle book at a later date (Szirmai 1999, 237). Indeed, it is feasible that any appropriately sized book could be given a secondary cover, however, one is not convinced in this case or indeed in the case of the Cambridge Terrier. If the secondary cover was an afterthought, or a later addition, then the primary cover would surely have had a secondary endband: one may assert that because he was satisfied that the structure was complete, with its secondary cover extending at both head and tail, the binder left the endband covered but without a secondary endband.

Cambridge Terrier – the secondary cover and metal fittings

So, from seemingly having no binding at all, at its inception in the late fourteenth century, the parchment text block of the Cambridge Terrier has been given not one but two coverings of alum-tawed skin. The secondary cover extends at the head sufficiently to cover the edge of the text block at the head and a further 120mm at the tail. The secondary cover has envelope flaps which are sewn on and form an integral part of the

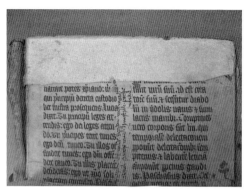

Fig. 7.20. *The Cambridge Terrier, CUL, Add 2601 – detail of the envelope flap.*

Fig. 7.21. *The Cambridge Terrier, CUL, Add 2601 – detail of the strap going through a series of slits.*

Fig. 7.22. *The Cambridge Terrier, CUL, Add 2601 – detail of strap, brass catch and pin.*

Fig. 7.23. *The Cambridge Terrier, CUL, Add 2601 – detail of brass pin on a brass mount.*

secondary cover (see fig. 7.20). The book has been eased into the resulting jacket and is held in securely by the envelope flaps. The extremely snug fit and the addition of the contemporary brass pin on a brass mount, fixed through the secondary cover on the back board, further suggests that the whole binding process is a complete entity. Attaching the secondary cover in this way means that it can extend in any direction and to the desired size. The sewing and the envelope flap survive on the backboard, whereas at the front the sewing threads are all but gone. However, the flap is still held adjacent to its original position by the strap, which goes through a series of slits in the secondary cover (see fig. 7.21). The secondary cover is not at all elegant. Unlike, for example, the aforementioned Spencer Ms 39, where it is pleated neatly as it leaves the text block area and extends to finish with a Turk's Head Knot. The reddish brown knot, combined with the once bright blue cover and bright yellow text block edges, would have looked stunning. The Cambridge Terrier has a much rougher, utilitarian appearance. However, its one concession to style is the strap and the brass catch and pin design (see figs. 7.22–7.24). The central strap is attached to the front board, in a fore-edge recess, by three brass nails. It passes through the edge of the envelope flap and through the secondary cover to the outside. Closure is achieved by the brass catch fitting over the brass pin. The metal fittings are quite intricate given the overall nature of the book. The strap is once again alum-tawed skin, but this time stained red and, when new, it would have been bright and bold. The red could possibly be produced from the insect kermes, although it was more likely achieved with Brazil wood or madder: the principles of the procedures used are outlined by Thompson (Thompson 1936, 116–117). Szirmai cites BL Sloane 345, dating from circa 1500 and published by Braekman (Braekman 1975, 173–181), wherein the staining procedures are described. The first known description of a bookbinder staining skin is as late as 1658. Dirk de Bray, when he was still an apprentice in the workshop of Passchier van Wesbusch, describes the staining of skin. Whilst his exposition on bookbinding is from well into the seventeenth-century, De Bray is describing techniques that had become well established in the trade:

> The red dye is boiled out of Brazil wood in water with a little potash to give it a slightly purple colour; you let it boil until it is dark enough – if no potash is added it becomes red – and colour… with this red dye. (De Bray 1658, LXXIII)

The extended secondary cover for the Cambridge Terrier has a sewn section which is possibly a repair and it finishes with a loose end. There is no finishing knot, as in Spencer Ms 39. Indeed, fifteen of the twenty-three aforementioned girdle books finish with a knot. Neither does the Cambridge Terrier have an

Fig. 7.24. The Cambridge Terrier, CUL, Add 2601 – detail of strap, catch and pin.

Fig. 7.25. The Cambridge Terrier, CUL, Add 2601 – detail of slits in secondary cover.

alternative belt attachment, namely a brass hook, witness the girdle book of the Museum Meermanno Westreenianum, in The Hague (Szirmai 1988). The Cambridge Terrier's skirt has been folded over and has two slits cut through the several layers of skin to probably facilitate an attachment to the belt (see fig. 7.25). Whether this was always the intended method of belt attachment, or is a crude adaptation as part of a possible repair, is not clear. The skin appears to be somewhat stretched in the area of the slits which suggests that it underwent some straining, probably as a result of hanging from the belt.

The Cambridge Terrier – the antecedents

Whilst the girdle book is a fifteenth and sixteenth-century phenomenon the practice of using a primary and secondary cover is well established. Indeed most, if not all, of the aforementioned twelfth-century books have the added protection of a secondary cover. The Romanesque secondary cover, or chemise, whilst not extending as much as their girdle book descendants, usually covered at least the thickness of the text block. Furthermore, the use of straps secured by pins and catchplates made it possible to enclose the book securely and to ensure as much protection as possible (see figs. 7.26 and 7.27). Thus, the craftsmen who made the Gothic girdle books have developed the heavy jacket of the Romanesque chemise into a more flexible, longer skirted variant.

Conclusion

As the research into girdle books advances and develops the primary issues of their structural qualities and idiosyncrasies will prompt wider cultural and social concerns. Indeed, even now one is asking such questions as, why were these books made; who

 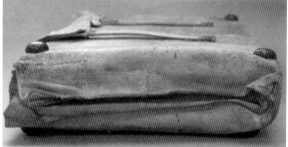

Fig. 7.26. Peterhouse Ms 13 – a large twelfth-century manuscript (470mm x 320mm).

Fig. 7.27. Peterhouse Ms 13 – detail of the secondary cover.

were they for; were they symbolic of status and did they carry other meanings? We may have a practical reason for the Cambridge Terrier to be a portable book. But why, at the other end of the spectrum, is St. Anthony, a saint from the third-century depicted in a sixteenth-century painting, carrying a girdle book? And why have they become known as belt or girdle books when most of the depictions in art have the owner carrying the book in his hand? One may, in time, be able to address such issues of status and symbol along with the practical and technical. However, at this stage in the proceedings the analysis is primarily on the structural components and, not least for the Cambridge Terrier, on the use of parchment and alum-tawed skin.

Acknowledgements

All images of CUL Add 2601 are reproduced by permission of the Syndics of Cambridge University Library. All images of Peterhouse Ms 13 and Peterhouse Ms 144 are reproduced by permission of the Master and Fellows of Peterhouse, Cambridge. All images of Corpus Christi College, Cambridge, The Eastfield Terrier, C.C.C XVIII–4 are reproduced by permission of the Master and Fellows of Corpus Christi College, Cambridge.

The author thanks the following people for their help, guidance and constructive criticism: Alan Farrant, Head of Conservation, Cambridge University Library (CUL); all my colleagues at CUL, especially Deborah Farndell for her help in understanding endband structures, in particular the secondary endband of C.C.C. XVII–4; Elizabeth Leedham-Green, Archivist of Corpus Christi College. Cheryl Porter, Course Director of the 'Montefiascone Project'. Margit Smith of the 'Medieval Girdle Book Project'. Special thanks to Rita.

I must especially acknowledge my friend and colleague, the late Dr. Nicholas Hadgraft. Nick is cited within this paper, but his influence is much greater than mere authorial acknowledgement. Nick first introduced me to book structures, in a meaningful way, over twenty years ago. His knowledge and understanding were matched by his enthusiasm and desire to share. Nick taught me to become a 'student of the book' and one strives to remember well and emulate his attitude of boldness and humility within such a learning process.

Bibliography

Baxandall, M. (1985) *Patterns of Intention: on the Historical Explanation of Pictures.* New Haven, Yale University Press.

Braekman, W. L. (1975) Medische en technische Middelnederlandse recepten [Medical and echnical Middle-Dutch recipes]. *Koninklijke Academie voor Nederlandse Taal-en Letterkunde (Gent),* Ser III, (40), 1–423.

Bray, D. de. (1658) *Kort onderwijs van het boeckenbinden? A Short Instruction in the Binding of Books* (facsimile reproduction edited by K. van der Horst and C. de Wolf, English translation by H.S. Lake), 1977, Amsterdam.

Bruckner, U. (1995) Beutelbuch-Originale. In R. Landwehrmeyer and H.-E. Teitge, (eds.) *Studien zum Buch- und Bibliothekswesen*, 9, 5–23.

Butler, L. Given-Wilson, C. (1987) *Medieval Monasteries of Great Britain*. London.

Clarkson, C. (1993) English monastic bookbinding in the twelfth century. In M. Maniaci and P. F. Munafo (eds.) *Ancient and Medieval Book Materials and Techniques* (Erice, 18–25 September 1992), vol 2, *Studi e Testi* 358, 181–200. Citta del Vaticano, Biblioteca Apostolica Vaticana.

Federici, C. di Majo, A. and Palma, M. (1996) The determination of animal species used in medieval parchment making. In J. L. Sharpe (ed.) *Roger Powell The Compleat Binder*. Brepols, Turnout.

Gullick, M. (1991) From parchmenter to scribe: some observations on the manufacture and preparation of medieval parchment based upon a review of literary evidence. *Pergament. Geschichte. Struktur. Restauruerung. Herstellung*. P. Ruck. Sigmaringen, Jan Thorbecke Verlag. 2: 480.

Hadgraft, N. (1997) *English Fifteenth Century Book Structures*. PhD Thesis, University College, London.

Hadgraft, N. (1997b) A glimpse at fifteenth-century book structures and the physical archaeology of the book. In G. Fellows-Jensen and P. Springborg (eds.) *Care and Conservation of Manuscripts*. Copenhagen.

Hall, C. P. and Ravensdale, J. R. (eds.) (1976) *The Westfields of Cambridge*. Cambridge.

Ker, N. R. (1954) *Fragments of Medieval Manuscripts Used as Pastedowns in Oxford Bindings with a Survey of Oxford Binding c. 1515–1620*. Oxford, Oxford Biblographical Society.

Lander, J. R. (1974) *Conflict and Stability in Fifteenth-Century England*. London.

Pollard, G. (1962) The construction of English twelfth-century bindings. *The Library*, Fifth Series, 11, 71–94.

Reed, R. (1972) *Ancient Skins, Parchments and Leathers*. London and New York, Seminar Press.

Roberts, M. T. and Etherington, D. (1982) *Bookbinding and the Conservation of Books: a Dictionary of Descriptive Terminology*. Washington, Library of Congress.

Spencer, M. and Howe, C. J. (2004). *Authenticity of Ancient-DNA Results: A Statistical Approach*. Electronically published June 15, 2004. *American Journal of Human Genetics,* 75, 240–250, 2004, © 2004 by The American Society of Human Genetics.

Szirmai, J. A. (1988) The girdle book of the Museum Meermanno-Westreenianum. *Quarendo*, 18, 17–34.

Szirmai, J. A. (1999) *The Archeology of Medieval Bookbinding*. Aldershot, England and Brookfield, Vermont, Ashgate Publishing.

Thomas, S. Clarkson, L. A. Thomson, R. (1983) *Leather Making in the Middle Ages*. Northampton.

Thompson, D. V. (1936) *The Materials and Techniques of Medieval Painting*. London, New York.

Chapter 8

The Shifting use of Animal Carcasses in Medieval and Post-Medieval London

Lisa Yeomans

Introduction

The supply and use of post-mortem products obtained from animal carcasses in the high and late medieval are compared to that in the post-medieval periods. The purpose of extending the discussion beyond the conference theme of the Middle Ages is to demonstrate a change in the supply of animal carcasses to urban craftsmen. Raw material distribution networks, location of workshops, scale of production and manufacturing methods can all influence how animal carcasses were used. Such factors were affected by practical issues such as supply but they were also influenced the organisation of work in the urban environment and the wider socio-economic climate. A considerable amount of historical research has focused on the economic developments between the medieval period and the modern day. It is therefore interesting to examine how the industries processing the carcasses of animals did or did not adapt as the regulated crafts were eventually replaced by an industrial and capitalist economy. These industries are of particular significance since the production of goods from animal carcasses remained essentially the same technologically throughout this period suggesting that external pressures were largely responsible for any changes in production strategies.

The results presented in this paper demonstrate how important the supply of raw materials was to the urban craftsmen in the medieval and post-medieval periods. Agricultural developments and enclosure of common land in the countryside had an impact on the animals that were available to the urban population. Supply between craftsmen was also a major influence as was the changing economic structure of late medieval and early post-medieval London.

Craft and industry

Comparing the cultural norms of medieval guild controlled production to the industrial factory based methods of manufacture that fully emerged during the 19th century gives an impression of the extent of organisational change in the processing of animal carcasses. Much of this development occurred between the late medieval period and 18th century, a time which marked a divide between two very different manufacturing strategies (c.f. Marshall 1929). In many industries the change was not just related to the organisation of the work, changing manufacturing processes allowing production on a larger and larger scale. Such technical developments must have fuelled the changes in the organisation of production but alone they could not have been responsible. The carcass processing industries in which the basic methods were not improved upon until the 19th century demonstrates this.

Medieval guilds were supposedly governed by strict regulations, recorded in numerous ordinances, aimed at protecting the interests of members who practiced similar trades. It is easy to assume that this role was the main function of the organisations because it formed the documented objective. The actual situation was probably somewhat different and a lack of strict coherence to the guild ordinances is often demonstrated by wills and court rolls showing the wide-range of employment that men, as well as women, undertook. The Statute of 1363, which stated that every merchant was to keep to one trade and every artificer but one mystery, was regularly not observed. Numerous documentary sources illustrate how individuals varied their employment through life or on a seasonal basis. Recently, a number of historians have argued that the power of the guilds in organising work in the towns was less effective than previously suggested (Rosser 1997). Nevertheless guild regulations, even if not always completely successful, did regulate industries to a certain extent. One aspect that would have been taken more seriously was preventing individual men or trades from controlling production. Therefore, tanners and butchers were often specifically targeted because they supplied many other craftsmen with raw materials and were potentially in a powerful position to monopolise distribution (Kowaleski 1990). The organisation of urban work tended to divide up the production process preventing its control. Different craftsmen were given the right to inspect goods, thus helping to ensure that consumers were not being deceived by poor standard work.

The spatial expansion of London and the increase in its population from the 16th century have often been cited as crucial factors in the declining power of the guilds, necessitating a change in the organisation of work. Such changes are clearly evident in both the archaeological evidence and historical sources which reflect the relocation of industries from medieval cities to more suburban areas. In London, for instance, no more than 40 men of the leather-trades were to be found in the City in 1619 whilst 3000 were said to inhabit the suburbs (Unwin 1963). Suburban growth and the rise of outwork had the effect of reducing the independence of the individual craftsman who could not always rely on the power of a guild to ensure fair access to raw materials and equal opportunities in the sale of produce. An investigation into three types of industrial craftsmen, the tanners, the leatherdressers (who treated mainly sheep and goat hides with oil or alum to produce a lighter leather) and the horners, show how the organisation of work altered as supply of raw materials and control of production were effected by the move of the industries away from the City.

The heavy (tanned) leather industry

In the late medieval period a greater demand for leather was generated by the proliferation of craftsmen using it as a raw material. This diversification of the leather trades led to increased efforts to regulate and inspect the tanners' goods. In response to the increased tension between manufacturers and consumers, tanners moved away from areas controlled by the urban authorities. Complaints about the pollution of streams by tanners encouraged decisions that led to the relocation of the trade as it was being forced out of the City (Sabine 1933). At the same time the reduced export market for hides effectively lowered the status of tanners. Cheaper land in the suburbs was an added incentive. The growth of small towns also allowed tanners to operate away from the major urban centres which had, in the medieval period, provided the main source of hides and therefore determined the location of leather production (Kowaleski 1990).

The development of regional specialisation during the 16th and 17th centuries bolstered the success of some tanners. In several provincial towns the increased status of tanners is apparent with one such craftsman becoming mayor of St Albans in 1554 (Saunders 1977). In late 16th century Leicester a tanner was appointed mayor on three separate occasions (Kowaleski 1990). This indicates the prosperity and level of power that men in this craft could attain although such cases were probably men engaged in trade rather than manufacture.

In London the tanners benefited from laxer control over their industry. Curriers (who were responsible for treating tanned leather with oils) and cordwainers (shoemakers) continued to exercise limited searches over the quality of leather but often tanners, who organised their own supplies of hides from butchers, tended to be less constrained by the activities of the guilds. Technologically the manufacturing process remained unchanged. This prevented a few individuals from saturating the market entirely because large quantities of leather took too much time and space to produce.

The light leather industry

Turning to light leather production, from the late 15th century the majority of the leatherdressers had moved out of the City of London into the suburbs. The leatherdressers craft was not as pungent as that of the tanner but their presence in the City still gradually decreased. Since these general craftsmen were no longer shopkeepers, (Unwin 1963) their need to pay high rents in order to be close to customers became less crucial. Leatherdressers had long been affiliated with the Company of Leathersellers but gradually the traders lost touch with the craftsmen and the growing gulf between the two is evident in the leatherdressers repeated petitions for a charter to allow them greater trading rights. The technical differences between the light and heavy leather trades meant that the former could produce larger quantities of goods. However, their activities were limited by the leathersellers supplying hides and taking the sale of their produce out of their hands (Unwin 1963).

As with the heavy leather industry the manufacturing processes involved in light leather production did not evolve throughout the 16th or 17th century. At the end of the 18th century there is evidence for a dramatic increase in the number of leatherdressers in the leather-producing parishes of Southwark in south London (fig.

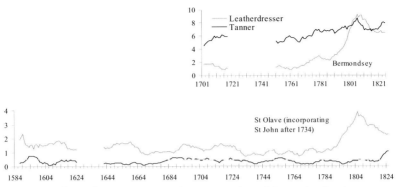

Fig. 8.1. Frequency of men (seven-year-moving average) working as leatherdressers and tanners in Bermondsey and St Olave (incorporating the parish of St John after 1734) based on the parish baptism registers.

8.1). This suggests that there was a significant development in the industry with the scale of production increasing. It may reflect a change in the organisation of the light leather industry as large operations of a factory type started to develop and the 'industrial revolution' took hold of the industry. A similar development did not occur in the tanning industry until the later part of the 19th century when the use of chromic acids drastically reduced the time needed to produce leather (Gomersall 2000). Comparison of faunal assemblages from earlier post-medieval leatherdressers' workshops across the country indicates a relatively standard way of processing skins. For example an assemblage dated 1450–1600 excavated in Leicester (Baxter 2004) was very similar to the bone from an early 18th century deposit in York (O'Connor 1984) and remains at many of the London sites indicate similar methods for processing the hides. When the industry developed into a large-scale operation, as in London at the end of the 18th century and early 19th century, the changing level of production would probably affect the way that bone waste was dealt with. If the hides were still brought to the site with the bones attached then large quantities of bone waste would have to be cleared more systematically. Many of the 19th century timber-lined pits excavated in Southwark appear contain minimal quantities of animal bone although selective archaeological recovery from late post-medieval deposits may also be a factor.

The horn-working industry

The third industry utilizing parts of the animal carcass is hornworking. The London Horners Company had an extensive set of rules that were frequently modified and added to over the course of the 16th and 17th centuries (Compton 1879; Rosedale 1911, 1912; Fisher 1936). Many of these additions and amendments were aimed at ensuring the supply of raw material. These counteracted the many factors that meant that the industry was wide-open to competition. The horners' produce was a useful

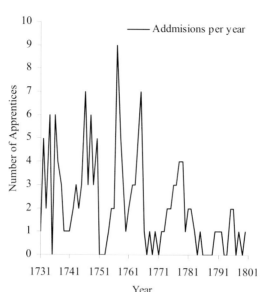

Fig 8.2. The decline of the London horn industry illustrated by falling apprenticeships.

commodity although in London there would never have been any overwhelming demand that could not be met by the quantity of horn available from the carcasses of animals brought into the City to feed its population. These factors made it difficult for individual producers to control the industry. In effect the "simplicity of the tools, the cheapness of the raw materials, and the limited market for the finished product all made hornworking a trade peculiarly unfitted for the large capitalist" (Fisher 1936, 7–8). The Horners Company was prepared to undertake legal action against those who tried to undermine its control. An example of this occurred in 1689 when a comb-maker was prosecuted for pressing horns (Compton 1879). Entry into the Company was strictly under apprenticeship allowing the Company to limit the number of horners in London in accordance with the level of demand. Additionally, master horners were allocated their share of a joint stock of horn according to their length of service, along with the greater allowance given to members who undertook duties to ensure the running of the guild. All these factors helped ensure that the Company members were able to earn a living. By the end of the 18th century the industry had gone into decline with cheaper glass production further reducing demand for the horners' produce. This is reflected in the number of apprentices starting their training (fig. 8.2) and, unlike the apprentice registers of some other companies (Walker 1986), the reduction in numbers in the later 18th century reflects the lowering demand for the horners' produce rather than the waning of guild control. Tracing the decline of the industry from zooarchaeological evidence is not as accurate because dating of the contexts where horners' waste have been found is not precise enough and the lack of deposits from specific dates may just reflect the extent of fieldwork rather than an actual change in the industries importance.

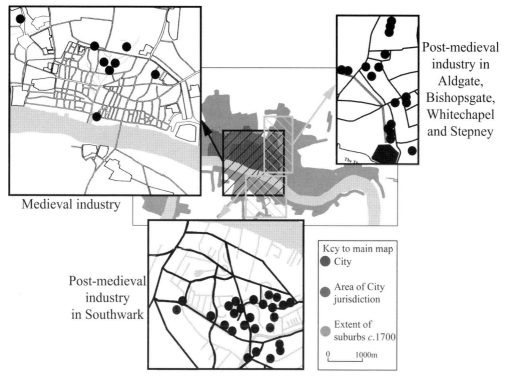

Fig 8.3. Zooarchaeological evidence for the location of industries processing animal carcasses in medieval and post-medieval London. In the eastern parishes the evidence is mainly from the horn-working industry and south of the river the evidence is largely remains of the leather industry.

Changing organisation in carcass-processing industries

These three cases show how the two types of leather producers and hornworkers were crafts whose organisation was altered in different ways by the frequently cited decline of the guilds and rise of capitalist production. Decisive factors seem to have been how effective individual craftsmen were at keeping control over raw material supplies and sale of produce. In the hornworking industry this was achieved because the profits never attracted capitalists and the guild remained in control. Prospects in the tanning industry were limited to certain extent by the production methods rather than market demand and this did not change until the 19th century. The craftsmen in light leather industry, however, did not retain as much control over their work. They suffered at the hands of the traders who began commanding the supply and sale of produce although their petitions against the leather-sellers controlling their industry may be somewhat exaggerated (Unwin 1963). The way that these industries dealt with economic change associated with the end of the medieval period aids our understanding of factors that were important to craftsmen in the medieval period and earlier.

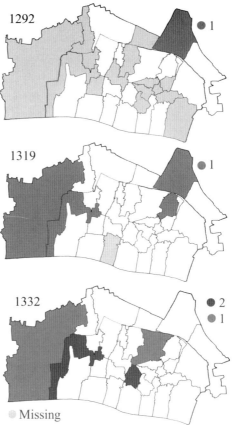

Fig 8.4. Occurrence of horners in the Lay Subsidy Rolls indicating the centres of hornworking in the medieval period (based on data in Curtis 1918 and Ekwall 1951).

Archaeological evidence for industrial relocation

Comparison of archaeological evidence from the Middle Ages through to the post-medieval period clearly shows the change in the geography of industries within London. The focus of leather production shifted towards the southern suburbs and, although significantly less so and not yet reflected by archaeological remains, into the eastern suburbs close to the river (fig. 8.3). The centre of hornworking, previously seen in the City or just outside the City wall, shifted into the eastern districts centred on Petticoat Lane with a smaller group continuing around the Fleet where archaeological evidence indicates a second concentration of the industry in the medieval period (fig. 8.4). Interestingly, only one horner has been identified in a study of the parish baptism registers of Bermondsey and St Olave in Southwark where raw materials would have been easily obtained from local tanning-yards. This provides further evidence that guild control over hornworking was still strong providing reason for members to congregate spatially rather than follow the availability of raw materials. The frequent

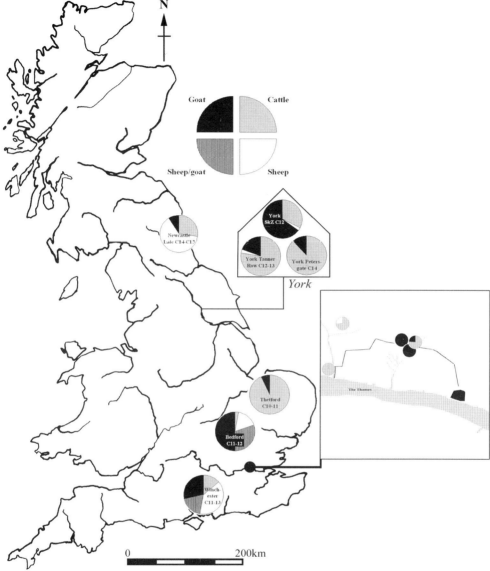

Fig 8.5. Selection of horn used by medieval horners.

cattle horncore-lined pits found in Southwark therefore contained reused waste from tanneries rather than waste from hornworking, although the tanners often sold the horn-sheath on to horners. This also fits with a detailed examination of the horncores which, in Southwark, lack examples with sawn-off tips or sawn segments of horncore which are found in the horners' waste assemblages of East London. A manuscript from 1641 listing members of the Horners Company and a study of occupations found in the East London parish registers, confirm the archaeological evidence for horners in East London.

Supply networks and use

Changes in the supply of animals coming into the City and used in the industries can also be identified in the archaeological record. Evidence for the hornworking industry has been found at a number of urban sites in England. The pie charts shown on Figure 8.5 illustrate the selection of raw materials by horners during the medieval period. The data is taken from faunal reports where hornworking was given as the most probable interpretation of horncore accumulations (Biddle 1990, Clutton-Brock and Armitage 1978, Drummond-Murray and Liddle 2003, Grant 1983, Jones 1984, O'Connor 1984, 1988, Rackham 1981, Ryder 1970). The hornworking craftsmen in urban centres evidently went to a great deal of effort to obtain goat horn since goats were a minority species even in rural areas (Grant 1988). This differs substantially to the evidence for the post-medieval centuries (fig. 8.6) when cattle and sheep were the main source of raw material for hornworking (Armitage 1978, Cram 1982, Hutchins and Steadman 1999, Noddle and Harcourt 1985, O'Connor 1991, Rackham 1981, Weinstock 2002). The graphs shown on this map (fig. 8.6) are based on evidence from sites dated to between the 16th and 18th centuries suggesting that horners in the post-medieval period were utilising horn supplied from different sources. The map only includes sites where horners' waste was given as the interpretation of the faunal assemblage and there is substantial evidence to suggest that sheep (but extremely rarely goat) horn was used by less specialised craftsmen. In London, historical evidence suggests that sites south of the river (see above) were not actually occupied by horners but that men in other trades such as the tanners, leatherdressers and butchers were removing horn for sale to the horners who occupied the area to the east of the City. Use of goat horn did not completely cease but there was a definite change. Some sixteenth century deposits in both Newcastle and London have produced evidence of goat horn working indicating the continued use of this animal for commercial production in towns.

Factors affecting supply

The effect of the traders' monopoly over animal products and distribution of raw materials to the manufacturers may be a possible explanation for the decreasing use of goat horn. In the early 17th century, for example, the leatherdressers had complained that for the past 20 years it had been practically impossible to find goat or kid leather unless they purchased it from one of three merchants of whom one was a freeman of the Leathersellers Company whilst the other two were not even leathersellers but members of the Haberdashers Company (Unwin 1963). This was, no doubt, an exaggeration on the part of the leatherdressers who were trying to make a point but it shows the effect that the control of trade could have on the supply of raw materials

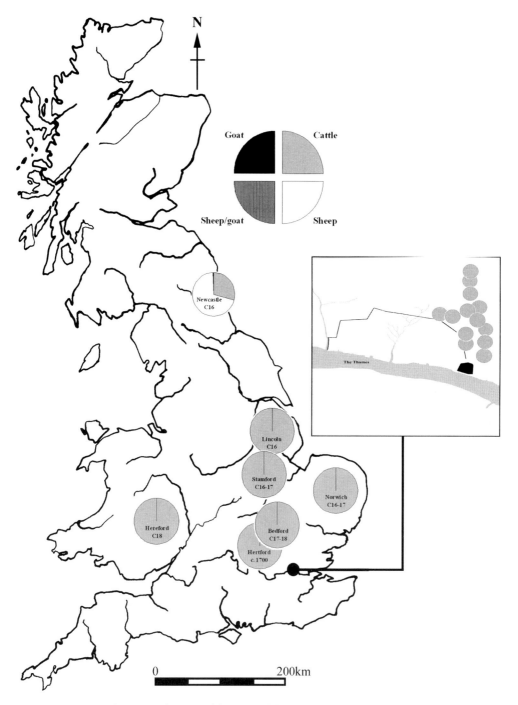

Fig 8.6. Selection of horn used by post-medieval horners.

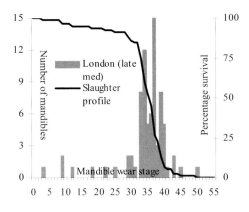

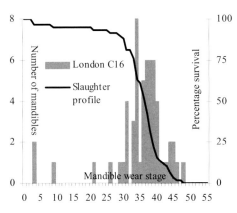

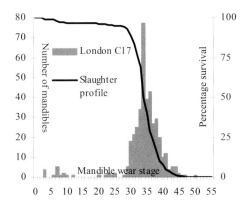

*Fig 8.7. Mortality profiles of sheep slaught-
ered in London over the late medieval and
earlier post-medieval periods.*

to manufacturers. Another factor may
have been the process of enclosure. The
16th century witnessed the conversion of
much common land into fields for sheep
which offered greater profits from their
wool yield and in turn their meat. The
increase in sheep flocks and the reduction
of common land for individuals to graze
their own animals may have had an impact
on the availability of products from other
species.

The effect that changes in the countryside were having on the animal carcasses
processed in towns is also notable in the
ages of the animals driven into the City.
The graphs shown in Figure 8.7 amal-
gamate evidence of mandible wear stages
from late medieval, 16th and 17th century
sites within London and its suburbs that
have been analysed during the course of
the research to date. More work is needed
to compare the profiles from different
sites but at this stage the graphs crudely
illustrate that sheep consumed in London
were older animals. This reflects how the
supply of animals into London and other
urban centres (*e.g.* Oxford and Exeter
(Wilson 1994, Maltby 1979)) was influenced by the increase in the rural wool
and cloth industries from the late
medieval period. Once a sheep's fleece
yield had started to decrease because of
age, the animal would be driven to market
and sold for meat. The results are similar
to those obtained from the well-known
wool producing area of Ypres (Ervynck
1998). There may have been a very slight
increase in the proportion of older sheep
killed in the London slaughterhouses in
the early post-medieval period but it
seems more likely that this just reflects
sample size. Additional work is needed
on faunal remains from the earlier
medieval sites in London to indicate when
there was a change in the age of sheep

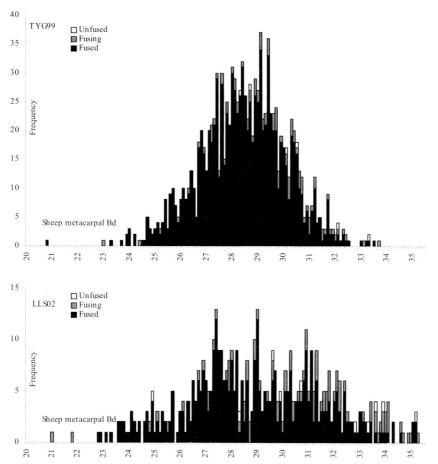

Fig 8.8. Sheep metacarpal measurements from two large assemblages of leatherdressers' waste reused to construct floor surfaces in Southwark.

consumed inferring either a significant change in the rural use of sheep or the supply of meat animals to the City.

A number of post-medieval deposits in London also suggest the presence of wethers again reflecting the importance of animals kept specifically for wool. This is best demonstrated by measurements taken on two large accumulations of leather-dressers' waste from Southwark that had been reused to construct floor surfaces (fig. 8.8). Both accumulations date to the 18th century and show that many of the largest bones (particularly at LLS02) were still fusing or even unfused (in the few cases where the epiphysis was recovered complete). These were probably bones from weathers whose bone fusion had been delayed by castration allowing them to continue growing. It is also interesting that the spread of measurements at the two sites is different. The higher variation in the LLS02 measurements suggests that some leatherdressers had access to a greater range of sheep probably from a variety of breed types.

Restrictions in use of local raw materials

In the post-medieval period people started to import large quantities of raw materials from distant sources such as ivory and horn from Africa and India, yet the use of animals locally available became more restricted. The most notable aspect of this change is the almost nonexistent use of antler. This had been a widely used raw material particularly during the early medieval period but its importance gradually declined. By the post-medieval period, by-products from livestock supplied most of the animal materials used in towns. Animal products were also subjected to a widening range of production processes with craftsmen finding new ways of manipulating the carcasses of sheep and cattle to produce artefacts. One example is the changing typology in combs (as antler and bone forms were replaced by horn examples) which testifies to the changing use of animal carcasses (for example see Dunlevy 1972; Biddle 1990).

Carcass utilisation in post-medieval London

The evidence briefly described above as well as other zooarchaeological and historical data have been used in an attempt to model the variety of ways that animal carcasses were used in post-medieval London and the distribution of raw materials between craftsmen. The aim is compile further evidence from the medieval period in the future allowing comparison of the way in which animal carcasses were used. Changes

Fig 8.9. Cattle metacarpals that were off-cuts from bone working with holes drilled down through the medial side of the proximal articulation indicating they had passed through a tannery.

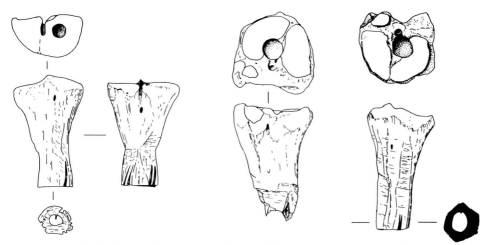

Fig 8.10. Pinners' bones manufactured from tannery waste (scale 1:4).

in the way that animal carcasses were processed reflect socio-economic developments around the medieval/post-medieval transition since the governing regulations had to adapt to the changes in the organisation of work and production. The changing use of species is also a reflection of the agricultural developments at this time suggesting how the urban population focused on farmed animals with wild animals rarely used.

Industries processing animal carcasses were dependant upon one another for their raw materials. This is evident in the spatial location of butchers, tanners, leather-dressers and horners reconstructed through the parish registers and confirmed by modifications to bones. Using this data it is possible to suggest the networks that divided and used parts of the animal carcass. For instance, numerous sites have produced sheep skulls, frequently chopped down the line of the sagittal suture with the horncores chopped off by means of cleaver blows directed to their base. These occur in deposits where the faunal assemblage has been interpreted as both butchers and leatherdressers waste suggesting that the process was not confined to one tradesman. The trade in sheep horn was widespread and it seems that the opportunity to sell this part of the carcass on was rarely missed. Similarly, tanners sold cattle horn on to horners occasionally leaving evidence of horn removal but also historical references mention the profits that could be made from this activity (Burridge 1824, Hartridge 1955). Figure 8.9 shows a group of typical bone working waste with the proximal and distal ends of the metapodials sawn off and found together in one context. The hole drilled through the proximal articulation suggests that the bone-worker had been supplied from a tanner who probably drilled the hole to aid in the stretching of the hides. Such modifications have been identified at many tannery sites and in locations where there was no subsequent processing of the bone suggesting that some aspect of the tanning process must have been responsible. Similar modifications have been found on pinners' bones (fig. 8.10) indicating another way in which animal bones passed between craftsmen in different trades. Pinners were

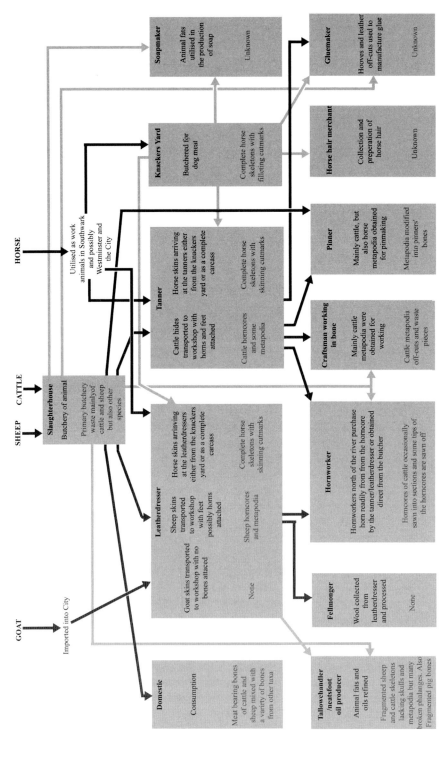

Fig 8.11. Flow diagram showing use of animal carcasses in post-medieval Bermondsey. Distribution networks identified from zooarchaeological and historical evidence are show by black arrows, potential distribution networks shown by grey arrows and characteristics of faunal assemblages shown by grey text.

groups of craftsmen who made pins and would use grooves sawn into bones to hold pieces of wire as they sharpened them into pins.

A model of animal carcass use in the leather-producing suburbs in Southwark was generated on the basis of the types of evidence presented above. This is shown in Figure 8.11 illustrating the many uses that animal carcasses could be put to and the complicated distribution network allowing the different trades to obtain the parts of carcasses they needed or could use. The faunal assemblages that accumulated at different workshops are also shown based on the analyses from Southwark since they may prove useful to others working on industrial waste.

Conclusions

To conclude, the use of animal carcasses in medieval and post-medieval cities was affected by the organisation of work both in urban centres and in the countryside. It is just as important, therefore, to look at evidence for how production was controlled and the changes that occurred at the end of the medieval period to understand how carcasses were transformed into items of material culture during the medieval period. The supply of animal goods was partly affected by changes in the rural economy and, in the post-medieval period, by the desire for new and exotic materials. Post-medieval faunal evidence shows the complex distribution network needed to ensure that all the craftsmen gained access to raw materials. Similar supply systems must have operated in medieval London and it will be interesting to compare the two when more evidence is analysed.

Acknowledgements

The work presented in the paper is part of an ongoing student research project supported by the AHRC and supervised by Drs. Jane Sidell and Louise Martin. The London Archaeological Archive and Research Centre, Kevin Rielly and Pre-Construct Archaeology provided access to assemblages and grey literature. The London Metropolitan Archive and the Guildhall Library provided additional help. Thanks also to the reviewer for commenting on the paper.

Bibliography

Armitage, P. L. (1978) Hertfordshire cattle and London meat markets in the 17th and 18th centuries. *London Archaeologist* 3, 217–223.

Baxter, I. L. (2004) Animal, bird, reptile and amphibian bones. In N. Finn *The Origins of a Leicester Suburb: Roman, Anglo-Saxon, Medieval and Post-medieval Occupation on Bonners Lane*, 132–148. Oxford, British Archaeological Reports, British Series.

Biddle, M. (1990) The nature and chronology of bone, antler and horn working in Winchester. In M. Biddle (ed.) *Object and Economy in Medieval Winchester, Volume II*, 252, 264. Oxford, Claredon Press.

Burridge, J. (1824) *The Tanner's Key*. London.

Clutton-Brock, J. and Armitage, P. L. (1977) Mammal remains from trench A. In (T. R. Blurton), Excavations at Angle Court, Walbrook, 1974. *Transactions of the London and Middlesex Archaeological Society* 28, 88–97.

Compton, C. H. (1879) The horners of the City of London. *British Archaeological Journal* 35, 372–379.

Cram, L. (1982) The pits and horn cores. In C. Mahany, A. Buchard and G. Simpson (eds.) *Excavations in Stamford, Lincolnshire, 1968–1969*, 48–51. The Society for Medieval Archaeology Monograph Series No. 9.

Curtis, M. (1918) The London Lay Subsidy of 1332. In G. Unwin, (ed.) *Finance and Trade Under Edward III*, 35–60. Manchester, The University Press.

Drummond-Murry, J. and Liddle, J. (2003) Medieval industry in the Walbrook valley. *London Archaeologist* 10, 87–94.

Dunlevy, M. (1972) Some comb forms of the fifteenth to eighteenth centuries. *North Munster Antiquarian Journal* 15, 22–27.

Ekwall, E. (1951) *Two Early London Subsidy Rolls*. Lund, C.W.K. Gleerup.

Ervynck, A. (1998) Wool or mutton? An archaeological investigation of sheep husbandry around late medieval Ypres. In M. Dewilde, A. Ervynck and A. Wielemans, (eds.) *Ypres and the Medieval Cloth Industry in Flanders: Archaeological and Historical Contributions*, 77–88. Flanders, Institute for Archaeological Heritage.

Fisher, M. A. (1936) *A Short History of the Worshipful Company of Horners*. London.

Gomersall, M. (2000) Departed glory: the archaeology of the Leeds tanning industry 1780 1914. *Industrial Archaeology Review* 22, 133–144.

Grant, A. (1983) The animal bones. In J. Hassall Excavations in Bedford 1977 and 1978. *Bedfordshire Archaeological Journal* 13, 70–72.

Grant, A. (1988) Animal resources. In G. Astill and A. Grant (eds.) *The Countryside of Medieval England*, 149–187. Oxford, Blackwell.

Hartridge, R. J. (1955) *The Development of Industries in London South of the Thames 1750 to 1850*. Unpublished MSc Thesis, University of London.

Hutchins, E. and Steadman, S. (1999) Evidence for 17th and 18th century cattle improvements. *Environmental Archaeology* 4, 87–92.

Jones, G. (1984) Animal bones. In A. Rogerson and C. Dallas (eds.) *Excavations in Thetford 1948–59 and 1973–80*, 187–192. Dereham, East Anglian Archaeology Report No. 22.

Kowaleski, M. (1990) Town and country in late medieval England: The hide and leather industry. In P. J. Corfield and D. Keene (eds.) *Work in Towns: 850–1850*, 57–73. Leicester, Leicester University Press.

Maltby, M. (1979) *Faunal Studies on Urban sites: the Animal Bones from Exeter 1971–1975*. Sheffield, University of Sheffield, Department of Prehistory and Archaeology.

Marsall, T. H. (1929) Capitalism and the decline of the English guilds. *Cambridge Historical Journal* 3(1), 23–33.

Noddle, B. A. and Harcourt, R. (1985) The animal bones. In R. Shoesmith (ed.) *Hereford City Excavations 3*, 84–94. London, Council for British Archaeology Research Report 56.

O'Connor, T. P. (1984) *Selected Groups of Bones from Skeldergate and Walmgate*. York: York Archaeology Trust.

O'Connor, T. P. (1988) *Bones from the General Accident Site, Tanner Row*. York, York Archaeology Trust.

O'Connor, T. P. (1991) The animal bone. In D. Stocker (ed.) *St. Mary's Guildhall, Lincoln: the Survey and Excavation of a Medieval Building Complex*, 88–91. Lincoln, City of Lincoln Archaeology Unit, The Archaeology of Lincoln Vol. XII–1.

Rackham, J. (1981) The animal remains. In (B. Harbottle and M. Ellison) An excavation in the castle ditch, Newcastle upon Tyne, 1974–6. *Archaeologia Aeliana* 21, 229–243.

Rosedale, H. C. (1911) *Some Notes on 'The Old Book' of the Worshipful Company of Horners.* London, The Worshipful Company of Horners.

Rosedale, H. G. (1912) *A Short History of the Worshipful Company of Horners.* London, Blades, East and Blades.

Rosser, G. (1997) Crafts, guilds and the negotiation of work in the medieval town. *Past and Present* 154, 3–31.

Ryder, M. L. (1970) The animal remains from Petergate, York, 1957–58. *Yorkshire Archaeological Review Journal* 42, 418–428.

Sabine, E. L. (1933) Butchering in medieval London. *Speculum* 8, 335–353.

Saunders, C. (1977) A sixteenth century tannery in St Albans. *Herefordshire Past* 3, 9–12.

Unwin, G. (1963) *Industrial Occupations in the Sixteenth and Seventeenth Centuries.* London, Frank Cass and Co, Ltd.

Walker, M. (1986) *The Extent of Guild Control in England c.1660–1820.* Unpublished PhD Thesis, University of Cambridge.

Weinstock, J. (2002) The medieval and post-medieval bone remains. In M. Atkin, and D. H. Evans. (eds.) *Excavations in Norwich 1971–1978 Part III,* 220–230. East Anglian Archaeology Reports No. 100.

Wilson, B. (1994) Mortality patterns, animal husbandry and marketing in and around medieval and post-medieval Oxford. In A. R. Hall and H. K. Kenward (eds.) *Urban-Rural Connections: Perspectives from Environmental Archaeology*, 103–115. Oxford, Oxbow.

Chapter 9

Hunting in the Byzantine Period in the Area Between the Danube River and the Black Sea: Archaeozoological Data

Luminiţa Bejenaru and Carmen Tarcan

Introduction

This study discusses archaeozoological data from five fortified settlements, built during the period of Byzantine domination over the Dobrudja province (fig. 9.1). The occupational history covers a short time span, from the 10th to 13th centuries. Dobrudja is a tableland area between the lower Danube River and the Black Sea, with

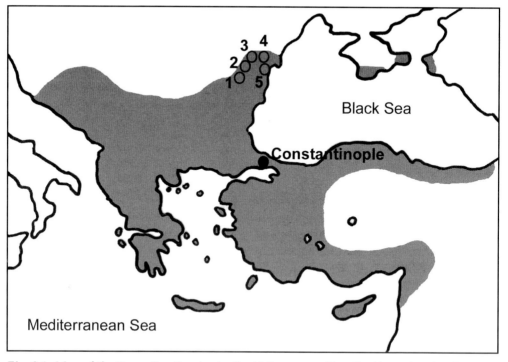

Fig. 9.1. Map of the Byzantine Empire in the 12th century (1 – Capidava; 2 – Carsium; 3 – Dinogetia; 4 – Noviodunum; 5 – Prislava).

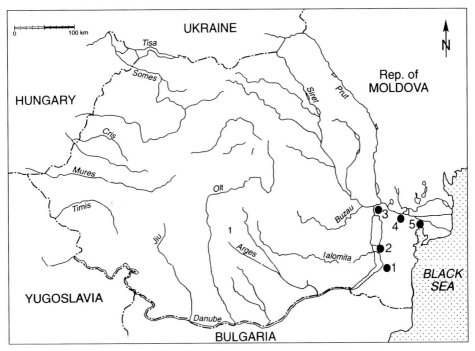

Fig. 9.2. *Map of Romania showing the Byzantine sites analyzed archaeozoologically (1 – Capidava; 2 – Carsium; 3 – Dinogetia; 4 – Noviodunum; 5 – Prislava).*

altitudes fluctuating between 0 to 400 m (Ghinea 2002). The Danube flows into the Black Sea through three river arms forming a delta (fig. 9.2).

A brief summary of the political history in the region between the 7th century BC and the Middle Ages will be described below. In the 7th and 6th centuries BC, this land, originally inhabited by the Dacians, was first colonized and several Greek colonies were founded. In the 5th century BC, the Thracians from the south established their rule over Dobrudja. After being conquered by Alexander the Great in the 4th century BC, the territory was brought under Macedonian domination for a short period of time. The 3rd century BC brought Dobrudja under the Scythians. Later, in 46 BC, the province became an annex of the Roman Empire, known as Scythia Minor. The Romans built the Trajan's Wall, a double fortification wall extending from the city of Constanta, on the Black Sea to the Danube River, to defend this strategically important territory. As part of the Roman and later of the Byzantine Empire, Dobrudja suffered frequent invasions by Goths, Huns, Avars, and other migratory tribes. Mongol Tartar raids were common in the 13th century A.D. The province became autonomous in the 14th century, when it came under the rule of the Walachian prince Dobrotici, from whom the name Dobrudja derives. The region was conquered by the Ottoman Turks in 1411 and remained under Turkish occupation for the next five centuries (Georgescu 1992).

Table 9.1. Relative importance of wild species.

NISP	Capidava	Carsium	Dinogetia	Noviodunum	Prislava
Total mammals	1028	781	2961	1680	543
Wild mammals	66	57	261	97	79
Hare, *Lepus europaeus*	1	-	3	-	-
Beaver, *Castor fiber*	1	1	-	-	-
Wild boar, *Sus scrofa*	28	26	56	33	60
Red deer, *Cervus elaphus*	27	20	184	58	17
Roe deer, *Capreolus capreolus*	8	7	6	1	1
Elk, *Alces alces*	-	-	1	-	-
Aurochs, *Bos primigenius*	-	-	1	4	-
Fox, *Vulpes vulpes*	-	2	2	-	-
Wolf, *Canis lupus*	-	-	-	-	1?
Marten, *Martes sp.*	-	1	-	-	-
Otter, *Lutra lutra*	-	-	1	1	-
Badger, *Meles meles*	1	-	5	-	-
Wild cat, *Felis sylvestris*	-	-	2	-	-

Archaeozoological analysis

The present analysis summarizes previous and recent archaeozoological studies in the area. In total, five archaeozoological samples will be discussed. The settlements from which faunal data were analyzed are as follows: Capidava (Haimovici and Ureche 1979), Hârşova-Carsium (Bejenaru 1995), Dinogetia (Haimovici 1989), Noviodunum (Bejenaru 2003) and Prislava (Bejenaru unpublished results).

The faunal assemblages are biased by taphonomic factors and recovery techniques. First, the samples were not sieved, which may have caused an overrepresentation of large animals such as red deer (*Cervus elaphus*) and wild boar (*Sus scrofa*). Consequently, the remains of small species such as hare (*Lepus europaeus*), beaver (*Castor fiber*), and otter (*Lutra lutra*) are scarce (see table 9.1). On the other hand, smaller carnivores such as fox (*Vulpes vulpes*), marten (*Marten* sp.), otter, badger (*Meles meles*), and wild cat (*Felis sylvestris*), mainly hunted for their furs, were probably skinned outside the habitation areas and as a result, their skeletal remains are also rare in the archaeozoological samples.

The wild mammals identified from the Byzantine settlements in Dobrudja and their proportions based on raw counts (NISP) are shown in table 9.1. In total, thirteen species, among which red deer, wild boar, and roe deer (*Capreolus capreolus*) are most frequent, were identified.

The frequencies of wild mammals, derived from the total number of identifiable mammal remains (fig. 9.3), range between 5.46% at Noviodunum and 12.7% at Prislava, with a mean that is 7.81% higher compared to values found at other

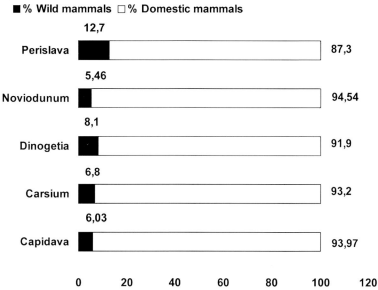

Fig. 9.3. *The relative importance of wild and domestic mammals.*

contemporary civilian settlements in southern Romania, such as Bucov – 2.22% (Haimovici 1979) or Dridu 1.48% (Necrasov and Haimovici 1967).

There is variation in the proportions of wild mammals between settlements. For example, red deer remains are predominant in two of the settlements (Dinogetia and Noviodunum), those of wild boar at three other sites (Capidava, Carsium and Prislava). Overall, large mammals (red deer, wild boar, and roe deer) are well represented, which suggests that these species were mainly hunted as a source of food. Smaller wild species were also consumed, as indicated by the butchering marks found on the bones (*e.g.* fox).

Details concerning the butchery processes could be obtained from the analysis of red deer remains from Noviodunum. The high variability in the types of cut marks (table 9.2) suggests that different butchery processes took place including evisceration, disarticulation and dismemberment, carcass partitioning into smaller pieces, and filleting. The location and frequency of butchery marks are schematically represented in table 9.2 and Figure 9.4. The analysis also indicates that different cutting tools were used including knives and chopping tools. Evisceration marks are present on the cranium; sagittal and transverse cuts were inflicted on the head for the extraction of the brain (fig. 9.5a). Disarticulation at the joints is indicated by marks on the articular ends of the bones. The articulations affected are: the humero-radioulnar (elbow) and radio-carpal (wrist) joints. The articulations between vertebrae and ribs were also severed. Antlers were detached from the cranium, but shed antlers were also found. Carcass apportionment into smaller portions is indicated by cut marks on scapulae (detachment of the proximal end), pelvis bones (fragmentation into three portions:

Table 9.2. Location and frequency of the butchering marks on reed deer remains (NISP=42).

Element	Anatomical description of butchery marks	NISP
Cranium	a. sagittal cut of cranial vault	3
	b. transversal cut on frontal bone	1
	c. transversal cut on parietal bone	1
	d. transversal cut on cornular process of frontal bone	1
	e. breach of maxilla	5
	f. oblique cut to M3 tooth with breach of mandible angle	5
	g. transversal breach on mandible body to P4 tooth	7
Vertebra	a. oblique cut on caudal end of the atlas transverse process	1
Rib	a. superficial, thin cuts on the extern face of shaft	1
	b. oblique cut of vertebral end	1
Scapula	a. transversal breach of the neck	1
Humerus	a. oblique cut on infer-medial end of the distal extremity	1
Radius	a. oblique breach on the proximal third of diaphysis	2
	b. oblique breach on the half of diaphysis	2
Pelvis	a. breaches on the borders of acetabulum	1
Tibia	a. breach on the distal third of diaphysis	2
Metacarpal	a. breach on the proximal third of diaphysis	1
	b. breach on the half of diaphysis	1
	c. breach on the distal third of diaphysis	3
Metatarsal	a. breach on the proximal third of diaphysis	1
	b. breach on the half of diaphysis	1
	c. breach on the distal third of diaphysis	1
Phalange III	a. cut on the lateral end of plantar surface	2

acetabular, pre-acetabular and post-acetabular), and some of the long bones such as radio-ulna, metacarpus, tibia, and metatarsus. The purpose of processing long bones was twofold: to obtain smaller size portions of meat and to extract the marrow inside the bones. That could explain the high degree of fragmentation of metapodials, bones that do not bear meat. Filleting, i.e. taking the meat off the bones, is indicated by fine cut marks on the ribs and the shafts of radii. The utilization of red deer bones as raw materials in manufacturing was observed in the sample from Noviodunum. The skin was probably used in the tannery industry, but this would be difficult to recognize

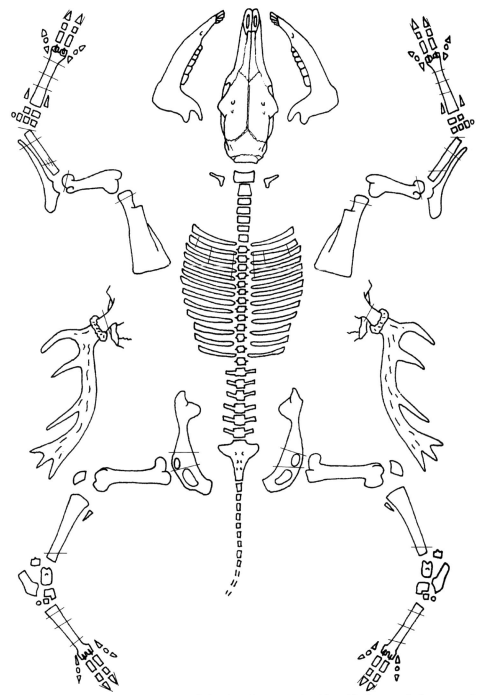

Fig. 9.4. Schematic representation of the butchery marks identified on red deer remains (skeleton diagram from Helmer 1987).

Fig. 9.5. Cervus elaphus *remains from Noviodunum: a. skull fragments with evisceration* marks; b. antler fragments with processing marks.

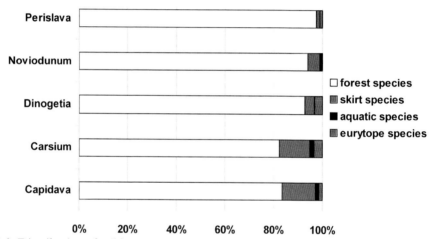

Fig. 9.6. *Distribution of wild mammal remains based on ecological parameters of the species.*

archaeozoologically. A large number of cut marks on antlers indicate that these elements were used as raw materials in the tool industry. In total, 57 antler fragments found at Noviodunum show marks resulting from tool manufacturing. These fragments were not included in the quantitative list since they are the result of tool production (fig. 9.5b).

Wild animals have different ecological requirements and the remains found in archaeological contexts might indicate the exploitation of a certain biotope. The animals were therefore grouped according to their ecological characteristics into forest species (*Cervus elaphus, Alces alces, Sus scrofa, Felis sylvestris*), skirt (transitional zone between forest and steppe) species (*Capreolus capreolus, Lepus europaeus, Bos primigenius*), aquatic species (*Castor fiber* and *Lutra lutra*), and eurytope species (*Vulpes*

vulpes, Canis lupus, Meles meles). Marten (*Martes* sp.) remains were excluded because they cannot be easily identified to species. As Figure 9.6 shows, in all assemblages, forest species are predominant. This suggests that large forests were present around settlements. These data correlate well with the information described in documentary sources. For example, a document from 1281 mentions that a large forest was present in the northern area of Dobrudja and that this forest was intensively exploited even in later times (Giurescu 1976). Red deer, a species currently found only in the Carpathian Mountains (Cotta 1982), had broader ranges and higher frequencies during the Byzantine period in the area between the Danube River and the Black Sea. The only bone of elk (*Alces alces*) found at Dinogetia probably comes from an animal that passed through the region during its migration from the north-east. Remains of aurochs (*Bos primigenius*), a species now extinct, were identified at Noviodunum in samples from the 12th–15th century. The presence of aurochs in this area correlates well with archaeozoological data from sites in the adjacent region at the north dated between the 14th and 15th centuries (Bejenaru *et al.* 2004). Medieval documents indicate that the aurochs disappeared from the Moldavian fauna probably at the beginning of the 17th century (Nedici 1940). Beaver has low representation in the archaeozoological sample. Beavers also became extinct in Romania in the 19th century. Records indicate that beavers were last present at Moldova Veche on the bank of the Danube, in 1823 and in 1853 it has been noted that beavers did no longer inhabit the Danube Delta (Nania 1991).

Conclusions

A relatively increased emphasis on hunting in the Byzantine settlements analyzed suggests that wild animals made a significant contribution to the diet. Large wild mammals such as deer and wild boar were mainly hunted for food. Remains of small carnivores, beaver, and hare have lower representation in the faunal assemblages, but these data must be interpreted with caution because the samples were subject to taphonomic destruction and were not sieved.

Thirteen species of wild mammals were identified, among which the remains of wild boar and red deer were most frequent. These species are characteristic to dense forest environments and were probably abundant in the area between the lower Danube River and the Black Sea at the beginning of the second millennium. Towards the end of the Middle Ages, the environment in the area underwent rapid changes due to human exploitation, especially deforestation. As a result, the range of some species such as red deer and wild cat changed. The intensification of hunting might have also been a contributing factor in the extinction of some species such as beaver and aurochs.

The relatively large number of wild species identified indicates that game was a rich environmental resource. Hunting was practiced because of both social and environmental reasons: all five settlements were military forts, located adjacent to large forests, in areas with fertile soil and plenty of game.

Some characteristics of the butchery patterns could be distinguished from the analysis of red deer remains from Noviodunum. The analysis indicates different stages of butchery, including evisceration, dismembering, apportionment, and filleting. In addition, red deer antlers were an important source of raw materials in tool manufacturing.

Bibliography

Bejenaru, L. (1995) Analiza unui material arheozoologic aparţinând Evului mediu timpuriu din Cetatea Hârşova *Arheologia Moldovei* 18, 321–328.

Bejenaru, L. (2003) *Arheozoologia spaţiului românesc medieval.* Iaşi, Editura Universităţii "Alexandru Ioan Cuza".

Bejenaru, L. Tarcan, C. and Stanc, S. (2004) Hunting in medieval Moldavia: archaeozoological data. *The Future from the Past. Archaeozoology in Wild Life Conservation and Heritage Management,* 97–102. Oxford: Oxbow Books.

Cotta, V. (1982) *Vânatul.* Bucureşti, Editura Ceres.

Georgescu, V. (1992) *Istoria românilor de la origini pînă în zilele noastre.* Bucureşti, Editura Humanitas.

Ghinea, D. 2002. *Enciclopedia geografică a României.* Bucureşti, Editura Enciclopedică.

Giurescu, C. C. (1976) *Istoria pădurii româneşti din cele mai vechi timpuri până astăzi,* Bucureşti, Editura Ceres.

Haimovici, S. (1979). Fauna din aşezările feudale timpurii (secolele VIII–X) de la Bucov-Ploieşti. SCIVA 30/2, 163–213.

Haimovici, S. (1989) Les caractéristiques des mammifères sauvages découverts dans le matériel archéologique provenu de la cité byzantine de Dinogetia (IXe–XIe siècles de n.e.). *Analele ştiinţifice ale Universităţii "Alexandru Ioan Cuza"* 35, Biologie, 51–53.

Haimovici, S. and Ureche, R. (1979) Studiul preliminar al faunei descoperite în aşezarea feudală timpurie de la Capidava. *Pontica* 12, 157–170.

Helmer, D. (1987) Fiches descriptives pour les relèves d'ensembles osseux animaux. *Fiches d'ostéologie animale pour l'archéologie,* série B: mammifères 1, 10.

Nania, I. (1991) *Vânatul pe teritoriul României.* Bucureşti, Editura Sport-Turism.

Necrasov, O. and Haimovici, S. (1967) Studiul resturilor osoase de animale descoperite în aşezarea feudală timpurie de la Dridu. In Zaharia, E. (ed.) *Săpăturile de la Dridu,* 202–241. Bucureşti, Editura Academiei R.S.R.

Nedici, Gh. (1940) *Istoria vânătoarei şi a dreptului de vânătoare.* Bucureşti, Tipografia ziarului "Universul".

Chapter 10

Chasing the Ideal? Ritualism, Pragmatism and the Later Medieval Hunt in England

Richard Thomas

Introduction

The hunt has long been recognised as an essential element of later medieval society (12th–15th centuries), serving a variety of symbolic and practical functions. At the most basic level, legitimate hunting provided dietary diversity to the aristocracy in the form of meat from non-domesticated animals, such as venison. It was also viewed as an important and pleasurable means of ensuring preparedness for war, relieving idleness and, concomitantly, sin (Almond 1994, 316; 2003, 13; Cummins 1988, 3–5; Thiébaux 1967, 260–261). Moreover, the fact that the right to hunt and possess the land upon which it took place was restricted to certain members of society meant that the act of hunting and the consumption of food procured in this way provided a means of social separation. Understanding the language and traditions of the hunt was thus an important element of what it meant to be an aristocrat, requiring both "socialisation and oral transmission" (Henrick 1982, 32). While this served the purpose of distancing the aristocracy from the peasantry, hunting was also used to negotiate socio-political relationships amongst the elite. The number of parks owned, for example, was an important marker of prestige. Lords were also "committed to the idea of *largesse*", which required the sending of gifts as a mark of friendship or deference to superiority (Dyer 1989, 69). Meats such as venison were an ideal gift (*e.g.* Hunt 1997, 110), since hunted animals were not intended to be marketable commodities (although see Sykes, this volume).

The hunt was also allegorical for many aspects of later medieval life, including courtly love, chivalric values of heroism and religious themes such as 'man's' dominance over nature and the hunting of errant souls (Cummins 1988; Klingender 1971). Furthermore, individual quarry species were emblematic of multiple, sometimes contradictory, symbols (Benton 1992, 104, 112). The hart (a male red deer), for example, was imbued with numerous Christian connotations, providing a symbol for eternal life and having associations with the Passion (with the hunter representing the devil; the hart, Jesus; the scenting hound, Judas; and the 'unmaking' and currée, the Crucifixion) (Cummins 1988, 68–70).

According to contemporary treatises, the medieval hunt was a highly ritualised activity, incorporating a number of distinct stages culminating in the symbolic 'breaking' of the animal (*e.g.* Hands 1975). However, Jean Birrell's (1991, 113) study of forest pleas has lead to the suggestion that although deer hunting occurred on a systematic basis, it was largely undertaken by servants. Indeed, she goes further by arguing that the management of deer in this period is deserving of the appellation 'farming'. This paper seeks to explore whether hunting rituals persisted in this context, or whether the medieval texts simply represented a literary ideal.

To address this issue it is valuable to consider primary data, thus, faunal evidence from a number of later medieval high status sites in England and Wales with secure archaeological contexts will be examined (fig. 10.1). This study will focus on three species of deer – red (*Cervus elaphus*), fallow (*Dama dama*) and roe (*Capreolus capreolus*) – and hare (*Lepus europaeus*). From a zooarchaeological perspective these species are particularly useful because their remains are relatively numerous on elite sites and they are not beset by some of the identification problems of other hunted animals, such as wild boar and fox, or inadequacies of sample size, as is the case for bear and otter.

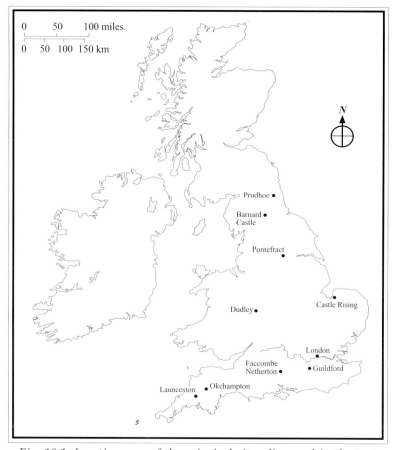

Fig. 10.1. Location map of the principal sites discussed in the text.

The anatomy of the medieval hunt

Hunting strategies

A thorough consideration of all the stages involved in the medieval hunt is beyond the scope of this paper and is covered in much more detail elsewhere (*e.g.* Almond 2003; Cummins 1988; Thiébaux 1967). In brief, there were two principal hunting techniques: *par force de chiens* and the bow and stable method. In the former method, a single hart was chosen and pursued by hounds, the place of death of animal was unknown, and depending on the efficiency of the hounds and the skill of the huntsmen, the whole process could cover large areas of countryside (Cummins 1988, 48). Hunting manuals indicate that this form of venery comprised a number of distinct stages (after Cummins 1988, 33): the quest, assembly, finding, chase, baying, death, unmaking and *currée* (the rewarding of the hounds). The second technique involved the driving of herds of deer towards standing huntsmen where they were brought down by archers in a set location (Almond 2003, 82). By the later medieval period, this latter method was becoming increasingly popular and was particularly associated with fallow deer in parks since it increased the viewing possibilities and displays of conspicuous consumption (Almond 2003, 82; Cummins 1988, 48–51, 87).

While many of the stages of the medieval hunt are archaeologically invisible, the following section seeks to outline two aspects that might be identifiable through the analysis of faunal remains: the choice of quarry, and the butchery and subsequent distribution of the carcass.

Quarry choice

As Almond (2003, 61–2) notes, the medieval system of classifying quarry species was somewhat complex; broadly, they were divided into the 'beasts of venery' (the hart, hare, wild boar and wolf) and the 'beasts of the chase' (the buck (male fallow deer), doe (female fallow deer), fox, marten and, lastly, roe deer). Historical documents make it clear that the hart was the most desirable of these animals (Almond 2003, 17; Cummins 1988, 84), although it has been recognised that fallow deer became more favoured during the later medieval period (Almond 2003, 17, 64–5; Birrell 1992, 30). The ideal hart for hunting was at least six years old with ten tines on its antlers, as anything younger than that was considered to be 'rascal' or 'folly' (Almond 2003, 63; Cummins 1988, 85). The hart was particularly associated with hunting *par force de chiens*. For bucks, the 15th-century *Boke of St. Albans* recommends pursuing those with "one branch antler on each, two advancers and twelve espelers" (Hands 1975, 126–7). Unfortunately, because antler development varies between different animals, it is not possible to equate this with an absolute age (Chapman 1975, in Sadler 1990, 487). There is less detail on the hunting ages for hinds (female red deer), does and roe deer in the historical literature. However, it is likely that these animals, and also younger male red and fallow deer, were taken using the bow and stable method.

The hunting manuals recommend the pursuit of pregnant hares in March and April when their location is more predictable because of the abundance of "easily acquired spring grazing" (Cummins 1988, 112). This suggests a preference for female adult animals, although given the long season for hare coursing – September to February or June (Almond 2003, 87) – this may not have been reflected in practice. While the hare was highly regarded for hunting, its value as a food animal was somewhat ambiguous (Cummins 1988, 110; Salisbury 1994, 52). It is probably for this reason that the Vienna *Tacuinum Sanitatis* – a late 14th or early 15th-century medical manuscript translated into Latin from an Arabic text – only recommends eating leverets caught by hounds (Cummins 1988, 119).

The 'unmaking' and the currée

The climax of the *par force* hunt was the 'unmaking', during which the quarry was systematically dismembered and distributed at the kill site. The *Boke of St. Albans* (1486) includes a detailed description of this process in a section entitled "How ye shall breeke an Hert" (Hands 1975, 76). Similar descriptions also occur in the 13th-century romance, *Sir Tristrem* (Brewer 1992, 85), in the 13th-century French text *La Chase dou cerf* (Almond 2003, 64) and in Gaston Phoebus' early 15th-century *Livre de la Chasse*. In brief, the dead hart was laid on its back, using the antlers to keep it upright, skinned, the internal organs removed, and then jointed, with the pelvis given to the raven, the left shoulder to the individual who 'unmade' the deer, the right shoulder to the forester, and the haunches to the lord. Many of the French hunting manuals stress the importance of the 'unmaking' being undertaken by a member of the aristocracy, however, in the early 15th-century *Master of the Game*, Edward Duke of York states that "there is no woodman nor good hunter in England that cannot do it well enough" (Almond 2003, 79–80).

It should be noted that not all hunted animals were similarly 'unmade'. For example, Gaston Phoebus states: "one must not skin [the roebuck] or unmake it as one does the hart" (Cummins 1988, 91). However, this is contradicted elsewhere, such as in the 14th-century *Les Livres du Roy Modus et de la Royne Ratio*, where it is stated that roe deer should be treated in the same way as a hart (Cummins 1988, 91).

In the case of hare, The *Boke of St. Albans* records that they should be 'unmade', but only the loins of the animal should be taken to the "keychn for the lordis meete"; the remainder of the carcass meanwhile was given to the hounds as a reward (Cummins 1988, 116; Hands 1975, 124).

The zooarchaeological evidence

Methods

Having outlined some of the recommendations for hunting deer and hare within contemporary medieval texts, it is now apposite to consider how zooarchaeological evidence can be employed to determine the extent to which these were observed.

With respect to quarry choice, the examination of the state of fusion of the post-cranial bones, and the eruption and wear of teeth, can be employed to determine the age at which the animals were hunted. The sex of red deer, fallow deer and hare can also be established through the biometrical analysis of long bones, since these animals are strongly sexually dimorphic (*e.g.* Chapman and Chapman 1975, 33).

The ritualised 'breaking' of the animals and the subsequent distribution of body parts following the hunt, are potentially identifiable through investigation of the range of skeletal elements recovered from sites. Butchery practice might also indicate the extent to which the prescribed division of the carcass was followed. For example, the removal of the lips, mouth and nose of a deer as part of this process – which were considered to be delicacies (Hands 1975, 145) – might leave characteristic marks on the cranium, as detected in cattle (Bartosiewicz 1995, 173, Plate 13). It must be acknowledged, however, that a skilled butcher could in fact leave very few traces on the skeleton.

In this paper, the zooarchaeological evidence from ten high-status sites across England has been studied in detail (fig. 10.1). These were selected because they have deer and hare present in sufficient quantities to provide a meaningful analysis of medieval hunting practices. Moreover, some of the faunal reports from these sites included detailed ageing, metrical and body part representation data. Inevitably, however, variability in recording strategies has resulted in problems of comparability – for example, deer phalanges were not recorded at four of the sites considered (figs. 10.5–10.7).

Choosing the quarry

Analysis of the bone fusion data for red deer at a number of later medieval sites (fig. 10.2) reveals that the majority of animals were hunted as adults (i.e. over approximately three years of age). This observation has also been noted at Okehampton Castle, Devon, where virtually all red deer were adult (Maltby 1982, 129). Unfortunately, it is impossible to establish whether any of these animals were over six years old, as recommended in the hunting manuals, since all bones fuse before this age is reached, and thre is also a paucity of ageable mandibles (see fig. 10.5 below). However, Figure 10.2 does reveal that some animals were less than two years of age when they were hunted.

Examination of these data also reveals marked inter-site and temporal variation in the age of red deer. For example, at Dudley Castle, West Midlands (Thomas 2002; 2005), there was a much higher proportion of younger animals compared to Barnard Castle, County Durham (Jones *et al.* 1985) or Prudhoe Castle, Northumberland (Davis 1987). In view of the small number of sites with available data, any conclusions drawn from this analysis of temporal variation must be considered tentative; however, at Dudley Castle (Thomas 2002; 2005) it is apparent that fewer younger animals were hunted in the later medieval period compared with the 14th century. While there was insufficient data from the medieval period, it is noteworthy that out of the 27 red deer specimens identified from Norman (980 – *c.*1204) deposits at Faccombe Netherton, Hampshire, six were noted as neonatal, five as juvenile and six as immature (Sadler 1990, 491).

Analysis of epiphyseal fusion data for fallow deer (fig. 10.3) reveals a marked

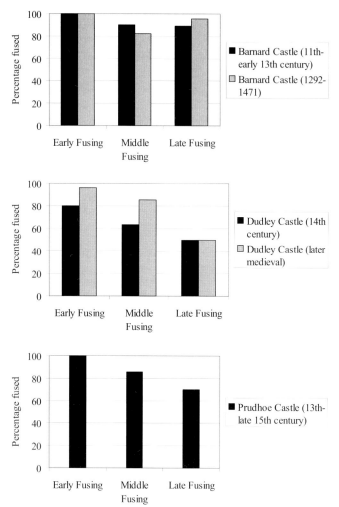

Fig. 10.2. *Analysis of bone fusion data for red deer at three medieval sites. Fusion categories follow Reitz and Wing (1999, table 3.5).*

degree of concordance with the pattern observed for red deer. The majority of animals appear to have been killed as adults, but at both Launceston Castle, Cornwall (Albarella and Davis 1996), and Okehampton Castle (Maltby 1982), fallow deer were present that were less than one to two years of age. Furthermore, at Dudley Castle (Thomas 2002; 2005) seven mandibles were recorded with deciduous dentition. Two of these were complete enough to determine the state of wear on the lower first molar using the method devised by Chaplin and White (1969): both fell into the 'group 1' age category and derive from animals in their first year. In medieval (c.1260–1356) deposits at Faccombe Netherton three fallow deer, out of a minimum number of 33, were estimated as being seven to eight months old, with four juvenile and one immature specimen also noted; only nine specimens were recorded as mature (Sadler 1990). While there was very little temporal change in the slaughter policy at Dudley Castle, at Okehampton Castle a greater number of younger animals were exploited in the 14th century than subsequently (Maltby 1982).

Little can be said regarding the age of roe deer due to the paucity of published fusion data – a problem doubtless exacerbated by the later medieval decline in the relative proportion of this species noted on archaeological sites (Thomas in 2006). At the two sites considered (Dudley Castle and Prudhoe Castle), while there was a preponderance of older animals, a small proportion was still slaughtered in their third or fourth year. At Dudley Castle, three mandibles deriving from phase 5 (1262– 1321) contexts also contained deciduous dentition (Thomas 2002; 2005).

The evidence for hare is similarly limited by small data sets. At Dudley Castle, although no deciduous teeth of hare were recorded, 17% (n=23) of the post-cranial bones were recorded as unfused (Thomas 2002; 2005). The greatest proportion of these was metapodials, suggesting that the animals from which they derived were very young in age (Habermehl 1985).

With respect to sexing, the metrical data for red deer, roe deer and hare are unfortunately insufficient to draw any conclusions regarding hunting preferences. This partly reflects the fact that the elements measured to distinguish sex occur too infrequently to make such an analysis possible. For example, only two red deer metatarsals with the greatest length were recorded at Dudley Castle (Thomas 2002, table A8.17; 2005) and only one from Launceston Castle (Albarella and Davis 1996, table 48). Moreover, at many sites, summaries of metrical data are published rather than the lists of raw values, which make these data impossible to re-evaluate (*e.g.* Jones *et al.* 1985, table 37). However, biometrical analysis of fallow deer metatarsal data reveals two clusters of data at each of the four sites considered in this analysis (fig. 10.4). This doubtless reflects the fact that this species is strongly sexually dimorphic and indicates a roughly equal exploitation of bucks and does in the later medieval period. Analysis of temporal variation in the relative proportion of male and female fallow deer reveals mixed patterns. At Dudley Castle, a greater proportion of males was slaughtered in the later phase (1397–1533), while at both Faccombe Netherton and Launceston Castle there appears to have been a greater number of does slaughtered in later periods.

The 'unmaking'

Analysis of body part representation for red deer at a number of later medieval sites (fig. 10.5) reveals a rather widespread and characteristic dominance of hind limb elements. Post-depositional degradation is unlikely to cause this pattern since bones of similar density, such as the metacarpal and metatarsal, should preserve equally well (see, for example, Lyman 1994, table 7.6). Recovery cannot be the cause of the bias either, since large bones such as the scapula and humerus are absent. It is more likely, therefore, that the distribution of body-parts reflects the selective butchery and

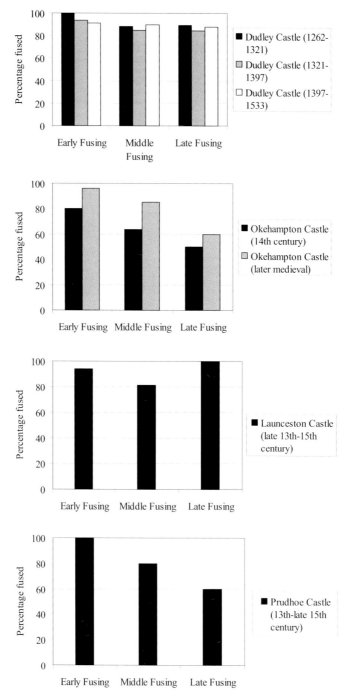

Fig. 10.3. Analysis of bone fusion data for fallow deer at four later medieval sites. Fusion categories follow Reitz and Wing (1999, table 3.5).

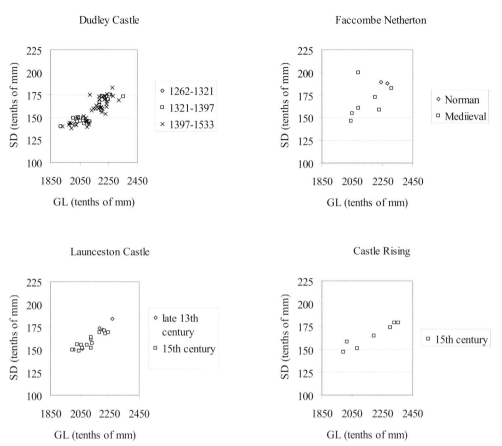

Fig. 10.4. Biometrical analysis of fallow deer metatarsal data from four medieval sites. All measurements taken using the criteria of von den Driesch (1976).

redistribution of deer carcasses, as outlined in contemporary hunting manuals. Thus, the predominance of hind-limb bones reflects the fact that these elements were taken to the lord's residence, while the absence of the forelimbs is consistent with the distribution of this part of the carcass to the forester and huntsman as rewards. The fact that some bones of the forelimb are present on all the sites considered in this study suggests that the systematic division of red deer, while common, was not always undertaken. The general paucity of pelves at Barnard Castle and the later phases at Dudley Castle (they were not recorded at Launceston Castle (Albarella and Davis 1996, 12) and Prudhoe Castle (Davis 1987)) may reflect the fact that this bone was selectively removed, although it is not a particularly dense skeletal element in deer (see, for example, Lyman 1994, table 7.6), and is therefore less likely to survive in the archaeological record.

While there is no apparent temporal variation in the body part distribution of red deer at Barnard Castle (Jones *et al.* 1985), this was not the case at Dudley Castle

Richard Thomas

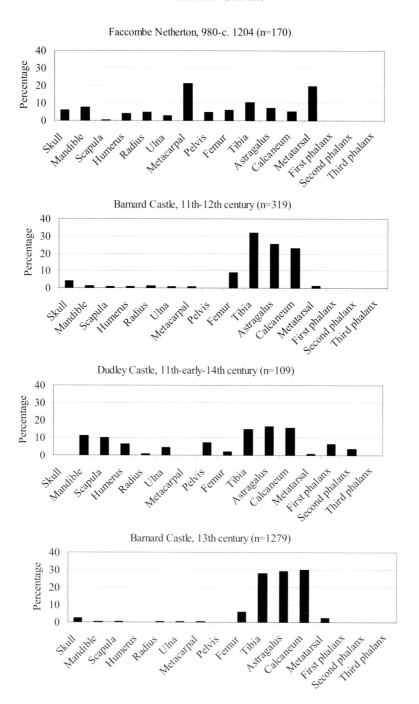

Fig. 10.5. Analysis of body part representation for red deer at five medieval sites. Continued overleaf.

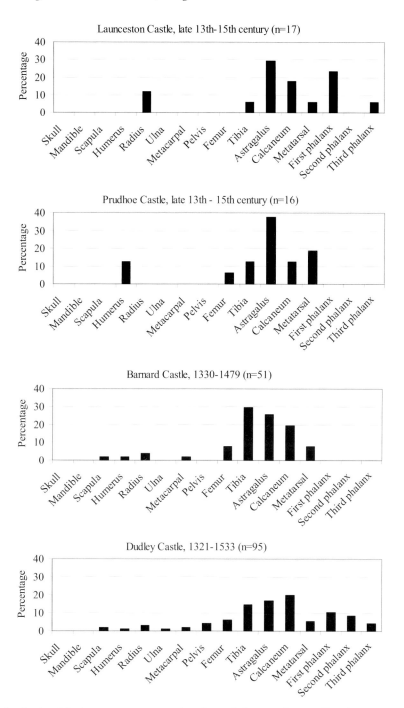

Fig. 10.5. Analysis of body part representation for red deer at five medieval sites. Continued from overleaf.

(Thomas 2002; 2005). At this site, in phases 1–5 (pre-1071–1321), virtually all body parts are represented, suggesting that the butchery of complete carcasses took place on site. However, in phases 6–9 (1397–1750) the distribution of body parts is much more akin to that witnessed elsewhere, with high proportions of hind-limb elements and an almost complete absence of teeth and bones of the forelimb. Earlier medieval deposits at Faccombe Netherton also revealed no predominance of hind-limb elements; unfortunately there were insufficient data from later deposits at this site to determine whether there was any subsequent change in practice (Sadler 1990).

Consideration of the proportion of butchery marks at Dudley Castle (which is the only site that had sufficient data in this regard) revealed that a change in practice also occurred alongside the change in body part representation. Between phases 1–5 and phases 6–9 there was a 10% decline in the proportion of cut post-cranial bones and a 5% rise in the overall proportion of chopped bones (Thomas 2002, table 9.6). It was noted, however, that the anatomical location of these marks did not change over time (Thomas 2002, 367).

Examination of the distribution of parts of fallow deer on six medieval sites (fig. 10.6) reveals a further bias towards the bones of the hind-limb and an almost complete absence of forelimb and cranial elements. This is a phenomenon that has also been noted at Castle Acre Castle, Norfolk (Lawrance 1982), Pontefract Castle, West Yorkshire (Richardson 2002) and Sandal Castle, West Yorkshire (Griffith *et al.* 1983).

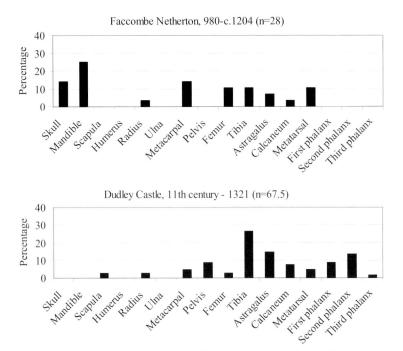

Fig. 10.6. Analysis of body part representation for fallow deer at six medieval sites. Continued over the next two pages.

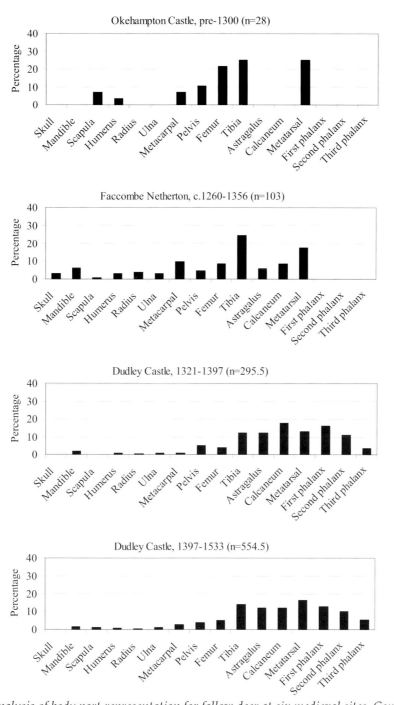

Fig. 10.6. Analysis of body part representation for fallow deer at six medieval sites. Continued from the previous page.

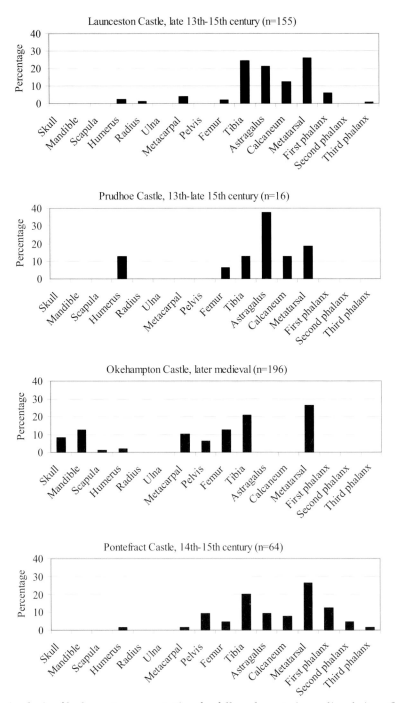

Fig. 10.6. Analysis of body part representation for fallow deer at six medieval sites. Continued from the two previous pages.

Again, this pattern is entirely consistent with the 'unmaking' process described in contemporary hunting manuals but, as with red deer, the presence of forelimb elements at all sites suggests that the prescribed redistribution of carcasses was not always adhered to. At Launceston Castle, Cornwall, although the pelvis was not a recorded element, the authors could not recollect observing any examples (Albarella and Davis 1996, 12). The fact that the pelvis is also less well represented than the hind limb elements at Dudley Castle suggests this bone may have been selectively removed.

With respect to temporal variation, Dudley Castle shows a slightly higher proportion of forelimb elements in the 11th to the early 14th century compared with later periods. This pattern is much more pronounced at Faccombe Netherton between the Norman (980–*c*.1204) and Medieval (*c*.1260–1356) phases and is also evident at Okehampton Castle (Maltby 1982, fig. 60), where pre-1300 levels exhibit a slightly higher proportion of forelimb elements, such as the scapula and humerus, than later medieval phases. Intriguingly, the same pattern occurs at the French site of Vatteville-la-Rue, where the body part distribution data were combined for all three species of deer (Sykes forthcoming).

Due to the smaller number of roe deer bones identified on castle sites it is much more difficult to determine the nature of their exploitation. However, analysis of body part distribution at four sites with sufficient data reveals a rather different pattern than that observed for fallow and red deer (fig. 10.7), with no particular predominance of bones of the hind limb. A comparable pattern was identified at Barnard Castle, Northumberland, although no temporal breakdown was given for these data (Jones *et al.* 1985, fig. 3.3).

Analysis of the element distribution for hare is somewhat precluded by the paucity of published datasets. Moreover, the small number of hare bones recovered on each site means that a meaningful analysis can only be achieved if multiple phases are combined; figure 10.8 shows the results of that analysis. What this diagram demonstrates is that the distribution of elements is strongly affected by recovery, with the smaller bones, such as the phalanges and astragalus, being present in much lower proportions than the long bones of the limb. Figure 10.8 also reveals that at the majority of the sites considered, all body parts are represented, suggesting that whole

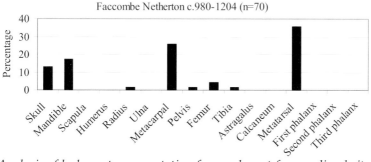

Fig. 10.7. *Analysis of body part representation for roe deer at four medieval sites. Continues on the next page.*

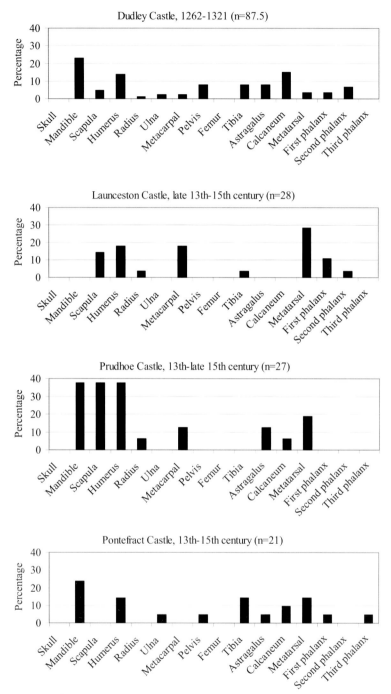

Fig. 10.7. Analysis of body part representation for roe deer at four medieval sites. Continued from the previous page.

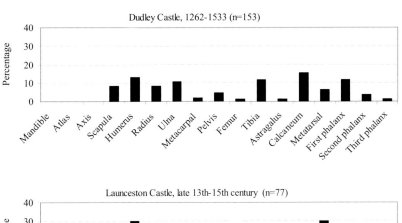

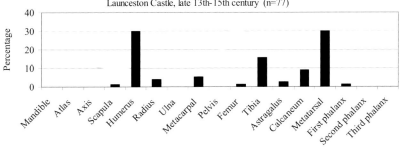

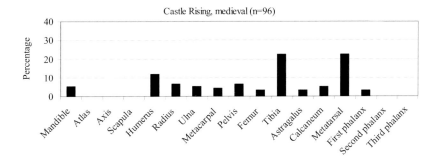

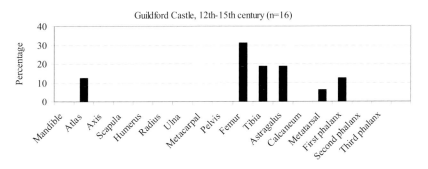

Fig. 10.8. Analysis of body part representation for hare at five medieval sites.

carcasses were processed on site. The same phenomenon was noted at slightly earlier dated deposits (11th –12th century) at Castle Acre Castle, where the skeletal remains consisted mainly of jaws, vertebrae and the bones of the fore- and hind-limb (Lawrance 1982, 283, 295). The data from Guildford Castle, Surrey, reveal an emphasis on bones of the hind-limb; however, this might just reflect the small size of the sample from this site.

Discussion

This analysis of the selected zooarchaeological evidence indicates that many of the recommendations outlined in contemporary hunting manuals do appear to have been exacted. Although it is not possible to determine their precise age, most deer were hunted as adults. The fact that a small proportion of young animals was hunted is also consistent with the historical evidence, if we presume that these were young males taken using the bow and stable method. While we may view the hunting of a hart with ten tines as a literary ideal, the fact that the majority of the deer hunted were adult might reflect deliberate stock management as much as symbolic preference. As Clutton-Brock and McIntyre (1999, 26) note, the mortality of calves in their first year is quite high, and 35–40% of yearlings can die in their first winter, where population density is high and the carrying capacity has been reached. Thus, the hunting of primarily adult red deer would have helped ensure the viability of the population. Similarly, because fallow deer usually only give birth to a single fawn each year (Chapman and Chapman 1975, 146), it would have been impractical to slaughter a high proportion of young animals without compromising the sustainability of the stock. The fact that the majority of roe deer were slaughtered as adults could also reflect the recognised need to maintain the population, especially since in some places neglect, malnutrition, prolonged heavy rain, and pneumonia can halve the population of first year kids (Fawcett 1997, 11). It was no doubt in the mind of the medieval estate managers to avoid such circumstances.

For hares, a much higher proportion of juvenile animals was killed, but given the dietary recommendations of the *Tacuinum Sanitatis*, this evidence is unsurprising. In addition to coursing, contemporary documents indicate that hares were trapped in snares and taken by falconers (Almond 2003); this may have resulted in the indiscriminant targeting of animals. Given the fact that hares, unlike deer, were not confined may have meant that medieval hunters were also less concerned with stock maintenance.

In terms of the sexual composition of the hunted stocks, the presence of roughly equal proportions of bucks and hinds at the four sites considered is more suggestive of bow and stable hunting, since this method was used to capture female deer, which were viewed as less suitable for *par force* hunting. This observation is consistent with the written record, since it is known that this technique was increasingly preferred in the later medieval period (Almond 2003, 82; Cummins 1988, 48–51, 87).

The rules for the 'unmaking' of quarry species similarly appear to have been largely adhered to. In fallow and red deer there is a clear predominance of hind-limb elements on many high status sites in the later medieval period. The fact that a hind-limb bias was noted at sites that appear to have practised the bow and stable method (*e.g.* Dudley Castle), suggests that the ritualised 'unmaking' may have occurred irrespective of the hunting technique employed. The presence of small numbers of cranial and forelimb elements on each site indicates that the rules may not have always been strictly followed. This might reflect that large numbers of animals were sometimes required for particular occasions, which may have necessitated less rigorous adherence to the distribution rites (Almond 2003, 18, 81). However, it is equally possible that members of the hunt who were allocated the 'lesser' joints of venison may have worked, and consumed food, within the castle. A further possibility is that some of the bones present at these sites were acquired illegally. While this is a practice largely associated with the peasantry (Birrell 1996), incidences of aristocratic poaching also exist. It is recorded in the Forest Pleas of 1286, for example, that in 1282 Roger de Somery, Lord of Dudley, whilst hunting in Baggeridge Chase, Cannock, put up a stag that fled into the Royal Forest of Kinver. Whilst in the Forest a member of Roger's household shot the stag and carried the venison to Roger's house at Swinford. Such an act contravened forest law and consequently Roger was fined 200 Marks (Birrell 1999, 119).

As noted, the hunting manuals indicated two approaches to the 'unmaking' of the roe deer. The identification of teeth, phalanges and limb-bones at the sites considered would suggest that complete carcasses were processed on site. Such a hypothesis accords well with the writings of Gaston Phoebus. However, it is possible that the preponderance of metapodials and cranial elements at Faccombe Netherton (Sadler 1990) is indicative of skinning waste. Perhaps because the roe deer was considered to be one of the lesser beasts of the chase in medieval hunting manuals it did not deserve such specialised treatment.

It is only hare, therefore, that were not 'unmade' according to the rules set out in the hunting treatises, since no predominance of hind-limb bones was noted at any of the sites studied. While hare coursing was highly considered, it did not require the preparation involved in deer hunting, and thus may have been a more informal or regular pursuit (Almond 2003, 67). Within this context, the selective butchery and redistribution of the small carcass may have been viewed as an unnecessary literary ideal.

Taking a functionalist perspective, the systematic division of deer carcasses, as outlined in the hunting manuals, provided a practical guide to butchery (Almond 2003, 81; Stringer 1714, 116–7). However, while the aristocracy may have expressed a dietary preference for haunches (Maltby 1982, 128), there were clearly other motivating factors behind the adherence to the rules of the 'unmaking'. Firstly, this ritualistic butchery enabled the aristocracy to express their dominance over nature, as well as converting a "worthy opponent" into food "worthy of consumption" (Salisbury 1994, 48). The ability to separate the carcass in a systematic way also required education and knowledge of a specialised vocabulary and thus provided a further means of separating aristocrat hunting from lower class imitations (Almond 2003, 89; Henrick 1982, 32; Sykes in press). Although if, as Birrell (1992, 113) suggests, hunting was carried out on a regular and systematic basis by servants "charged with

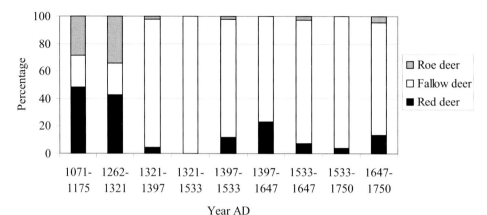

Fig. 10.9. *Relative proportion (%NISP) of red, fallow and roe deer at Dudley Castle, West Midlands, by phase (after Thomas 2002, Fig. 4.6).*

the task of supplying their employers with deer", they appear to have been well versed with the requisite techniques.

The fact that the various parts of the animal were differentially distributed also provides an indication that each part of the carcass had an implicitly understood status value. This may have served as an analogue for the hierarchy of medieval society and acted as a means of reinforcing social order, with the best portions of meat going to those at the top of the social scale. In this context, the allotment of the pelvis to the raven is intriguing because this bird was emblematic of the clergy in the medieval period in England (Klingender 1971, 353). This allocation may therefore have fulfilled an act of religious thanksgiving, for example, or satisfied one of the many allegorical aspects of the hunt (see above).

The clearest change in hunting practice over the later medieval period occurs around the 13th and 14th centuries. During this period, there is a shift towards the hunting of older red and fallow deer at a number of sites. In addition, there appears to be a shift in the distribution of body parts of both red and fallow deer at some sites, towards an increasing emphasis on hind-limb elements. Such evidence, while not substantial, tentatively indicates a growing adherence to the recommendations of the hunting manuals. In order to determine the cause of these phenomena it is necessary to consider the broader historical context.

The period under consideration witnessed a greater commodification of land. Part of this process saw an increase in the number of parks (Rackham 1986, 123) as a countermeasure against the decline in woodland, relaxation of forest law, a rise in status seeking, and the growth in the importance of local lords (Cantor 1965; Stamper 1988, 140). The development of parks may have also been facilitated by the extension of woodland and pasture at the expense of arable following the population decline in the middle of the 14th century (*e.g.* Dyer 1991, 80; Thirsk 1997, 11–12). In tandem, this period witnesses a shift in the relative proportions of the three deer species at many sites, from equal proportions of all three to a preponderance of fallow (fig. 10.9). This partly reflected the fact that fallow deer, being a communal, herd-dwelling species, were better suited to the park environment (Yalden 1999, 153).

Following the expansion of parks and the more widespread utilisation of fallow deer, the hunting and management of deer may have become much more strictly controlled and the development of 'park-hunting', which provided viewable entertainment (Cummins 1988, 57), may have necessitated greater emphasis of rituals. The importance of display was doubtless facilitated by the Edwardian chivalric revival in the 14th century (Almond 2003, 29). Thus, deer hunting became a stage on which the aristocracy performed according to a script – a phenomenon that may well be linked to the growing 'theatricality' of the tourney and jousting in this period (Henrick 1982, 23–4). The fact these changes coincided with the publication of four of the most 'influential' manuals on the hunt (Almond 2003, 146–7; Thiébaux 1967, 265) is perhaps unsurprising. Indeed, Sykes (forthcoming) has noted that it was only in the 13th century, following the publication of hunting treatises, that the characteristic hind-limb predominance on French archaeological sites is observed. The 13th and 14th centuries also witnessed a growing diminution of the boundaries between the aristocracy and the peasantry, as the former was increasingly drawing cash revenues from their manors and peasant rents, and there was a growing demand for wages (Thomas in press). One aristocratic response to this threat to their position was the invocation of Sumptuary Laws (*e.g.* Pickering 1762, 164) and property qualifications restricting those who could have the necessary equipment to participate in hunting (Henrick 1982, 26). The increased consumption and reliance of the elite on wild birds as status differentiators within the diet from the 14th century, also appears to reflect growing concern amongst the aristocracy with social climbers (Albarella and Thomas 2002, 29; Thomas in press b). As Henrick (1982, 34) notes, "the development of formality may be related to a group's need to solidify its identity". Given the fact the hunt provided an important means of social separation, the greater adherence to hunting rituals at some sites may have reflected an aristocratic attempt to reestablish social boundaries, and reaffirm their own identity, in response to the changing nature of later medieval society.

Conclusion

At the beginning of this paper I posed the question of whether the medieval hunt had a primarily functional or symbolic focus, given the way in which deer, for example, appear to have been extensively managed. On reflection, adopting a Cartesian dichotomy between these two interpretations is a gross oversimplification. As Pluskowski (2002, 167) has noted, it is not possible to separate conceptual and physical in the medieval period since the two were so interwoven. Clearly, animals were used as a means of creating and manipulating relationships through the acquisition and consumption of particular foods and in the participation of certain activities (see, for example, Soderburg 2004, 167) and through their symbolic associations (see, for example, Stocker and Stocker 1996). The hunt and its products were thus an important and active part of medieval material culture. It is evident from the zooarchaeological data that many of the recommendations of the hunting manuals were enacted. While these were pragmatically grounded, both the managed animals and the stages of the hunt were imbued with symbolic meanings. The fact that there may have been a growing concern to enforce hunting rituals around the 14th century is consistent with the view that the aristocracy were becoming increasingly insecure about their own position in this period.

Acknowledgements

I would like to thank the following people for helping me to complete this paper: Naomi Sykes, for allowing me sight of unpublished data from Castle Rising and Guildford Castle in addition to two forthcoming articles; Jane Richardson for access to unpublished data from Pontefract Castle; and Umberto Albarella, Neil Christie and Heidi Thomas and the anonymous reviewer for their helpful comments on earlier versions of this paper. I would also like to express my gratitude to the University of Leicester for granting me a period of study leave to conduct this research.

Bibliography

Albarella, U. and Davis, S. (1996) Mammals and birds from Launceston Castle, Cornwall: decline in status and the rise of agriculture. *Circaea* 12, 1–156.
Albarella, U. and Thomas, R. (2002) They dined on crane: bird consumption, wild fowling and status in medieval England. *Acta Zoologica Cracoviensia* 45, 23–38
Almond, R. (1994) Medieval deer hunting. *Deer* 9 (5), 315–318.
Almond, R. (2003) *Medieval Hunting*. Stroud, Sutton Publishing Limited.
Bartosiewicz, L. (1995) *Animals in the Urban Landscape in the Wake of the Middle Ages. A Case Study from Vác, Hungary*. British Archaeological Reports, International Series 109. Oxford, Archaeopress.
Benton, J. R. (1992) *The Medieval Menagerie: Animals in the Art of the Middle Ages*. New York, Abbeville Press.
Birrell, J. (1991) Deer and deer farming in medieval England. *Agricultural History Review* 40, 112–126.
Birrell, J. (1992) The forest and chase in medieval Staffordshire. *Staffordshire Studies* 3, 23–50.
Birrell, J. (1996) Peasant deer poachers in the medieval forest. In R. Britnell and J. Hatcher (eds.) *Progress and Problems in Medieval England: Essays in Honour of Edward Miller*, 66–88. Cambridge, Cambridge University Press.
Birrell, J. (ed.) (1999) The forests of Cannock and Kinver: select documents 1235–1322. *Collections for a History of Staffordshire* (Fourth Series) 18.
Brewer, E. (1992) *Sir Gawain and the Green Knight: Sources and Analogues*. Cambridge, Cambridge University Press.
Cantor, L. M. (1965) The medieval parks of South Staffordshire. *Transactions and Proceedings of the Birmingham Archaeological Society* 80, 1–9.
Chaplin, R. E. and White, R. W. G. (1969) The use of tooth eruption and wear, body weight and antler characteristics in the age estimation of male wild and park fallow deer (*Dama dama*). *Journal of Zoology* 157, 125–132.

Chapman, D. I. (1975) Antlers – bones of contention. *Mammal Review* 5 (4), 122–172.

Chapman, D. and Chapman, N. (1975) *Fallow Deer: Their History, Distribution and Biology.* Lavenham, Terence Dalton Ltd.

Clutton-Brock, T. and McIntyre, N. (1999) *Red Deer.* Grantown-on-Spey, Colin Baxter Photography Ltd.

Cummins, J. (1988) *The Hound and the Hawk: The Art of Medieval Hunting.* London, Weidenfeld and Nicholson.

Davis, S. J. M. (1987) *Prudhoe Castle. A Report on the Animal Remains.* London, Ancient Monuments Laboratory Report 162/87.

Driesch, A. von den. (1976) *A Guide to the Measurement of Animal Bones from Archaeological Sites,* Harvard University, Peabody Museum Bulletin 1.

Dyer, C. C. (1989) *Standards of Living in the Later Middle Ages: Social Change in Britain c.1200–1520.* Cambridge, Cambridge University Press.

Dyer, C. C. (1991) The West Midlands. In E. Miller (ed.) *The Agrarian History of England and Wales Volume III: 1348–1500,* 77–91. Cambridge, Cambridge University Press.

Fawcett, J. K. (1997) *Roe Deer.* Cheddar, SP Press.

Griffith, N. J. L., Halstead, P. L. J., Maclean, A. and Rowley-Conwy, P. A. (1983) Faunal remains and economy. In P. Mayes and L. A. S. Butler (eds.) *Sandal Castle Excavations 1964–1973,* 341–8. Wakefield, Wakefield Historical Publications.

Habermehl, H. (1985) *Altersbestimmung bei Wild- und Pelztieren.* Hamburg-Berlin, Paul Parey.

Hands, R. (ed.) (1975) *English Hawking and Hunting in* The Boke of St. Albans. Oxford, Oxford University Press.

Henrick, T. S. (1982) Sport and social hierarchy in medieval England. *Journal of Sport History* 9 (2), 20–37.

Hunt, J. (1997) *Lordship and Landscape: A Documentary and Archaeological Study of the Honor of Dudley c. 1066–1322.* British Archaeological Reports, British Series 264. Oxford, Archaeopress.

Jones, R., Sly, J., Simpson, D., Rackham, J. and Locker, A. (1985) *The Terrestrial Vertebrate Remains from The Castle, Barnard Castle.* London, Ancient Monuments Laboratory Report 7/85.

Klingender, F. (1971) *Animals in Art and Thought to the End of the Middle Ages.* London, Routledge and Kegan Paul.

Lawrance, P. J. (1982) Animal bones. In J. G. Coad and A. D. F. Streeten (eds.) Excavations at Castle Acre Castle, Norfolk, 1972–77, country house and castle of the Norman earls of Surrey, 275–296. *Archaeological Journal* 139, 138–301.

Lyman, R. L. (1994) *Vertebrate Taphonomy.* Cambridge, Cambridge University Press.

Maltby, M. (1982) Animal and bird bones. In R. A. Higham, J. P. Allan and S. R. Blaylock (eds.) Excavations at Okehampton Castle, Devon, 114–135. *Devon Archaeological Society* 40, 19–152.

Pickering, D. (ed.) (1762) *The Statutes at Large from the Fifteenth Year of King Edward III to the Thirteenth Year of King Hen. IV. Vol. II.* Cambridge, Joseph Bentham.

Pluskowski, A. G. (2002) Hares with crossbows and rabbit bones: integrating physical and conceptual studies of medieval fauna. *Archaeological Review from Cambridge* 18, 153–182.

Rackham, O. (1986) *The History of the Countryside: The Classic History of Britain's Landscape, Flora and Fauna.* London, J. M. Dent.

Reitz, E. J. and Wing, E. S. (1999) *Zooarchaeology.* Cambridge, Cambridge University Press.

Richardson, J. (2002) The mammal bones. In I. Roberts (ed.) *Pontefract Castle. Archaeological Excavations 1982–86,* 363–385. Yorkshire Archaeology 8. Exeter, West Yorkshire Archaeology Services.

Sadler, P. (1990). Faunal remains. In J. Fairbrother (ed.) *Faccombe Netherton. Excavations of a Saxon and Medieval Complex II*, 462–508. London, British Museum Occasional Papers No. 74.

Salisbury, J. E. (1994) *The Beast Within: Animals in the Middle Ages.* London, Routledge.

Skinner, A. (1714). The Experienced Huntsmen. Belfast, Blow.

Soderburg, J. (2004) Wild cattle: red deer in the religious texts, iconography, and archaeology of early medieval Ireland. *International Journal of Historical Archaeology* 8 (3), 167–183.

Stamper, P. (1988) Woods and parks. In Astill, G. and Grant, A. (eds.), *The Countryside of Medieval England*, 128–148. Oxford, Basil Blackwell Ltd.

Stocker, D. and Stocker, M. (1996) Sacred profanity: the theology of rabbit breeding and the symbolic landscape of the warren. *World Archaeology* 28 (2), 265–272.

Sykes, N. J. (2005) Hunting for the Anglo-Normans: zooarchaeological evidence for medieval identity, 73–80, in A. Pluskowski (ed.) *Just Skin and Bones? New Perspectives on Human-Animal Relations in the Historic Past.* British Archaeological Reports, British Series. Oxford, Archaeopress.

Sykes, N. J. (forthcoming) *The Norman Conquest: a Zooarchaeological Perspective.* British Archaeological Reports, British Series. Oxford, Archaeopress.

Thiébaux, M (1967) The medieval chase. *Speculum* 42 (2), 260–274.

Thirsk, J. (1997) *Alternative Agriculture. A History from the Black Death to the Present Day.* Oxford, Oxford University Press.

Thomas, R. (2002) *Animals, Economy and Status: The Integration of Historical and Zooarchaeological Data in the Study of a Medieval Castle.* Unpublished Ph.D. thesis, University of Birmingham.

Thomas, R. (2005). *Animals, Economy and Status: The Integration of Zooarchaeological and Historical Evidence in the Study of Dudley Castle, West Midlands (c.1100–1750).* BAR British Series 392. Archaeopress, Oxford.

Thomas, R. (2006) Of books and bones: the integration of historical and zooarchaeological evidence in the study of medieval animal husbandry. In M. Maltby, (ed.), *Integrating Zooarchaeology.* Oxford, Oxbow.

Thomas, R. (in press) Food and the maintainance of social boundaries in medieval England, in K. Twiss (ed.), *We Are What We Eat: Archaeology, Food, and Identity.* Carbondale, Center for Archaeological Investigations Occasional Publication No. 31.

Yalden, D. (1999) *The History of British Mammals.* London, T and A D Poyser Ltd.

Chapter 11

Taking Sides: the Social Life of Venison in Medieval England

Naomi Sykes

Introduction

In 1159 John of Salisbury complained that 'In our days, the scholarship of the aristocracy consists in hunting jargon' (*Policraticus* 1.4, I.23). He was referring to the strict social etiquette and Gallicised terminology that, following the Norman Conquest, came to surround aristocratic hunting (Sykes 2005). Knowledge of these new hunting rituals was deemed to mark a person as noble, a belief that both persisted and intensified through the later medieval period (Rooney 1997, 12). Because of this, and the body of historical evidence surrounding it, there has arisen a tendency to view hunting as an activity significant only for the medieval elite. Certainly the aristocracy was fanatical about hunting but it was this preoccupation which drew in all social classes and made hunting central to popular culture – in practice it was far from socially exclusive.

The ritualised nature of noble deer hunting, but also the social mixing it entailed, is perhaps best exemplified by the 'unmaking' – the climax of the hunt when the quarry was skinned, disembowelled and butchered in a ceremonial fashion (see Thomas this volume). Several hunting manuals depict unmaking scenes and illustrate the high level of non-aristocratic involvement: that shown in Gaston Phoebus' *Livre de chasse* (MS fr. 616 Ch. 40, fol. 70), for example, indicates that just three of the ten huntsmen are noble, the remaining seven being hunt-servants or yeomen. Not only were these lower-status men active participants in the hunt, it seems that they would have been entitled to a share of the venison. Medieval hunting manuals suggest that body-part gifting was an integral part of the unmaking process, with certain portions and sides of the carcass being given to particular individuals. Instructions vary considerably between manuals (for examples see Thiébaux 1967; Cummins 1988, 180) but in general, as Thomas (this volume) has already outlined, hunting dogs received much of the offal, the '*corbyn*' bone (the pelvis) was cast away as an offering to the '*corbyn*' (crow or raven) and, more significant for this paper, the shoulders (upper forelimbs) were also gifted: one side – the left according to the *Tretyse off Huntyng* (Rooney 1987) – was as presented to the forester or parker as his fee, with the other going to the best hunter or the breaker of the deer.

Evidence that the unmaking procedure, in particular the gifting of shoulders, was carried out in the manner suggested by hunting manuals is provided by household accounts and recipe books, which frequently refer to haunches of venison but seldom mention shoulders, indicating that these joints did not arrive back at aristocratic residences (Birrell forthcoming). More recently, zooarchaeological studies (Grant 1988; Sykes 2001; Thomas this volume) have confirmed the absence of 'gifted' portions in deer-bone assemblages from elite sites: those dating to the mid-eleventh to mid-12th century show a dearth of pelvic bones and a clear under-representation of meat-bearing elements from the forelimb, a pattern which becomes more defined through the course of the medieval period. The possibility that that these patterns are an artifice of inter-element variation in preservation, recovery or identification can be entirely discounted on the basis that multi-period assemblages, in particular those spanning the pre- and post-Conquest periods, record their appearance only after 1066, demonstrating that their arrival is both linked to Norman influence and reflects a true shift in cultural practices (Sykes 2005 and forthcoming a).

If it is accepted that only two thirds of each deer was regularly transported to a lords residence then, by concentrating exclusively on elite sites, we are overlooking at least one third of all venison consumption that took place in post-Conquest England. This oversight is even greater if the quantities of illegally-obtained venison are taken into account: according to Birrell (1982, 124) the numbers of deer poached annually from parks could be very high. In this paper I hope to redress the balance and shine a light on the lower social life of venison in later medieval England. To do this, I will be examining the body part data for red deer (*Cervus elaphus*) and fallow deer (*Dama dama*) assemblages from keepers' residences, villages and towns. I shall also consider documentary evidence collated by historians such as Jean Birrell (1982, 1992, 1996, 2001 and forthcoming) and Roger Manning (1993). By marrying these two sources of evidence together, I shall attempt to argue that deer hunting and venison consumption were as meaningful to the lower classes as they were to the elite: creating social cohesion on the one hand, facilitating acts of subversion on the other, but always playing a role in the construction of peasant identity.

The legitimate

Before the data from other site types are examined it is worth rehearsing briefly the evidence from elite assemblages. Figure 11.1 shows the combined body-part patterns for red and fallow deer from three later medieval sites – Guildford Castle (Sykes forthcoming b), Faccombe Netherton (Sadler pers. comm.) and Stafford Castle (Sadler pers. comm.) – assemblages selected due to the availability of siding data. As would be expected from the historical evidence, they show a clear scarcity of elements from the upper forelimb: the scapula, humerus, radius and ulna are all under-represented by comparison to hindlimb elements. Otherwise elite assemblages are entirely uniform, exhibiting parity in the representation of left and right elements.

The final destination of the gifted shoulder joints is, on the surface, difficult to ascertain from the archaeological record, since there are few obvious deer assemblages which show an over-representation of forelimb elements. But this is perhaps to be

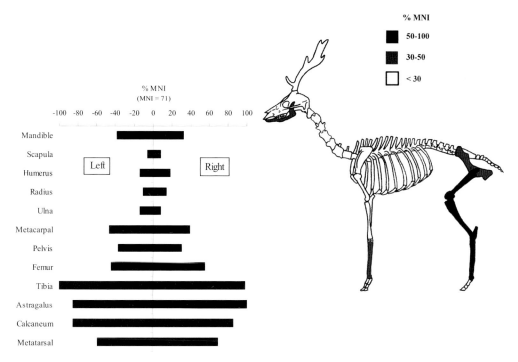

Fig. 11.1. Anatomical representation of deer from elite sites.

expected within the context of venison gifting, as the meat from the forequarters would have been distributed far more widely than that from the haunches (fig. 11.2). Such circumstances would potentially result in a range of contexts containing forelimb elements in low frequencies, perhaps too low to attract attention from zooarchaeological researchers. Another possible reason for the apparent absence of forelimb-dominated assemblages is that the type of sites where shoulders of venison were consumed may have been little investigated by archaeologists. Credence is added to the latter suggestion when the zooarchaeological evidence from forest workers' residences are examined. Few of these site types have been excavated but examples include Lodge Farm in Dorset (Locker 1994 and n.d), Donnington Park Lodge in Leicestershire (Bent 1977–8) and the site of Stanstead Lodge in Essex, which has recently been investigated by Framework Archaeology (Bates n.d.). One further site can tentatively be added to these – the tower from Ascot Doilly Castle, which appears to have been occupied by workers of the Doilly estate (Jope 1959). Interestingly, the assemblages from these sites contain an abundance of deer remains, their frequency being far higher than is commonly seen on elite sites (fig. 11.3). In terms of anatomical representation, their deer body-part patterns are in complete opposition to those from most high-status settlements: when the data are viewed together (fig. 11.4) they demonstrate an over-representation of forelimb elements and a scarcity of those from

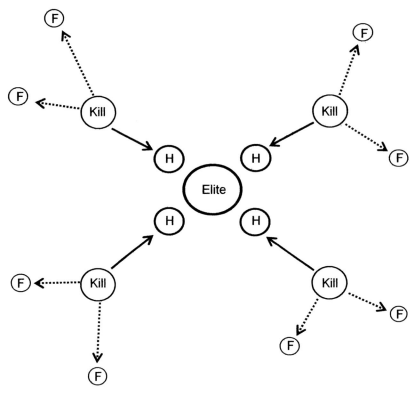

Fig. 11.2. Landscape model showing the concentration of deer hindlimbs (H) versus the dissipation of forelimbs (F) as they move from the kill-site (kill).

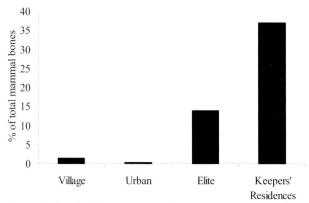

Fig 11.3. Inter-site variation in the representation of deer remains, shown as a percentage of the total count of mammal bone fragments.

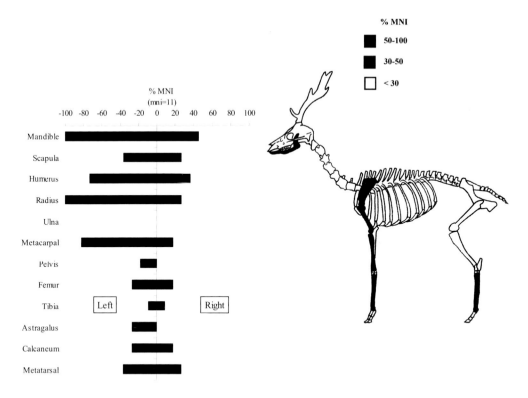

Fig. 11.4. Anatomical representation of deer from keepers' residences.

the hind-limb – indeed, of the 80 or so fallow deer fragments from Stanstead Lodge none was from the hindlimb (Bates n.d.). Furthermore, each of the assemblages was skewed towards the left side of the carcass; application of the Chi-squared test suggests this to be statistically significant. Taken together this is strong evidence to suggest that, as outlined in the *Tretyse off Huntyng*, the parkers regularly received their allotted shoulders of venison. Indeed, if the data in Figure 11.3 are representative of the true situation, it would appear that venison made a substantial contribution to the meat diet of forest workers, and one wonders how prized venison would actually have been in this context: hunting and venison consumption was perhaps less prestigious to those for whom it constituted their livelihood and daily fare.

Having determined the fate of the left shoulders, what then of the hunters and their shoulder joints? Unlike foresters and parkers, hunters did not receive accommodation as a perquisite of office. As has been mentioned above, many of them were yeomen and most would have lived within the rural community. Animal-bone assemblages from medieval rural sites are notoriously scarce and are often badly preserved. With the exception of that from Lyveden in Northampton (discussed below) few village assemblages contain deer bones in any number. Fewer still is the number of zooarchaeological reports providing details of deer anatomical representation, so it

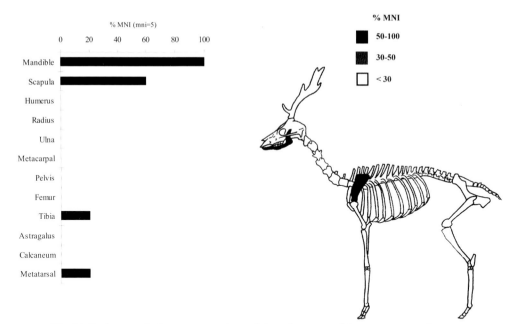

Fig 11.5. Anatomical representation of deer from rural low status settlements.

has been difficult to obtain a reasonable sized dataset. Despite this, the evidence gathered from five village assemblages – those from Seacourt in Oxfordshire (Jope 1961–2), Boteler's Castle in Leicestershire (Pinter-Belows 1997), Gomeldon in Wiltshire (Harcourt 1986) and the two Northamptonshire sites of West Cotton (Albarella and Davis 1995) and Brixworth (Coy *et al.* 1977) – is interesting.

Figure 11.5 shows that the mandible is the best-represented element in these assemblages. Quite plausibly this over-representation could be explained in terms of differential preservation – the jaw being the most robust element in the skeleton. However, we know from even the earliest hunting manuals that portions of the carcass were given to 'the poor' (Almond 2003, 77; Manning 1993, 40) and it seems possible that the head formed part of this gift. Certainly head bones tend to be under-represented in assemblages from elite sites (fig. 11.1), and it seems possible that, with the exception of those fed to the dogs or used as hunting trophies, heads could have been redistributed in this way.

In rural assemblages the only other element that is well represented is the scapula (fig. 11.5). Although the sample size is small, the significance of its presence becomes more apparent when the data are considered against the backdrop of elite assemblages. For instance, from the village of Boteler's castle, the only post-cranial deer bone recovered was a red deer scapula; at the village of Seacourt four deer bones were recovered and three of these were scapulae. By contrast, of the 784 specimens from Faccombe Nertherton, just two shoulder blade fragments were identified. Thus even with this limited dataset, rural assemblages appear to contain a greater proportion of scapulae than those from elite residences. Stretching the evidence even further, it is interesting to note that most of the elements from rural sites come from the right side of the body (all three of the scapulae from Seacourt were rights), which is what might be expected if village-dwelling hunters were receiving their dues. Considering how structured the body part patterns of elite and hunting lodges assemblages are, it is perhaps not entirely surprising that village assemblages show equally rigid patterning.

Indeed, it is this rigid structuring that embodies the legitimate procurement, distribution and consumption of venison. At every stage of the process people knew, and were reminded of, their place within society: different ranks had different roles within the hunt itself; the cut of venison they were given (be it haunch, shoulder or head) would have been a meaty symbol of social position, and even at the level of consumption different people were offered different venison dishes according to rank – the saying to 'eat humble pie' is derived from the social humiliation attached to the consumption of the offal, or 'numbles' (Goody 1982, 142). This status-based structuring is often considered in negative terms, as having been socially divisive (Rooney 1993; Sykes 2005b). To be sure, the framework was hierarchical and an individual would have known his place, but it was a place *within* a group. Legitimate hunting, venison distribution and consumption had the ability to create community and could actually narrow the gap between lord and peasant; participants would have perceived themselves to be on the same side. A parallel is easy to find in modern day fox hunting. From the outside it is often seen as an elitist activity and, again, it does contain elements of hierarchy, but all participants (riders and foot-followers) would argue that the hunt is entirely egalitarian and is central to their lifestyle and identity (Howe 1981; Milbourne 2003). I would argue that the medieval deer hunt, together with the rituals that surrounded the distribution and consumption of venison, was similarly important to all, not just the elite, who participated in it.

Whilst many members of society were undoubtedly involved in hunting, and profited from it, there would have been others who were either excluded from or objected to the social group that practiced it. For them, the structured nature of legitimate hunting could be manipulated for their own ends, providing the perfect opportunity for expressing defiance and subverting authority. Birrell (1982, 2001) and Manning (1993) have shown clearly that members of the gentry and nobility regularly often employed poaching in this way, but the discussion below concentrates on evidence pertaining to the lower classes of rural and urban society.

The illicit

It was an established unwritten rule that venison was priceless – a perk of office or something that was gifted as a demonstration of royal or aristocratic largesse – it certainly should not be bought or sold (Birrell, 1992, 114). One way of undermining control was then, simply to sell gifted portions. Historical evidence demonstrates that under-paid and disgruntled forest workers were occasionally caught flogging their

Naomi Sykes

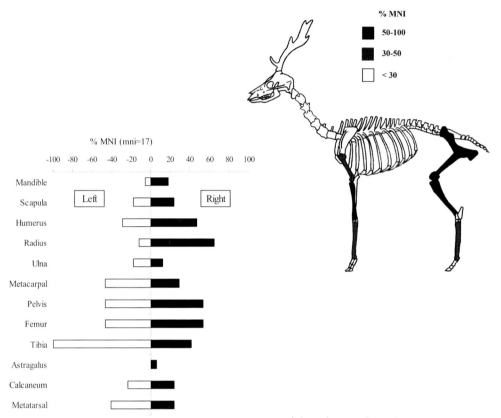

Fig 11.6. Anatomical representation of deer from urban sites.

share (and more) on the urban black market (Birrell 1982, 16; Manning 1993, 28–32). That this occurred is supported by the zooarchaeological evidence: Figure 11.6 shows that bones from the forelimb are well-represented, especially when compared to the mandible and foot bones, suggesting that quantities of pre-butchered venison did, indeed, percolate into towns. When examined side by side, the source of some of these portions can be conjectured. All five of the urban assemblages considered here – two from sites in Reading (Sykes n.d. a and Emma-Jayne Evans, pers. comm.), one from Carlisle (Emma-Jayne Evans, pers. comm.), one from Sussex (Sykes, n.d. b) and the last from Oxford (Sykes n.d. c) – demonstrated a forelimb distribution skewed to the right-hand side; perhaps the hunter's share?

   The over-riding impression provided by the body part patterns, however, is that they do not conform to the structured anatomical representation seen on other sites and it would seem that venison was brought into towns through a variety of mechanisms, some legitimate but perhaps the majority illicit. Individuals (keepers or hunters) may have brought a shoulder here or a haunch there, but a few complete carcasses must also have arrived – this is suggested by the presence of at least some mandibles and foot bones but also the pelvis, an element that ought to have been discarded had the unmaking rituals been observed. The acquisition, manhandling and distribution of a whole carcass would have been beyond a single individual, requiring a greater degree of collusion and cooperation. We must surely be looking at zooarchaeological evidence for the organized poaching gangs that operated out of urban taverns and alehouses, where they also consumed and sold their bag (Manning 1993, chapter 6; Birrell 1982, 14). The method and meaning of this form of venison procurement, distribution and consumption was, in many ways, different to that surrounding the aristocratic hunt: usually operating at night to avoid detection, poaching gangs would have moved within a darker, shadier and, perhaps more exciting, landscape and their hunting would have carried feelings of social defiance and thus personal empowerment. Although often undertaken for commercial ends, we should not assume that this type of hunting was without ritual – Manning (1993) has demonstrated that the success of these gangs was that they had their own codes of conduct which, for them, legitimized their actions and tied them together. Within the safety of the tavern, the communal consumption of their ill-gotten venison, together with the drinking, story telling and general bravado it entailed, would have cemented the fraternity in much the same way it did for legitimate hunting groups. The difference between the two was simply that they were on opposites sides, each viewing one-another with contempt.

Moving on to the less flamboyant side of poaching, Jean Birrell (1982, 1996) has shown that peasants used a variety of methods to obtain venison. Few of these methods – such as the setting of traps or the collection of dead, wounded and diseased animals – constituted true hunting but they were, nevertheless, illegal activities. A classic example of peasant poaching comes from the village of Lyveden, a settlement where poaching is attested by both the historical (Birrell 1982, 21) and zoo-archaeological (Grant 1971) record. The animal-bone assemblage from the site contained not only a heavily-butchered red deer skeleton which was 'hidden' down a well but also a range of other deer bones from all parts and sides of the body, a pattern in no way suggestive of the unmaking procedure. In this case it would seem that the acquisition and breaking of the carcass was governed more by the need for stealth, to avoid capture by patrolling foresters, than to play out any kind of social performance. But again, we should not see peasant poaching and venison con-sumption as devoid of social significance. Whilst it is often stated that peasants poached as an act of desperation, because they were hungry, it seems wholly unlikely that this was generally the case: Manning (1993, 20) has found little evidence to support such assumptions. As has already been explained, hunting and venison consumption were part of popular culture, and their significance would not have been lost on rural peasants. They too had a sense of occasion and sought to include venison on their festive menus (Birrell, 1996, 84). Deer were often taken specifically for these events, the poachers gifting the venison throughout their community (Manning 1993, 153; Birrell 1996, 84–5). Whether for reasons of defiance or emulation, this poaching, redistribution and consumption of venison allowed rural peasants to engage with and participate in wider social practice – it was important to them.

Conclusion

Medieval deer hunting and venison consumption has often been described as simply a pastime or luxury restricted to the upper classes. Venison was, without doubt, a currency of power – its procurement and redistribution both a reflection and prescription of social order – but it was not solely the preserve of the elite and could be used to subvert and challenge the very institution that established it as a prestige item.

This paper has sought to demonstrate that the methods and meanings of venison procurement, distribution and consumption were varied, multifaceted and context-dependent. Indeed, the unmaking tradition actually allowed venison from a single carcass to be consumed within a variety of social scenes – the haunches arriving at the aristocratic table, the shoulders forming part of the daily diet of a forest-worker and, if gifted shoulders were sold on the urban black market, it was even possible for venison to move from the legitimate to the illicit.

Currently the zooarchaeological data pertaining to lower-status venison procurement and consumption are scarce with few reports providing specifics concerning skeletal representation, let alone siding information. As a result, the sample size on which this study is based is woefully small, demonstrating the need for rigorous reporting on wild animal remains so that the models presented here might be tested and developed.

Acknowledgements

I am indebted to Andrew Bates, Emma-Jayne Evans and Peta Sadler for supplying me with unpublished data – this paper would not have been possible without their help. My thanks go also to Jean Birrell, David Hinton and Dale Serjeantson for reading and commenting upon an earlier draft of the text.

Bibliography

Albarella, U. and Davis, S. (1994) The Saxon and medieval animal bones excavated 1985–1986 from West Cotton, Northamptonshire. Unpublished Ancient Monuments Laboratory Report 17/94.

Almond, R. (2003) *Medieval Hunting*. Stroud, Sutton.

Bates, A. n.d. The animal bones from the Stanstead excavations 1999 to 2001, unpublished report for Framework Archaeology.

Bent, D. C. (1977–78) The animal remains, 14–15 in P. Liddle (ed.) A late medieval enclosure in Donnington Park. *Transactions of the Leicestershire Archaeological and Historical Society* LIII, 8–29.

Birrell, J. (1982) Who poached the Kings deer? A study in 13th century crime. *Midland History*, 7, 9–25.

Birrell, J. (1992) Deer and deer farming in medieval England, *Agricultural History Review* 40, II, 112–126.

Birrell, J. (1996) Peasant deer poachers in the medieval forest. In R. Britnell and J. Hatcher (ed.)

Progress and Problems in Medieval England: Essays in Honour of Edward Miller. 68–88. Cambridge, Cambridge University Press.

Birrell, J. (2001) Aristocratic poachers in the Forest of Dean: their methods, their quarry and their companions. *Transactions of the Bristol and Gloucestershire Archaeological Society* 119, 147–54.

Birrell, J. (forthcoming) Procuring, preparing and serving venison in late medieval England. In C. Woolgar, D. Serjeantson and T. Waldron (eds.) *Food in Medieval England: History and Archaeology*. Oxford, Oxford University Press.

Coy, J., Bramwell, D. and Jewell, J. (1977) Animal bones, 119–122 in R. Cramp, P. Everson and D. N. Hall (ed.) Brixworth Archaeological Research Committee. Excavations at Brixworth 1971 and 1972. *Journal of the British Archaeological Association* 130, 52–122.

Cummins, J. (1988) *The Hound and the Hawk: the Art of Medieval Hunting*. London: Weidenfield and Nicholson.

Goody, J. (1982) *Cooking, Cuisine and Class: A Study in Comparative Sociology*. Cambridge: Cambridge University Press.

Grant, A. (1971) The animal bones, 90–93 in G. F. Bryant and J. M. Steene (ed.) Excavations at the deserted medieval settlement at Lyveden. A third interim report *Journal of the Northampton County Borough Museum and Art Gallery* 9.

Grant, A. (1988) The animal resources. In G. Astill and A. Grant (eds.) *The Countryside of Medieval England*. 149–187. Blackwell: Oxford.

Harcourt, R. (1986) Animals bones, 166–69 in J. Musty and D. Algar, Excavations at the deserted medieval village of Gomeldon, near Salisbury, *Wiltshire Archaeological and Natural History Magazine* 80, 127–169.

Howe, J. (1981) Fox hunting as ritual, *American Ethnologist* 8 (2), 278–300.

John of Salisbury, *Policraticus I–IV* ed. K. S. B. Keats-Rohan (1993), Turnholt: Brepols.

Jope, M. (1959). Animal bones, 269–70 in E. M. Jope and R. I. Threlfall, The twelfth-century castle at Ascot Doilly, Oxfordshire. *Antiquaries Journal* 39, 219–272.

Jope, M. (1961–2) The animals bones, 197–201 in M. Biddle, The medieval village of Seacourt, Berkshire. *Oxoniensia* 26–27, 70–210.

Locker, A. M. (1994) Animal bones, 107–110 in M. Papworth, Lodge Farm, Kingston Lacy estate, Dorset. *Journal of the British Archaeological Association* 147, 57–121.

Locker, A. M. (n.d) The animal bones from Lodge Farm. Archive Report held at the Kingston Lacey estate.

Manning, R. B. (1993) *Hunters and Poachers: A Cultural and Social History of Unlawful Hunting in England 1485–1640*. Oxford, Clarendon Press.

Milbourne, P. (2003) Hunting ruralities: nature, society and culture in 'hunt countries' of England and Wales, *Journal of Rural Studies* 19, 157–171.

Pinter-Belows, S. (1997) Animal Bone, 65–73 in C. Jones, G. Eyre-Morgan, S. Palmer and N. Palmer (eds.) Excavations in the outer enclosure of Boteler's Castle, Oversley, Alcester, 1992–93. *Transactions of the Birmingham and Warwickshire Archaeological Society* 101.

Rooney, A. (ed.) (1987) *The Tretyse off Huntyng* (Medieval and Renaissance texts and studies 19) Brussels, Scripta.

Rooney, A. (1993) *Hunting in Middle English Literature*. Cambridge: Boydell Press.

Sykes, N. J. (2005) The zooarchaeology of the Norman Conquest, *Anglo-Norman Studies* 27, 185–197.

Sykes, N. J. (2005b) Hunting for the Normans: zooarchaeological evidence for medieval identity. In A. Pluskowski (ed.) *Just Skin and Bones? New Perspectives on Human-Animal Relations in the Historical Past*, 73–80. British Archaeological Report, British Series, Oxford, Archeopress.

Sykes, N. J. (forthcoming a) The impact of the Normans on hunting practices in England. In C. Woolgar, D. Serjeantson and T. Waldron (eds.) *Food in Medieval England: History and Archaeology*. Oxford, Oxford University Press.

Sykes, N. J. (forthcoming b) The animal bones. In R. Poulton (ed.) *Guildford Castle and Royal Palace*. Surrey Archaeological Society Monograph.

Sykes, N. J. (n.d. a) The animal remains from Reading Oracle sites 12 and 29. Unpublished report to Oxford Archaeology.

Sykes, N. J. (n.d. b) The animal bones from Marlipins Museum, Shoreham, Sussex. Unpublished report to Sussex Archaeological Society.

Sykes, N. J. (n.d. c) The animal bones from Codrington Library, All Souls College, Oxford. Report to John Moore Heritage Services.

Thiébaux, M. (1967) The medieval chase, *Speculum* 42, 260–274.

Chapter 12

Animals as Material Culture in Middle Saxon England: The Zooarchaeological Evidence for Wool Production at Brandon

Pam Crabtree

Introduction

Trained as an archaeolozoologist in the early 1970s, at the height of the processual movement in archaeological theory, I began my career as a dyed-in-the-wool paleoeconomist. My research focused on the use of faunal remains for the reconstruction of Anglo-Saxon diet, animal husbandry practices, and hunting strategies. When I applied for my first university teaching position, one of the social anthropologists, Gananath Obeysekere, asked me what kinds of information could be gleaned from animal remains other than information on past economic practices. I found the question difficult to answer, and it forced me to begin to think about the non-dietary roles of animals in early medieval societies. I have spent the past 20 years trying to answer Professor Obeysekere's question. I am delighted that the theme of this volume is animals as material culture in the Middle Ages. In this short paper, I plan to show how the animals from Brandon, a Middle Saxon site in East Anglia, were used as material culture in three different ways. I will briefly examine the role of horses in ritual and the ways in which animals were used to express social status. The bulk of the paper will focus on the role of sheep in textile production at Brandon.

Archaeological background

Between 1979 and 1988, the Suffolk County Archaeological Unit, under the direction of Bob Carr and Andrew Tester, carried out eight seasons of excavation at the at the Middle Saxon settlement site at Staunch Meadow, Brandon, Suffolk (fig. 12.1), in advance of the construction of athletic fields (Carr *et al.* 1988). The site is located on a small island which was never plowed, ensuring excellent preservation of the Middle Saxon remains. Approximately 13,000 square meters of the site were excavated, revealing 34 timber buildings marked by postholes, plus at least 20 fence lines, 35 ditches, pits, hearths, and a church and cemetery. An industrial area was identified around the waterfront on the north of the island.

The artifactual evidence and structural evidence from Brandon indicates that it was a wealthy, Christian community (Carr *et al.* 1988). While some researchers have

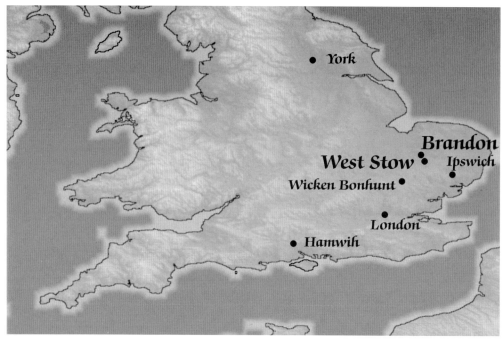

Fig. 12.1. Map of southern Britain showing the location of the sites mentioned in this paper.

suggested that Brandon might represent an early monastic community, there is no clear archaeological or documentary evidence to support this assertion. Ceramics and other dating evidence indicate that Brandon was occupied during the Middle Saxon Period. The site was initially occupied around A.D. 650, about the time that the nearby early Saxon settlement of West Stow was abandoned (West 1985; Crabtree 1990). The Middle Saxon occupation At Brandon ended by around A.D. 900, possibly as a result of flooding. Recent detailed analyses of the Brandon pottery have provided little evidence for occupation of the site between 850 and 900 A.D., suggesting a somewhat earlier date for the end of the Middle Saxon occupation.

   The excavations at Brandon yielded a large and well preserved faunal collection, including more that 158,000 fragments of mammal and bird bone. Most of the faunal remains were recovered from a general cultural layer, about 10–15 cm thick, that covered the site. As a result, few bones could be assigned to specific chronological phases within the Middle Saxon period. The vast majority of the faunal remains were those of domestic animals, including sheep, cattle, pigs, horses, chickens, and geese. Although most of the animals bones were the remains of domestic animals, a diverse range of wild birds and mammals was recovered from the Staunch Meadow site including red deer (*Cervus elaphus*), roe deer (*Capreolus capreolus*), hare *(Lepus europaeus)*, otter (*Lutra lutra*), badger (*Meles meles*), grey seal (*Halichoerus gryphus*)a small whale or dolphin, diver (*Gavia stellata*), bitterne (*Botaurus stellaris*), swan (*Cygnus olor*), and the extinct East Anglian crane (*Grus* sp.).

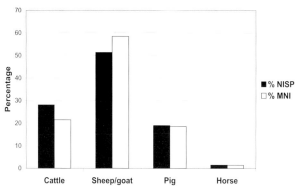

Fig. 12.2. *Species ratios for the large domestic mammal remains from the Middle Saxon site at Staunch Meadow, Brandon.*

The role of horses in ritual

Horse bones are relatively rare at Brandon; only 702 horse bones were identified from the entire Brandon faunal collection. Horses make up about 1.5% of the large domestic mammal remains on the basis of NISP and 1.4% on the basis of MNI (fig. 12.2). However, horse bones appear to have played an important role in certain ritual contexts.

A horse skull was found in the door pit leading into the chancel of the Brandon timber church that was constructed around A.D. 700. This archaeological context also produced a number of other associated horse bones, including fragments of the mandible, vertebrae, and ribs. The male horse was an elderly animal. The teeth are more heavily worn than any horse teeth that were recovered from early Saxon West Stow, and two of the vertebrae show slight lipping and fusion.

A second, possibly similar, deposit was recovered from context 9151 at Staunch Meadow. Although a horse skull was not present, this context produced the remains a horse's mandibles, ribs, vertebrae, and pelves. These finds come from an area that produced a very small amount of rubbish, but it is directly above a complex of entryway pits and postholes to the Saxon phase of the chapel enclosure. This find is still under study, but it is possible that these finds are the redeposited remains of a deliberate partial horse burial.

These data suggest that horse skulls and other axial elements may have been placed symbolically under doorways. I am still searching for parallels and antecedents, but the evidence from East Anglia suggests that the burial of horse skulls under doorways may be traced as far back as the Roman Period (Andrew Tester, personal communication). There is substantial evidence for the burials of horses, including horse heads, in ritual contexts from the Early Anglo-Saxon Period in eastern England. The burial of a horse head, including tack, was recovered from the pagan Anglo-Saxon cemetery at Snape. The horse head was associated with a wealthy burial, Grave 47. In addition to the Snape find, horse burials are known from the sites of

Icklingham, Sutton Hoo, and Lakenheath in Suffolk (Filmer-Sankey and Pestell 2001, 256). Filmer-Sankey and Pestell (2001, 259) note that horse burials are more than simple markers of high status; they "arguably fulfilled deeper ritual associations." The Brandon data suggest that these ritual associations may have continued into the Middle Saxon Period, even after the adoption of Christianity.

Animals as markers of social and economic status

The most striking feature of the bird assemblage from Brandon is the presence of a nearly complete skeleton of a peregrine falcon (*Falco peregrinus*). The presence of this bird at Brandon is significant for three reasons. First, it represents the earliest archaeological example of a peregrine falcon from medieval England. Vandervell and Coles (1980, 29), for example, note that, "The history of hawking in England probably goes back to the seventh or eighth century, but the actual dates are not clear." Second, since peregrines' natural habitats are cliffs and upland areas (Lascelles 1892, 236), the Brandon falcon most probably represents a captive bird. Peregrines, however, do occasionally occur in East Anglia as non-breeding visitors (Heinzel *et al.* 1972). Third, falconry is traditionally a sport of the upper classes. For example, *the Boke of St. Albans* (1486) describes the peregrine falcon as suitable for an earl (Hands 1975). The rich artifactual evidence recovered from Brandon indicates that the site was occupied by a comparatively wealthy population in Middle Saxon times. The presence of a peregrine falcon further documents the wealth and status of the Brandon community. A single bone of hawk or buzzard (*Buteo buteo*) was also identified in the Brandon bird collection, and this bird might have been used for hawking as well.

Sheep and textile production

While exotic species such as falcons provide important information about Anglo-Saxon Brandon, nearly all the animal bone remains recovered from Brandon were identified as domesticates. The most common mammals were sheep, cattle, pigs, and horses. Sheep remains made up the majority of the large domestic mammal bones on the basis of both fragment counts and minimum numbers of individuals. Sheep bones make up 51.4% of the large mammal NISP and 58.5% of the Minimum Numbers of Individuals (MNI) (see fig. 12.2). While these species ratios are similar to the ratios seen at the nearby early Saxon site of West Stow (figs. 12.3a and b), they are very different from the species proportions seen at other Middle Saxon sites in East Anglia (fig. 12.4). Sheep play only a minor role in the faunal assemblages from the Middle Saxon emporium at Ipswich in Suffolk (fig. 12.4b) and the Middle Saxon rural site of Wicken Bonhunt in Essex (fig. 12.4c). Cattle are the most common animals at Ipswich (Crabtree n. d. 1), as they are at other Middle Saxon emporia including AnglianYork (O'Connor 1991), Hamwic (Bourdillon and Coy 1977; 1980), and Middle Saxon London (West 1989). Pigs predominate at Wicken Bonhunt, which appears to have been a specialized Middle Saxon site, possibly a site where food rents were collected (Crabtree n. d. 2).

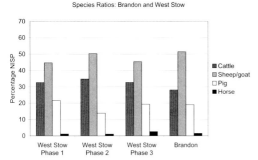

Fig. 12.3a. Comparison of species ratios (based on NISP) for Brandon and the Early Anglo-Saxon site of West Stow, Suffolk. At West Stow, Phase 1 is fifth century, Phase 2 is sixth century, and Phase 3 is late sixth and early seventh century.

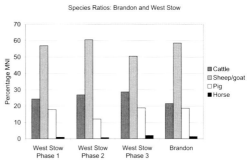

Fig. 12.3b. Comparison of species ratios (based on MNI) for Brandon and the Early Anglo-Saxon site of West Stow, Suffolk.

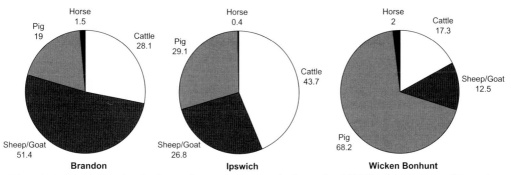

Fig. 12.4. Species ratios for large domestic mammals from the Middle Saxon sites of Brandon (a), Ipswich (b), and Wicken Bonhunt (c).

While the Brandon and West Stow faunal assemblages are both dominated by sheep, measurement evidence and ageing data indicate that the sheep played very different roles at the two sites. Measurements on a range of complete long bones were used to calculate withers heights for the sheep from Brandon and the 6th century contexts at West Stow, following the recommendations of von den Driesch and Boessneck (1974) (fig. 12.5). While the West Stow sheep had an average estimated withers height of 61.9 cm, the average Brandon sheep stood only

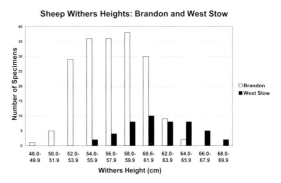

Fig. 12.5. Distribution of withers heights for sheep from Middle Saxon Brandon and sixth century (Phase 2) West Stow.

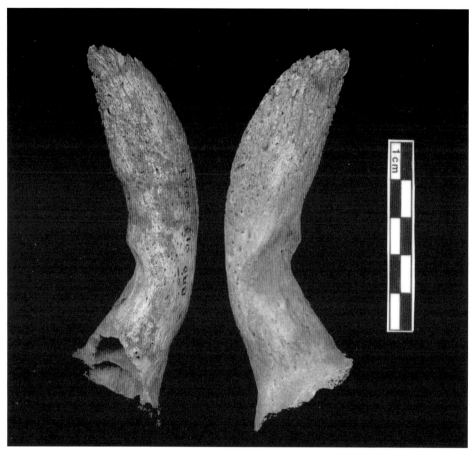

Fig. 12.6. Sheep horn core from Brandon showing possible signs of malnutrition.

56.6 cm at the withers. In short, the average West Stow sheep was over 5 cm taller than the typical Brandon sheep. These differences are significant at the p = 0.01 level, based on a Student's t-test.

In order to test the significance of these size differences more systematically, t-tests were used to compare the Brandon and the West Stow sheep, based on a series of individual measurements on the limb bones, following von den Driesch (1976). The greatest lengths (GL) of the metacarpus, metatarsus, calcaneus, and the distal breadth (Bd) metatarsus are all significantly smaller in the Brandon sheep (p = 0.05). In short, detailed measurement analyses suggest that the Middle Saxon Sheep from Brandon were generally smaller than their early Saxon counterparts from West Stow.

The small stature of the Brandon sheep may be explained in several ways. First, it is possible that overgrazing and poor nutrition may have led to a decrease in sheep size at Brandon. Several female sheep horn cores from Brandon showed the "fingerprint" depressions that may reflect poor nutrition (fig. 12.6). Alternatively, it is possible that the West Stow sheep maintained some of the size increase that was

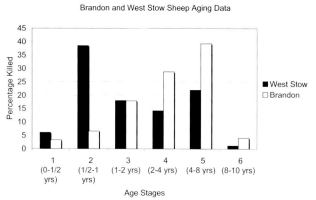

Fig. 12.7. *Age profiles based on dental eruption and wear for sheep from Middle Saxon Brandon and Early Anglo-Saxon sheep from West Stow.*

introduced to Britain by the Romans, as seen in the very large sheep from the nearby Roman site of Icklingham (Crabtree 1991). However, the ageing data suggest another possibility. The small Brandon sheep may, in fact, reflect the introduction of a new breed of sheep, possibly a more specialized wool producer. Future comparisons of measurements on teeth from Brandon and West Stow may allow us to determine whether these size differences are genetic or environmental in nature.

The ageing data, based on dental eruption and wear (Payne 1973; Grant 1982), show that the majority of the Brandon sheep survived to adulthood (fig. 12.7). The West Stow assemblage includes a higher proportion of animals killed during the first two years of life, while the Brandon collection includes a much higher proportion of mature animals. When the two age profiles are compared using a Kolmogorov-Smirnov test, the differences are significant at the $p = .001$ level. The increasing important of wool production would certainly explain the increased numbers of adult animals in the Brandon faunal assemblage (Payne 1973). In a wool-producing flock, we might also expect to find a substantial proportion of adult males, since castrated males or wethers are excellent wool producers. Of the 521 sheep horn cores and pelves from Brandon whose sex could be determined with reasonable certainly, 309 or approximately 59% were male. To conclude, the ageing and sexing data for the Brandon sheep can be used to make a strong circumstantial case for the development of specialized wool production in Middle Saxon East Anglia. This archaeological evidence for wool production from Brandon does not exist in isolation. Botanical evidence for flax, hemp, and dye plants indicates that textile production and dyeing also took place in the waterfront industrial area at Brandon (Carr *et al.* 1988).

Conclusion

While the final publication of the Brandon site report is more than a year away, the faunal data from this important site provide clear evidence for the varying roles that animals played in Anglo-Saxon material culture. Although horses were a minor component of the Brandon faunal assemblage, they clearly played a role in ritual in the early Christian community. Peregrine falcons and other birds of prey may have played important roles as markers of social and economic status. Sheep appear to have been kept as specialized wool producers at Brandon. This marks an important change from the early Anglo-Saxon period when sheep were kept for a variety of purposes including meat, milk, and wool (Crabtree 1990, 83–83; see also Archer 2003, 42). This specialization may be linked to the development of more complex societies in the Middle Saxon period in eastern England.

Acknowledgements

This research was carried out in collaboration with Douglas V. Campana. It was supported by the US National Endowment for the Humanities and English Heritage.

Bibliography

Archer, S. (2003) *The Zooarchaeology of an Early Anglo-Saxon Village: The Faunal Assemblage from Kilham, East Yorkshire*. M. Sc. Thesis, Department of Archaeology, University of York.

Bourdillon, J. and Coy, J. P. (1977) Statistical Appendix to Accompany the Animal Bone Report on Material from Melbourne Street (Sites I, IV, V, VI, and XX) Excavated by the Southampton Archaeological Research Committee Between 1971 and 1976. Unpublished ms. available at the Archaeology Department, University of Southampton.

Bourdillon, J. and Coy, J. P. (1980) The animal bones. In P. Holdsworth (ed.) *Excavations at Melbourne Street, Southampton, 1971–76*, 79–121. London, Council for British Archaeology Research Report No. 33.

Carr, R. D., Tester, A., and Murphy, P. (1988) The Middle-Saxon settlement at Staunch Meadow, Brandon. *Antiquity* 62, 371–377.

Crabtree, P. J. (1990) *West Stow: Early Anglo-Saxon Animal Husbandry*. East Anglian Archaeology, Report No. 47. Ipswich, Suffolk County Planning Department.

Crabtree, P. J. (1991) Roman Britain to Anglo-Saxon England: the zooarchaeological evidence. In P. J. Crabtree and K. Ryan (eds.) *Animal Use and Culture Change*, 32–38. Philadelphia, MASCA Research Papers in Science and Archaeology, Supplement to Volume 8.

Crabtree, P. J. (n. d. 1) The Animal Bone Remains from Ipswich Suffolk Recovered from Sixteen Sites Excavated Between 1974 and 1982. Unpublished manuscript on file at English Heritage.

Crabtree, P. J. (n. d. 2) Animal Bones Recovered from Wicken Bonhunt Essex. Unpublished manuscript on file at English Heritage.

Driesch, A. von den (1976) *A Guide to the Measurement of Animal Bones from Archaeological Sites*. Cambridge, Harvard University, Peabody Museum Bulleting No. 1.

Driesch, A. von den, and Boessneck, J. (1974) Kritische Anmerkungen zur Widerristhohen-berechnung aus Langenmasses vor- und frühgeschichtlicher Tierknocken. *Saugetierkundliche Mitteilungen* 22: 325–348.

Filmer-Sankey, W. and Pestell, T. (2001) *Snape Anglo-Saxon Cemetery: excavations and Sruveys 1824–1992*. East Anglian Archaeology, Report No. 95. Ipswich, Suffolk County Council Archaeological Service.

Grant, A. (1982) The use of tooth wear as a guide to the age of domestic ungulates. In B. Wilson, C. Grigson, and S. Payne (eds.) *Ageing and Sexing Animal Bones from Archaeological Sites*, 91–108. Oxford, British Archaeological Reports, British Series, No. 109.

Hands, R. (1975) *English Hawking and Hunting in The Boke of St. Albans*. Oxford, Oxford University Press.

Heinzel, H. Fitter, R. and Parslow, J. (1972) *The Birds of Britain and Europe*. London, Collins.

Lascelles, D. (1892) Falconry. In H. Cox and G. Lascelles (eds.) *Coursing and Falconry*, 217–371. The Badminton Library. Boston, Little, Brown.

O'Connor, T. P. (1991) *Bones from 56–54 Fishergate. The Archaeology of York*, Volume 15/4. London, Council for British Archaeology and the York Archaeological Trust.

Payne, S. (1973) Kill-off patterns in sheep and goats: the mandibles from Aşvan Kale. *Anatolian Studies* 23, 281–303.

Vandervell, A. and Coles, C. (1980) *Game and the English Landscape: The Influence of the Chase on Sporting Art and Scenery*. New York, Viking.

West, B. (1989) Birds and mammals from the Peabody site and National Gallery. In R. L. Whytehead and R. Cowie, Excavations at the Peabody Site, Chandos Place, and the National Gallery. *Transactions of the London and Middlesex Archaeological Society* 40, 150–168.

West, S. (1985) *West Stow: The Anglo-Saxon Village*. East Anglian Archaeology, Report No. 24. Ipswich, Suffolk County Planning Department.

Chapter 13

Animal Bones: Synchronous and Diachronic Distribution as Patterns of Socially Determined Meat Consumption in the Early and High Middle Ages in Central and Northern Italy

Marco Valenti and Frank Salvadori

Introduction

The Medieval Archaeology Section of the University of Siena has been engaged in the study of early medieval rural settlements for more than twenty years. Research has followed a strategy based on landscape surveys (so far we have covered about 9% of Tuscany), detailed catalogues of all published material and a number of long-term open area excavations. This has led to the elaboration of the "Tuscan model", as it is often defined by the Italian archaeological community: a historiographical model that is frequently discussed and considered to be a crucial point in the early medieval settlement debate. Its main points can be resumed as follows:

a – gradual decline of the *villa* system and of the rural population between the 5th and 6th centuries;

b – early medieval village formation around the beginning of the 7th century, when nucleated settlements become dominant;

c – aristocracies play a weak role until the mid 7th century and show a more incisive influence on the organisation of rural areas only from the 8th century;

d – transformation of many villages into private estates, through the adaptation of the *curtis* model to pre-existing settlements, during the 9th century;

e – evolution of the villages into castles during the 10th century, when estate organisation is maintained and strengthened by territorial dominium;

f – definitive transformation of castles into seats of power, with a territorial lordship exercised over a subordinate district, between the end of the 11th century and the 12th century.

Our efforts have mainly been concentrated on identifying a number of material indicators that would allow us to focus on interpretative matters connected to the socio-economical nature of villages in a diachronic perspective. The goal of this work is to better understand the affirmation of local powers through the interpretation of data on the rural productive class; this in turn leads us to a better understanding of the transformations in the administration and management of the land itself and of the means of production employed.

Analysis of settlement centres has therefore been based on residential features, on the functional use of buildings and open spaces, on the settlement's morphology, on the traces of production activities, and on diet and food distribution. The combination in space and time of all these factors allow us to determine the typology of each village, its productive vocation, the economic context in which it existed and the presence of internal hierarchies between the Lombard age and the Carolingian – Ottonian period.

Within this methodological framework, the study of archaeobotanical and archaeozoological remains takes on particular importance; early medieval society was, in fact, mainly rural and excavations have clearly shown the relevance of such material sources. Their analytical study therefore plays an important role in drawing up population patterns. Knowing about the control, availability and distribution of food supplies helps our understanding of productive activities and yields information about the allocation of "riches". In this sense, the amount of information derived from more traditional archaeological indicators such as pottery is far less significant, if not totally lacking.

In this paper we will deal with questions related to the study of animal bones from rural centres showing settlement phases of the 9th 10th centuries, a period for which we actually have the most consistent osteological samples. There are two main methodological issues at the basis of our work: the creation of sophisticated digital recording-processing systems and the primary focus of creating a socio-economic interpretation of data. Moreover, we will constantly compare what has been proposed by historical literature, based on written sources, with the knowledge produced by archaeology, underlining every point of convergence as well as the divergences in the models based the two different kinds of sources. Written sources for the early medieval period are generally almost inexistent, and therefore material evidence becomes of primary significance. Over the last 30 years archaeological research has finally produced a large amount of data, especially through its planned interventions, and the interpretative perspectives on rural societies (until now mainly based on laws and chronicles for the Gothic and Lombard age and on histories, lives of saints and, mainly, private documents between the 9th and the 10th centuries) have been markedly widened. The written sources have often been interpreted through a retroactive process, in some cases influenced by consolidated historiographical paradigms that can, at times, be seen as very strict grids (Valenti 2005).

As a consequence of our approach, we can identify three classes of data which have been used together in order to throw new light on the history of food consumption in early medieval rural communities in Northern and Central Italy, and especially on Tuscan sites: historiographical elaborations based on the interpretation of written sources, data from archaeological research, and osteo-zoological information.

Written sources

The economic organisation of early medieval Italian rural spaces is a theme that has been consolidated in the historical literature of the last 30 years. Nonetheless, it is quite difficult to form a synthesis of settlement patterns, forms of landscape population and production activities. The information is more detailed only in the case of some large monastic estates and is mainly limited to the period between the 9th and the 11th century, when juridical, social and economic viewpoints were favoured. In general, for Northern and Central Italy we do not have reliable economic and settlement patterns for the period preceding the formation of large landed estates (*latifundia*). We know about the existence of large fiscal territories and landed estates, which are sometimes interpreted as a direct derivation from the late Roman land management system, but our knowledge about them is very poor and it is impossible to understand their form and their real impact on the landscape.

The models proposed by historians are based on systematic studies of four kinds of documents: the goods inventories *(polittici)* of some large monastic Northern Italian *curtes*, the deeds of sale, the juridical disputes between lords and peasants, and all the laws of different periods. In brief, the trends recognized by these studies point towards some prominent economic-alimentary characteristics: diet was very varied, agriculture and the exploitation of uncultivated land were equally important, silvopastoral activities had a primary role in the socio-economic life, and hunting was practiced without distinction of social level.

The impression we get is that of a generalisation based on few and not entirely reliable data. With the partial exception of the *polittici*, none of the documents used explicitly deals with the aspects related to production and to food consumption. While the *polittici* register information limited to the great monastic properties, this cannot be applied to the most common type of settlement, smaller villages-estates, for which the excavated Tuscan examples show different production strategies and relationships. Duby himself clearly underlines the nature of early medieval goods inventories: "These *polittici*, in truth, project a very particular and probably deforming light on the realities of the countryside. This happens mainly for three reasons. First of all, the inventories describe only the agricultural estates submitted to the authority and the economical power of an owner. Nonetheless we are sure that there were also independent estates, but we will never know about their number, location and consistence because sources are missing. Also, nothing proves that the roles mentioned in the *polittici* about the fees due by the dependents always match the real repartition of land possession in the *ager*, since, in order to simplify the collection, administrators of the lords responsible of the redaction of the inventories affectedly kept on counting the old roles, which did not correspond anymore to reality. Finally, a *politico* is not a cadastre" (English translation of Duby 1984, 46–47).

A study conducted by Francois Bougart in 1995 (Bougart 1995) allows us to quantify the private written documents of this period (while royal degrees and papal bulls are extremely rare). If we consider Tuscany alone, the 8th century provided 308 documents, the 9th century 859 documents, and the 10th century 1,104 documents. Altogether there are 2,207 pieces, representing an apparently important source of information. But, if we look more closely, we can see that most of the documents come from the city of Lucca (1,730, corresponding to 88.27 %); this clearly represents a severe limit to the detection of trends to be considered valid for the whole region. If we continue with this basic statistical approach, it is possible to get an idea of the informative potentials of this dataset in the reconstruction of socio-economic and settlement dynamics. In Tuscany (an area of 22,290 km^2) we have one document every 74 km^2 in the 8th century, one every 26.76 km^2 in the 9th century and one every 22.10 km^2 in the 10th century. The results are even more discouraging for other regions, for which historiography has however managed to produce apparently solid syntheses. The analysis of written sources alone is therefore insufficient to explain the birth of early medieval settlements, their configuration, what material form the economic and social (if not organizational) changes took and, finally, the real history of production and of food consumption.

Archaeological sources

Archaeology has finally reached a methodological precision that allows the formulation of historiographical models, prompting renewed discussion of settlement trends. This also means reconsidering the written sources available within a framework composed of multiple elements of evaluation. In fact, archaeological models must remain independent from those proposed by historians: we should never force archaeological readings in order to fit suggestions derived from written sources. This is the main challenge of Medieval Archaeology, a discipline that is not yet fully taken into consideration by historiography. The latter remains substantially indifferent to the contribution made by material evidence, despite the fact that it is «surely able to "challenge" what has been outlined by the mere written sources», as recently highlighted by Francovich (Francovich 2004).

Over the last few years, research in Medieval Archaeology has focused on four main issues: how the end of late Roman landscapes came about; how the same landscapes changed in relation to the early medieval settlement types; what forms early medieval landscapes took; what role aristocracies played. The debate is particularly intense and is centred mainly on the territory of Tuscany and on part of Northern Italy. However, if we leave out the Tuscan cases, the formation of settlements in the early medieval countryside is only supported by significant data for a brief period immediately following the demise of the Roman *villae*, while the settlement patterns as well as their nature and evolution remain substantially obscure for the later centuries.

The archaeological record for Tuscany is based on a large number of excavations in villages with wooden buildings, preserved underneath the deposits of castles (fig. 13.1). This fact clearly shows how, in order to comprehend the formation, the transformation and the social and economic features of early medieval communities, it becomes of primary importance to study successful settlements which rappresent an example of the *globalisant* phenomenon. We can affirm that rural society in early medieval Tuscany was organized around nucleated settlements, set within a network of local economies. This was the dominant form of settlement, and we can understand the dynamics of economic and patrimonial relationships much better than political-institutional features through the urbanistic and structural transformations, which are clearly shown by archaeology.

The village can be compared to a stage on which all the productive forces of the countryside played a role in the mid 6th–10th century and where we can identify the

Fig. 13.1. Miranduolo (Chiusdino – Siena), aerial view of the excavation: early medieval evidence found underneath the castle.

material evidence of socio-economic relationships, the formation of rural *elites* and their long and arduous process of consolidation. With the creation of *curtes,* the hegemonic patrimonial basis was formed, determining the clear hierarchization of rural society that lies at the origin of territorial lordship.

The villages that have been found underneath Tuscan castles reveal the material form of the productive organisations existing in this period, showing how the *curtis* started from a system of pre-existing rural centres, which were urbanistically transformed as a consequence of the presence of an owner. In fact, with the transformation into the *curtis* organizational model, the settled area of the countryside was subject to marked reorganization, probably including a new method of labour management. The seats of power belonging to the settlement leaders appear as a very well arranged complex, sometimes surrounded by defence structures and physically separated from the houses of peasants; they are often located at the centre of the settlement or on hilltops. Another sign of change in the appearance of villages is the existence of buildings (stores and granaries) that clearly show the presence of a *possessor* who rationalized the agricultural produce. The same figure also had enough power – to centralize the productive structures for material goods (especially forges and furnaces) or for agricultural goods (ovens for cereal drying, grinders, and buildings used for the slaughtering and butchering of animals); to demand services from the peasants (building of palisades or walls, excavation of ditches; fig. 13.1); or to demand fees payable in kind; or, finally, to recruit skilled workers for specific tasks (building of churches).

Fig. 13.2. The Carolingian age village at Poggio Imperiale (Poggibonsi – Siena).

We can describe the *casa dominica* as a relatively small residential area, formed of the dwelling of the owner or of his agent, surrounded by stores, granaries, open spaces, stables and enclosures for animals, structures used for the production of artisan goods or for the processing of farming produce (fig. 13.2). In this context, diet and food consumption represent the most significant indicators in recognizing any kind of social differentiation. In conclusion, the definition of archaeological interpretative grids allows zooarchaeological research to contextualize the bone samples within an assortment of settlements, which differ in typology as well as in chronology.

Material sources

In this paper, based on the study of faunal remains, we have tried to identify analogies and divergences derived from the finds, which could somehow yield information about the economic and social characteristics of early medieval Tuscan rural communities; this has been done through a diachronic and synchronic comparative analysis of bone samples found in several medieval sites excavated by the Medieval Archaeology Area of the University of Siena.

Using this kind of approach, we have looked in particular at the different factors that determine the formation of a bone sample. The complexity of the whole process, called taphonomy in zooarchaeological literature, is well known. Taking into account all the interpretative difficulties, here we intend to focus on the three stages that are most intimately linked to material culture: the biotic, thanatic, perthotaxic processes (O' Connor 2000). The distribution of *taxa* and of the relative anatomical elements, observed through an intra-site perspective widened by inter-site correlations, are the indicators used in developing the interpretative grid relating to the three stages mentioned above.

The first type of information is derived from the evaluation of the arrangement of osteological segments within the archaeological space; specifically, we compared the bone samples of some Carolingian age structures excavated at Poggio Imperiale (figs. 13.3 and 13.4). In fact, this is not the first attempt to use spatial distribution of finds to draw archaeological conclusions (see, for example, Davis 1987 regarding the reconstruction of religious practices) or to understand how natural agents can concur in deposit formation dynamics (Tagliacozzo *et al.* 1999).

The second kind of synchronic analysis involved the anatomical state of preservation of swine bones found in 9th–10th century Tuscan villages. Observing which animal portions are better preserved and trying to explain the reasons behind these isolated data is a delicate deductive process, which cannot be done following a univocal interpretation criteria. If man is, in most cases, the main cause of the creation of archaeological deposits, anatomical distribution can give us important information on methods of butchering and dietary habits. Even taking into account the fact that that we were working on a sample, and therefore only a part of the whole productive process, this deductive methodology aims to go beyond the contrast between production and consumption that was formalised in the past (Clark 1997).

The third analysis has a diachronic perspective and regards the comparison between faunal composition of long-term settlements, through the examination of samples from early medieval villages and the later castles.

The case of Poggio Imperiale

Within the grounds of the Medicean fortress of Poggio Imperiale (Poggibonsi – Siena), an open-area excavation has revealed the presence of a settlement of wooden buildings dating from the mid 9th century to the beginning of the 10th century. The village topography shows an organized space which can be interpreted as the centre of a *curtis*, with a dominant central longhouse (hut 3) next to some functional structures, such as a large granary and what was probably a hen-house (or a sort of straw stack); a slightly sunken road departs from the longhouse and is bordered by several smaller huts (fig. 13.2; Valenti 2004).

The analysis of osteological finds was focused on a comparison between the different structures. This method is based on the axiom that the spatial dispersion of bones is the result of a combination of animal and anthropic factors, as part of a long process which transforms the original living animal population into a fossilized sample (King 1994): therefore the study of their spatial distribution means understanding the dynamics of deposit formation.

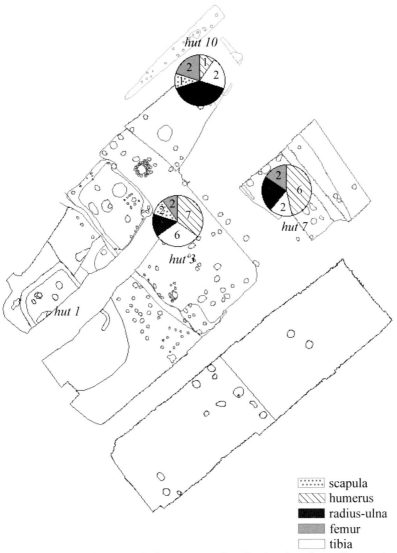

Fig. 13.3. Poggio Imperiale GIS platform: Bos, *distribution based on diagnostic areas (see legend), bone fragments per structure.*

Data processing was done within a GIS solution developed at the LIAAM (Laboratory of Information Technology applied to Medieval Archaeology), consisting of a relational database (Boscato, Fronza, Salvadori, 2003) and a GIS platform (Nardini, Salvadori, 2003). The use of GIS as an advanced analysis tool turned out to be extremely useful in the production of thematic maps where the frequency results obtained through the DBMS are efficiently visualized. This kind of approach directly

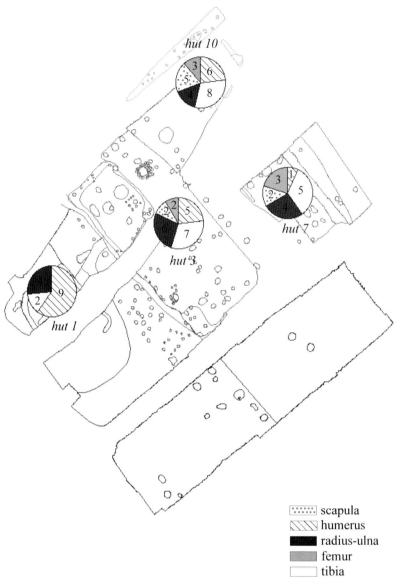

Fig. 13.4. Poggio Imperiale GIS platform: Ovis-Capra, *distribution based on diagnostic areas (see legend), bone fragments per structure.*

influenced our research, allowing easy spatial reading of the context and a consequent improvement in the possibility of evaluating and interpreting the deposits.

The anatomical consistence of ox remains, analysed by taking significant "diagnostic areas" (in this case only long bones; fig. 13.3), into consideration shows a clear disparity between the huts of the village. In hut C1, for example, there were no

Table 13.1. Bone fragmentation related to ox limbs from huts C3 and C10 of Poggio Imperiale.

Osteological segment	hut C3	hut C10
humerus_distal	1	
humerus_medial	1	
humerus_medio-distal	1	
humerus_proximal	3	1
radius_medial	1	
radius_proximal	1	
radius_medio-proximal		2
radius-ulna_medio-distal		1
ulna_proximal	2	1
femur_distal	1	
femur_medio-proximal	1	
femur_medial		2
tibia_distal	1	1
tibia_medial	2	
tibia_medio-distal	2	
tibia_proximal	1	1

ox limbs, while we found a few bone segments related to the lowest quality cuts of meat (phalanges, teeth). Differences are also evident between the huts C3 and C10. First of all in terms of frequency, as it seems to be indicated by the 16 limb anatomical segments found in hut C3, against the 9 fragments found in hut C10. It may also be that the quality of meat cuts was different between the two structures, if we accept the bone fragmentation (table 13.1) as a valid indicator for the comprehension of alimentary customs. A comparison between the two structures shows differences especially in the presence of medial parts; these are frequent in hut C3 and are almost completely absent in hut C10, where we find more fragments related to limb extremities. In conclusion, the finds seem to show a lower bovine meat consumption by the inhabitants of hut 10, probably related to low quality cuts.

The same processing method was applied to osteological segments of sheep/goats; we were able to identify anomalies that derived directly from the dietary customs of the inhabitants of the village in this case too.

In hut C1 the absence of bovine meat seems to be compensated by the presence of sheep/goat bones. However, also in this case, the evidence shows an almost complete lack of forelimbs (fig. 13.4). In fact, the anatomical distribution in other dwellings appears to be more complete and the samples from different huts are quite homogeneous, also in their state of fragmentation.

Hut C7 is a different case, where the archaeological evidence suggests that it was a functional structure dedicated to slaughtering and the allocation of meat cuts amongst the inhabitants of the village. The bone samples from this building have strong analogies with the distribution in hut C3, except for the higher presence of bones with clear signs of slaughtering and a significant number of fragments related to slaughtering waste (cranial parts, teeth, small bones).

On the basis of archaeological and faunal information, the site of Poggio Imperiale can be interpreted as a socially structured village, where the quantity and quality of meat clearly reflects its organisation. The material indicators of these customs are bovine meat and the hind quarter cuts of goats/sheep, which allow us to understand the methods of food sharing between the inhabitants. If hut C1 seems to be the house of a servant (*prebendario*), the food remains indicate the almost exclusive consumption of sheep/goat forelimbs and of bovine meat waste. In contrast, the inhabitants of hut C10 appear to have had access to better cuts of meat, though still of low quality. The family living in hut C3 consumed the best cuts and in larger quantities.

The large estate property organised on the land-management model of the *curtis* became widespread in Italy during the 9th century. In its classical form, this model was composed of two complementary parts: the *massaricium* and the *pars dominica* (Montanari 1990). The village of Poggio Imperiale has all the characteristics of a dominical centre, which is the part of the *curtis* directly managed by the lord and inhabited by the *prebendari* servants. The name *prebendari* derives from the fact that the servants were directly dependent on the lord who provided their food (Bloch 1976; Montanari 1990). Therefore, in our case meat would have had a socially distinctive value, as it was used by the lord to show off his condition and his control over individual subjects.

Inter-site correlation: the anatomical distribution of pigs

We have not so far considered the distribution of pig bones within the buildings of Poggio Imperiale. This is due to the substantial homogeneity between the samples in all buildings and, even more so, to the low incidence of the species in the total sample. The most significant data regard the very low frequency of hind limbs as compared to the number of forelimbs; moreover, femoral fragments were not found and cranial elements were rare (Poggio Imperiale, fig. 13.5).

The problem of the anatomical integrity of animal species within archaeological deposits (and not only there) is often dealt with in archaeozoological literature (O' Connor 2000). The schlep effect has been referred to in order to explain different anatomical distributions regarding single species. The concept has mainly been applied to pre- and protohistoric contexts, as the result of an idea influenced by geographic and naturalistic determinism. In other words, anatomical disparities observed within a sample are thought to be mainly due to the size of the animal and to the distance between where the prey was killed and where it was consumed. The greater these values (weight and distance), the smaller the parts transported to the settlement will be (Alhaique 2000).

The greater complexity of medieval economic systems, in comparison to prehistoric periods, and the development of routes and means of communication introduce new variables in the explanation of possible differences in the anatomical distribution of species.

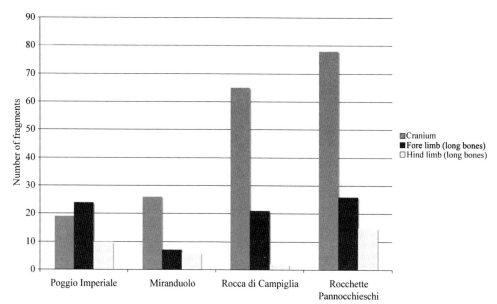

Fig. 13.5. Sus, anatomical distribution in Tuscan villages (9th–10th centuries).

To apply the schlep effect to medieval communities means also taking into account economic and social factors as crucial components in the process of formation of an osteological sample and, as a direct consequence, in the anatomical distribution of the respective *taxa*. As has been recently noted, there is no univocal method of counting anatomical parts for the evaluation of a bone deposit. It is the quality and quantity of data, associated with the archaeological and historical context, that make it possible to interpret each individual situation and draw a sufficiently reliable historical conclusion on that basis (O' Connor 2000). Therefore, in our case we considered disparities in the presence of anatomical segments of pigs, in particular the difference between fore and hind limbs and their relationship with the cranial parts, and came up with the hypothesis that the evidence could be due to this animal being imported into the village in the form of cuts of meat (specifically the shoulder). The suggestions that seemed to arise in this context were then compared to other settlements of the same period, where applying the same type of interpretation helped us to better understand to what extent our hypothesis was correct. The samples involved in the comparative study were all from the mid 9th–10th century and were from the Tuscan sites of Poggio Imperiale (1), Rocca di Campiglia (2), Miranduolo (3) and Rocchette Pannochieschi (4) (fig. 13.6).

The first and most evident data regards the differences in numbers of cranial bones in relation to other anatomical parts: on all sites except Poggio Imperiale this was the most commonly represented part (fig. 13.5). The presence of a high number of osteological fragments related to slaughtering waste, such as teeth, cranial parts and mandibles, is usually related to on-site slaughtering practices. This means that the

Fig. 13.6. The Tuscan villages of the 9th–10th centuries that were involved in inter-site correlation.

village of Poggio Imperiale clearly distinguishes itself from all the others, and in this case we believe that the general trends strengthen the hypothesis of importation. If we consider the relationship between hind and fore limbs, on the other hand, we can see a strong similarity between Poggio Imperiale and the site of Rocca di Campiglia. However, the prominence of cranial bones and the ages at death observed at Rocca di Campiglia suggest two opposing interpretations of the sites. We have already discussed the probable importation of shoulder cuts in the former, while the same meat was probably exported from the latter.

Trying to reconcile data emerging from material evidence with the more general historical background in which the village of Poggio Imperiale is set is certainly a complex process, but a necessary one if the ultimate aim of our research is to produce historical knowledge. It is therefore important to understand the economic processes behind the importation of pig portions to a specific site, the commercial network that the village belonged to, and the methods of exchanging goods with the neighbouring settlements.

The specific characteristics of the Carolingian age economy have been thoroughly discussed and explained by several historians on the basis of written sources (Duby 2004 for Central and Northern Europe; Andreolli, Montanari 1985 for Italy). The *curtis* system is the economic form that most strongly influenced the social and economic life of Europe in this period. From this point of view, we are convinced that Poggio Imperiale, as already mentioned above, can be interpreted as the administrative centre of a *curtis*: a site characterised by a complex social structure and a well organised topography, where the goods produced by the estate were gathered and stored.

In the early Middle Ages the relationship between the landed property and the dependent *mansi* was regulated in various ways, including manual labour on the land directly dependent on the *curtis* centre (*corvées*) and the payment of fees or rent either in kind or in money. In our case the existence of rent seems to be of particular relevance. Historians tell us that in the Romanized territories the tenants paid the lord mainly in kind or in money, while manual labour on the owner's land was a less common form of payment (Duby 2004). Some documents from Central and Northern Italy seem to partially confirm this trend (Andreolli Montanari 1985) but, above all, they provide a clear indication of the importance of pigs as an object of fiscal transaction in regulating land use, especially in relation to uncultivated land (Montanari 1990). The most significant reference, due to its obvious analogies with our case, is a form of tax (or donation) known as *amiscere* that dates back to the 10th century in Italy. This payment usually took the form of a pig's shoulder or a few coins (Andreolli Montanari 1985).

In conclusion, we cannot be absolutely sure that food waste reflects what is written in the documents, but the convergence between all the indicators involved (archaeological, zoological and documentary sources) concur in the interpretation of the settlement as the administrative centre of a *curtis* estate. Within this context the remains of pigs could, at least in part, be the material evidence of payment to the landowner by tenant peasants living in the farmsteads (*mansi*) or in other villages.

The role of hunting in the Early Middle Ages

Hunting requires separate treatment, since it was strictly tied to the evolution of early medieval society and subsequently turned into a custom of the *elite* when territorial lordship was established. This process is recognized by most historians, who tend to identify in the formation of local lordships and the feudal society a crucial moment, in which the differences in lifestyle and dietary habits of the hegemonic and subordinate social classes were already defined. Hunting started to have a decisive social role when it lost the traits of a common right, open to all social levels, to become a privilege reserved for a few people: an exercise of the dominant class that served to legitimise power and those who held power. Although the birth of hunting as described seems to be generally accepted by historiographers, there are several different points of view regarding the dynamics that led to such a transformation in the significance of venatorial activities.

According to Grand-Delatouche (Grand, Delatouche 1981), hunting was initially open to everyone but there were differences based on social classes: while the great landowners hunted large animals, peasants and small land owners did not have the necessary time or means to pursue such an activity. The history of venatorial activities in the Middle Ages is, in the opinion of these authors, a reflection of the evolution of rural societies and of the spread of agricultural practices. Therefore, in the early Middle Ages the only hunting interest for peasants was that of preserving the crops and livestock from the threat represented by wild animals; in the following centuries, when game became scarce as a consequence of the expansion of cultivated land, the wild animals themselves became the object of protection by the noble land owners.

The historiographical school of Bologna has developed a different model, in which hunting represented a crucial economical resource during the early Middle Ages: a real food supplement for both nobles and peasants (Montanari 1990; Fumagalli 1994). The evolution of venatorial activities is mainly explained under a social perspective. The opposing behavioural models of nobles and peasants, which became clear between the 8th and the 9th century, was much less obvious in the first centuries of the early Middle Ages because of the strong presence of a "mixed" social class composed of the farmer-warriors (Flandrin, Montanari 1997). The disappearance of this class, or rather the social levelling out that began early in the Middle Ages and ended only with the definitive attainment of a feudal society, was documented in the 9th century when the laic world was deliberately (but not yet institutionally) divided into *bellatores* and *laboratores*. The term *laboratores* does not mean generic "workers", but specifically "farmers" and people who worked on the land. From the 9th century the areas dedicated to venatorial activities, namely the woods and forests, began to be systematically closed to rural communities and were increasingly perceived as places reserved to nobles and to their hunting activities. This was where early medieval lords, who basically showed no interest in agricultural work and field management, found their true "productive" interest: in hunting (Flandrin, Montanari 1997).

Galloni expresses a last opinion on the subject. According to this scholar (Galloni 1993), the appropriation of hunting rights by nobles is the result of a process that started at the beginning of the early Middle Ages, when all men where virtually free to chase wild animals since there were no specific rules to forbid it in the barbaric laws; this situation does not seem to have been subject to any changes until at least the 11th century. The only exception is represented by the royal hunting reserves, known from documents of the 7th century onwards in France; in these places venatorial activities were prohibited to everyone (including nobles) without a specific authorisation issued by the king (Galloni 1993; Montanari 1990). The appropriation of venatorial rights by local lordships is explained as a process of acculturation of the aristocracies. In other words, there was a slow but constant acquisition of royal privileges from the beginning of the early Middle Ages; the process reached its highpoint immediately after the fall of the Carolingian Empire. After 1000 AD, with the definitive affirmation of a feudal society, venatorial activities were increasingly influenced by the will of *potentes*, who could decide to prohibit hunting, demand the payment of fees, or even personally reserve some species or parts of the prey captured (Galloni 1993). In the context of this debate, of which we have just sketched the main contours, a detailed analysis of the bone samples of all sites showing the presence of wild animals represents the significant historical contribution that archaeology and zoology can provide.

An initial overview, produced at the beginning of the 1990's (Baker, Clark 1993), showed that bones belonging to wild species were totally absent or extremely rare in all samples from the 6th–11th centuries. This information seemed to deny the important role of hunting for early medieval rural communities. In contrast, the systematic cataloguing of all published archaeozoological data for the Italian Middle Ages (a project which is currently in progress at the University of Siena) shows a constant presence of wild species in all Central and Northern Italian settlements that later became castles; the data is particularly clear if compared to different settlement types (fig. 13.7). Several faunistic samples from Italian castles register the presence of wild animals, sometimes in significant numbers, in the deposits linked to the appearance of the first stone buildings. This trend becomes even more impressive if we compare the data mentioned with those derived from early medieval villages of wooden huts, where such species were very often completely lacking.

A good example comes from the diachronic comparison between the deposits from the excavated Tuscan castles which are often founded on pre-existing early medieval settlements, as archaeological research has now clearly recognized (Francovich, Hodges 1990 and 2003; Valenti 2004). In Campiglia Marittima, for example, the oldest layers, related to a village of wooden buildings dating back to the 10th century, yielded no evidence of wild species, which were, on the contrary, present in the immediately subsequent phase associated with the construction of the first stone walls of the castle (11th century: the first documentary source is of AD 1004; Salvadori 2004). At Poggio Imperiale, where we have evidence of a village of wooden huts from the 6th century, there is no evidence of bones related to wild animals (Valenti, Salvadori 2003). The evidence at Miranduolo shows a different situation, where fragments of roebuck bones were found in the deposits dating back to the beginning of the 11th century, associated with the first stone circuit-wall that replaced a 10th century wooden palisade (the first written source is of AD 1004). The 8th–9th century deposits of the Montarrenti site yielded a few roebuck bone fragments, again corresponding to the period in which the oldest stonewall fortifications of the settlement were built; also in this case there is no evidence regarding wild animals in the previous phases (Clark 2003). Remains of roebuck and deer are associated with the first stone fortifications at the Rocchette Pannochieschi site (end of the 9th – beginning of the 10th century). The castles of Rocca San Silvestro and Scarlino have yielded fragments of roebuck and deer bones in the oldest deposits generically dated as 10th–13th century. An 11th century fill found inside the tower of the castle of Rocca Sillana contained a higher percentage of roebuck fragments than of any other species.

The same trend also seems to be traceable outside Tuscan territory. In Piedmont there are currently three cases: the castle of Manzano, Santo Stefano Belbo and San Michele di Trino (a long term settlement with continuity from the Roman period to the late Middle Ages). In the latter case the main concentration of wild species belongs to the 11th century deposits, related to a village of wooden huts with a well-made quadrangular stone building at the centre that does not appear to have been built by peasants. In Liguria there is evidence of deer remains, which represent the second

1 Montereale Valcellina
2 Rocca di Asolo
3 San Michele di Trino
4 Santo Stefano in Belbo
5 Castello di Manzano
6 Castello di Delfino
7 Poggio Imperiale
8 Rocca Sillana
9 Montarrenti
10 Miranduolo
11 Scarlino
12 Rocchette Pannoccheschi
13 Rocca San Silvestro
14 Campiglia Marittima

Fig. 13.7. Italy, GIS platform (elaboration by Federico Salzotti): sites with presence of wild species.

most common species in the 13th century and the oldest deposits at castle Delfino. In North-Eastern Italy, remains of wild species have been found in the 11th century contexts of the Rocca di Asolo in the Veneto region. In the region of Friuli, remains of large wild species came from the castle of Montereale Valcellina (for a bibliographical reference see Salvadori 2003).

The association between settlement typology and the presence of osteological remains related to wild species, as it appears to emerge from the evidence of castles and villages, prompts renewed reflection on the role played by venatorial activities in early medieval society in Central and Northern Italy. According to Chris Wickham, the *incastellamento* (castle formation) process in Tuscany, especially during the 11th century, represents the affirmation of a status symbol. In other words, a family owning a castle distinguished itself from the others. A castle became the necessary proof of membership of the "new aristocracy". Castles were clear signs of these attributes and represented the growing privatization of the structures of power (Wickham 1990).

On the basis of what we have discussed so far, it obviously becomes of vital importance to explain the meaning of the relationship between archaeological sequences, zoological evidence and information derived from written sources, in order to achieve an interpretation. The data we currently have at our disposal leads us to identify hunting as a mainly aristocratic prerogative. In fact, several material indicators show that the practice of hunting is strictly related to the presence of a person linked in some way to the military aristocracy, while peasants looked for other forms of subsistence activities. First of all the shift from wooden architecture to a new building technique characterised by the use of stone walls (albeit not particularly accurate or imposing at this stage). Secondly the appearance of wild species in the related contexts. Thirdly the change-over from a landed lordship to a territorial lordship that centralized public power and often made private use of it (*e.g.* the faculty of prohibiting hunting in reserves, forests or *garennes*).

Bibliography

Alhaique, F. (2000) *Schlep effect intrasito un esempio dai livelli del bronzo antico di Gerico (Palestina)*. In AA.VV. *Atti del III Convegno Nazionale di Archeozoologia*, c.s.

Andreolli, B. and Montanari, M. (1985) *L'azienda curtense in Italia. Proprietà della terra e lavoro contadino nei secoli VIII–XI*. Bologna, CLUEB.

Baker, P. and Clark, G. (1993) Archaeozoological evidence for Medieval Italy: a critical review of the present state of research. *Archeologia Medievale* 20, 45–77.

Bloch M. (1976) *Sviluppo delle istituzioni signorili e coltivatori dipendenti*. In Postan M. M. (ed.) *Storia economica Cambridge. Vol. I*. 288–354, Torino, Einaudi.

Boscato, P. Fronza, V. and Salvadori, F. (2003) Proposal of a faunal remains database. *Archaeofauna* 12, 113–126.

Bougart, F. (1995) *La justice dans le royaume d'Italie de la fin du VIII siècle au début du XI siècle*. Ecole francaise de Rome, Roma.

Clark, G. (1997) Monastic economies? Aspects of production and consumption in early medieval central Italy. *Archeologia Medievale* 24, 31–54.

Clark, G. (2003) *The mammal bone finds from Montarrenti*. In Cantini F. (ed.) *Il castello di Montarrenti*, 181–212. Firenze, All'Insegna del Giglio.

Davis, S. (1987) *The Archaeology of Animals*, London.

Duby, G. (1984) *L'economia rurale nell'Europa medievale. Francia Inghilterra Impero (secoli IX–XIV)*. Bari, Laterza.

Duby, G. (2004) *Le origini dell'economia europea. Guerrieri e contadini nel Medioevo*. Bari, Laterza.

Flandrin, J. L. and Montanari, M. (1997) *Storia dell'alimentazione*. Bari, Laterza.

Francovich, R. (2004) *Villaggi dell'altomedioevo: invisibilità sociale e labilità archeologica.* In Valenti 2004, IX–XXII.

Francovich, R. and Hodges, R. (1990) Archeologia e storia del villaggio fortificato di Montarrenti: un caso o un modello? In R. Francovich and M. Milanese (eds.) *Lo scavo archeologico di Montarrenti e i problemi dell'incastellamento medievale: esperienze a confronto,* 15–38. Firenze, All'Insegna del Giglio.

Francovich, R. and Hodges, R. (2003), *Villa to Village,* London, Duckworth.

Francovich, R. and Milanese, M. (eds.) (1990) *Lo scavo archeologico di Montarrenti e i problemi dell'incastellamento medievale: esperienze a confronto.* Firenze, All'Insegna del Giglio.

Fronza, V. (2003) Principi di database management in archeologia: l'esperienza senese. In SAMI, R. Fiorillo and P. Peduto (eds.) *III Congresso Nazionale di Archeologia Medievale,* 629–633. Firenze, All'Insegna del Giglio.

Fumagalli, V. (1994) *Paesaggi della paura. Vita e natura nel Medioevo.* Bologna, Il Mulino.

Galloni, P. (1993) *Il cervo e il lupo. Caccia e cultura nobiliare nel Medioevo.* Bari, Laterza.

King, A. (1994) *Mammiferi.* In P. Arthur (ed.) *Il Complesso Archeologico di Carminiello ai Mannesi, Napoli (Scavi 1983–1984),* 367–406. Galatina (Le), Congedo Editore.

Montanari, M. (1990) *L'alimentazione contadina nell'Alto Medioevo.* Napoli, Liguori.

Nardini, A. and Salvadori, F. (2003) A GIS platform dedicated to the production of distribution models of archaeozoological remains. *Archaeofauna* 12, 127–141.

O' Connor, T. (2000) *The Archaeology of Animal Bones.* Stroud, Sutton.

Salvadori, F. (2003) Archeozoologia e Medioevo: lo stato degli studi. In SAMI, R. Fiorillo and P. Peduto (eds.) *III Congresso Nazionale di Archeologia Medievale,* 176–181. Firenze, All'Insegna del Giglio.

Salvadori, F. (2004) *I reperti osteologici animali.* In G. Bianchi (ed.) *La Rocca di Campiglia Marittima. II Indagine archeologica.* 477–511, Firenze, All'Insegna del Giglio.

SAMI (2003), Fiorillo, R. and Peduto, P. (eds.) *III Congresso Nazionale di Archeologia Medievale.* Firenze, All'Insegna del Giglio.

Tagliacozzo, A. *et al.* (1999) Analisi Tafonomica dei reperti ossei del livello Alfa. In M. Piperno (ed.) *Nortarchirico. Un sito del Pleistocene medio–Iniziale nel bacino di Venosa (Basilicata).* I, 455–520, Osanna, Venosa.

Valenti, M. (2004) *L'insediamento altomedievale nelle campagne toscane. Paesaggi, popolamento e villaggi tra VI e X secolo.* Biblioteca del Dipartimento di Archeologia e Storia delle Arti – Sezione Archeologica Università di Siena, 10, Firenze, All'Insegna del Giglio.

Valenti, M. (2005) *La formazione dell'insediamento altomedievale in Toscana. Dallo spessore dei numeri alla costruzione di modelli.* In G. P. Brogiolo, A. Chavarria and M. Valenti (eds.) *Dopo la fine delle ville: evoluzione nelle campagne dal VI al IX secolo.* Mantova, Padusa, in press.

Valenti, M. and Salvadori, F. (2003) *Il periodo altomedievale di Poggio Imperiale (Poggibonsi – SI): dal villaggio all'azienda curtense.* In SAMI, R. Fiorillo and P. Peduto (eds.) *III Congresso Nazionale di Archeologia Medievale,* 325–330. Firenze, All'Insegna del Giglio.

Wickham, C. (1990) Documenti scritti e archeologia per la storia dell'incastellamento: l'esempio della Toscana. In R. Francovich and M. Milanese (eds.) *Lo scavo archeologico di Montarrenti e i problemi dell'incastellamento medievale: esperienze a confronto,* 79–102. Firenze, All'Insegna del Giglio.

Chapter 14

People and Animals in Northern Apulia from Late Antiquity to the Early Middle Ages: Some Considerations

Antonietta Buglione

Introduction

Northern Apulia is the focus of a multidisciplinary project carried out by the Department of Humanities of Foggia University (coordinated by Prof. G. Volpe) on the history and archaeology of towns (such as *Herdonia*-Ordona, *Canusium*-Canosa di Puglia) and rural settlements (*e.g.* Faragola- Ascoli Satriano) from an economic, social and environmental perspective, focusing particularly on the periods of Late Antiquity and the Early Middle Ages (fig. 14.1).

This paper considers only some aspects of the relationship between people and animals (husbandry, diet, bone working) in these periods, focusing on the animal remains collected in the area of the public baths in the Roman town of *Herdonia* (the end of the 5th–10th centuries AD), the bone finds from the area of Ecclesiastic complex of San Pietro at *Canusium* (second half of 7th century–post 9th/10th centuries AD) and the sample from the ruin layers of the roman *villa* of Faragola (the end of 6th–7th/8th

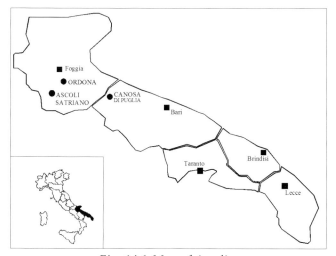

Fig. 14.1 Map of Apulia.

centuries AD). This data has to be considered preliminary: it hasn't been possible to integrate it with the data coming from other samples of the same sites in this paper substantially completed at the beginning of 2005 (get up to date seeing Buglione 2006).

Methodology

For all the contexts, bones were collected by hand. Several levels of identification were made: identifiable elements (ID) were distinguished from unidentifiable elements (UNID). All of the ID elements were quantified and studied to determine species, anatomical elements and where possible, proportion, side, age, sex, butchery marks and metrical information. From the UNID elements, ribs and vertebrae were subdivided into small or large-sized mammals, except for those from *Herdonia*, which were identified by M. Leguilloux. Where possible, caprine elements were identified as sheep or goat (Boessneck, Müller, Teichert 1964; Payne 1985; Prummel, Frisch 1986; Halstead, Collins, Isaakidou 2002). Long bones and teeth were used to identify horses and asses (Davis 1987, 34). The material has been quantified on the basis of the number of identifiable fragments (NISP) and of minimum number of individuals (MNI). MNI has been calculated (for each stratigraphical unit) by considering the number of right or left sides of bone; to this was added the number of animals which, on the basis of that same bone, must be from different animals. This number is increased by information from one side, proportion, age, sex and size.

Analysis of the ages at death of the animals has relied on fusion dental eruption and dental wear evidence (Barone 1974, Silver 1969, Bullock and Rackham 1982, Payne 1973, Bull, Payne 1982). Sexual data were recorded where possible according to morphological and size differences among bones (for cattle metapodials, Nobis 1954). This is the background to the summarized data presented here (for more details see Buglione, De Venuto in press and Buglione 2006).

Materials and discussion

Herdonia

Herdonia was an important ancient town with a successful economy in the Tavoliere (flat plain) area of Northern Apulia. The *Herdonia* sample (excavations of 2000) comes from the area of the Roman public baths after they had been abandoned (fig. 14.2). The archaeological contexts consisted of a) the period from the end of the 5th to the 7th century and b) the period from the 7th to the 10th century when the population of the city reformed and the settlement almost became a village (Favia, Giuliani, Leone 2000, 127–201; Volpe 2000, 507–554).

In total, 3461 animal remains were studied and 3015 were ascribed to element and species of animals (87.1% of the sample identified, vertebrae and ribs included). In both periods the remains of wild animals were in the minority, the majority being ascribed to domestic animals (cattle, sheep and goat, pig, horse and donkey, dog and chicken).

Fig. 14.2 Roman baths at Herdonia *by G. Volpe.*

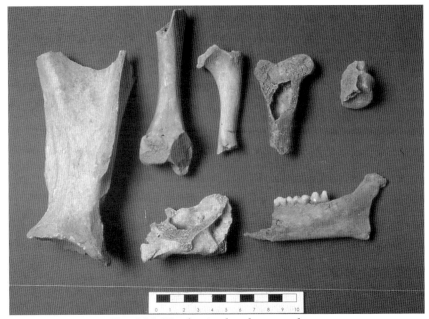

Fig. 14.3 Herdonia: *butchery marks.*

It seems there are no differences in fragmentation between the two periods (fig. 14.3). All the skeletal bones are present. Especially evident on cattle bones, these fine cut marks were probably caused by skinning the carcass or taking tendons, clear from cuts and hacks on metapodial ends and shafts, phalanges and calcaneus (Lignereux, Peters 1996, 60–64; Baker 1999, 430) and dividing it into joints (on humerus, shoulder or femur). Moreover the vertebrae were often cut laterally, on either side of the spine, probably to extract the entire back-bone; less frequently they were chopped transversely indicating the breaking up of the carcasses into sections. Only a few were bisected.

As far as the remains of sheep/goat are concerned, marks on the atlas could be attributed to slaughter by head-injury, and some knife hacks on the long bones are consistent with cutting away flesh and skin. Some bones from the legs of sheep/goat (calcaneus and tibia) have small holes which could have been made by dogs or, less probably, by humans in order to hang the carcass.

Regarding the pig-bones, there are cuts on the axis and frequent chops on the distal epiphysis of the humerus and scapula, indicating the separation of the front limb from the ribcage. There are also some butchery traces on bird bones, not observed on equid bones. The presence of a hole on some oyster-shells can be attributed to either predators (they could be perforated to enable the soft part to be eaten through the hole) or more likely to human action (fig. 14.4).

From the Late Antique context, 1012 remains were recovered, of which 918 were identified (90.7%). Of the three main kinds of domestic animals (cattle, sheep/goat, pig), cattle are the most represented according to NISP and MNI (table 14.1). They were primarily killed after the age of 24 months (many of these after 48–60 months)

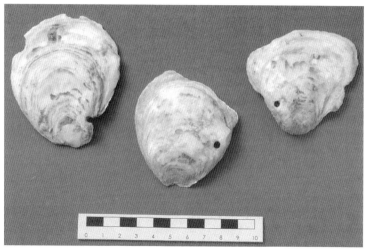

Fig. 14.4 Herdonia: *holed oysters.*

Table 14.1 Herdonia: *species represented by fragment count (NISP; %NISP) and by minimum number of individuals (MNI; %MNI) for Late Antiquity Age.*

Domestic animals	NISP	% NISP	MNI	% MNI
Equus caballus L.	42	4.57	8	8.88
Equus asinus L.	6	0.65	3	3.33
Bos taurus L.	653	71.1	30	33.3
Ovis vel *Capra*	118	12.8	18	20
Sus domesticus Erx	44	4.79	17	18.8
Canis familiaris L.	13	1.41	5	5.55
Gallus gallus L.	25	2.72	6	6.66
Anas domestica L.	1	0.1	1	1.11
Wild animals				
Cervus elaphus L.	7	0.76	2	2.22
Shells				
Ostrea edulis L.	9	0.98		
Total ID	918		90	
Total UNID	94			

and only a small minority before the age of 12–24 months (fig. 14.5). So they were primarily used for traction also helped by cows (71.4% among seven individuals); milk, meat, hides and manure may also have motivated the keeping of cattle.

The second most important *taxon* is represented by sheep/goats. 61.1% of these

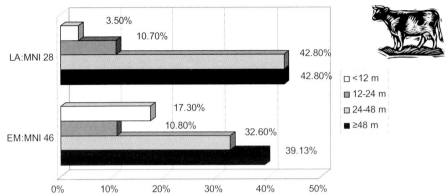

Fig. 14.5 Herdonia: *cattle mortality data (LA: Late Antiquity; EM: Early Middle Ages).*

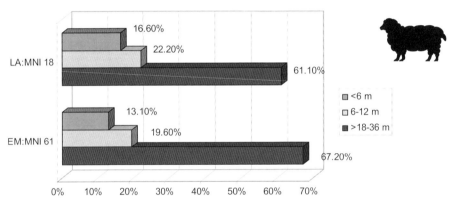

Fig. 14.6 Herdonia: *sheep/goat mortality data (LA: Late Antiquity; EM: Early Middle Ages).*

animals were killed after the age of 18–36 months, while 38.8% before 12–18 months, many of which at only a few months old; this pattern suggests that they were bred not only for meat and wool, but also for milk (fig. 14.6). Sheep are prevalent (57.1% among seven individuals). Pigs are the third most popular kind of domestic animals. The majority died before the age of 12 months (63%, some at only a few months old), the remainder after the age of 12–18 months (fig. 14.7). 5.2% of the sample is made up bones of equids. Poultry bones were identified, most of which were hens, which were probably bred both for meat and eggs. The only wild animal remains (0.76%) come from red-deer; these are all lower add limb bones (metapodials and phalanges), considered waste elements; probably discarded when skinning the deer for their hides. Although there are no signs of butchery on any of these bones, the possibility that the meat was eaten cannot be excluded.

For the Early Middle Ages 2449 bones were recorded, and 2097 identified (85.6%): as in the previous period cattle is the species most common, but only in terms of NISP

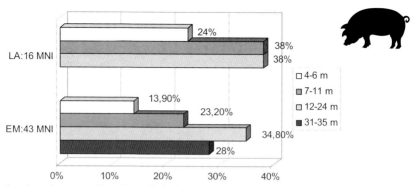

Fig. 14.7 Herdonia: *pig mortality data (LA: Late Antiquity; EM: Early Middle Ages).*

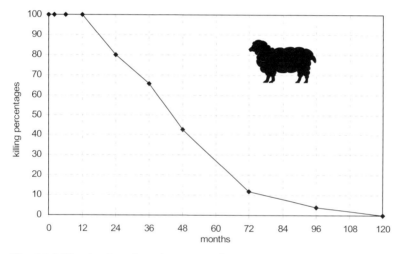

Fig. 14.8 Herdonia : *sheep/goat mortality curve for Early Middle Ages.*

(table 14.2). Almost all the cattle died after the age of 24–48 months and many after reaching 48–60 months (fig. 14.5). Among caprines, 67.2% of these animals were killed after the age of 18–36 months, and the remainder before 12 months (fig. 14.6). As is also clear from the mortality curve (in accordance with Payne 1977; figs. 14.8–14.9) based on the 25 mandibles recovered, sheep/goat was bred mainly for meat and wool but also for milk; most of them were killed between the ages of 24 and 36 months (a good age as far as the meat is concerned). Sheep dominate over goats (67.4% among 43 individuals). Of 43 individuals whose age was counted for pigs, 62.7% lived at least to the age of 12–24 months and longer, while the 37.2% died before they reached 12 months (fig. 14.7). Males are more numerous (61.5% among 13 individuals). Equids represent a small part of the sample again. Of the recovered birds, chicken is still the most prevalent domestic bird; there was an increase in the amount of domestic goose remains, probably also bred for its feathers and eggs. Wild animals continue to be

Antonietta Buglione

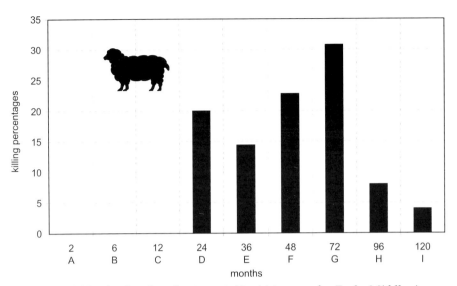

Fig. 14.9 Herdonia: *sheep/goat mortality histogram for Early Middle Ages.*

Table 14.2 Herdonia: *species represented by fragment count (NISP; %NISP) and by minimum number of individuals (MNI; %MNI) for Early Middle Age.*

Domestic animals	NISP	% NISP	MNI	% MNI
Equus caballus L.	57	2.71	8	3.98
Equus asinus L.	25	1.19	2	0.99
Bos taurus L.	780	37.2	46	22.8
Ovis vel *Capra*	712	33.9	61	30.3
Sus domesticus Erx	264	12.5	43	21.3
Canis familiaris L.	60	2.86	11	5.47
Gallus gallus L.	147	7.01	20	9.95
Anas domestica L.	12	0.57	2	0.99
Felis domestica L.	1	0.04	1	0.5
Wild animals				
Cervus elaphus L.	8	0.38	3	1.5
Capreolus capreolus L.	11	0.52	2	0.99
Lepus europaeus L.	2	0.09	2	0.99
Shells				
Ostrea edulis L.	16	0.76		
Unio elongatulus	1	0.04		
Donax trunculus L.	1	0.04		
Total ID	2.097		201	
Total UNID	352			

outnumbered by domesticates; along with some red-deer and roe-deer, hare appear to have been hunted occasionally.

The remains of shellfish are more numerous in the Early Middle Ages than in Late Antiquity: sixteen belong to *Ostrea edulis*, one to *Donax trunculus* and one to *Unio elongatulus*. Where perforated oysters have been found, they are often interpreted as pendants or amulets such as those collected at S. Antonino di Perti, also showing an erosion of surfaces (Murialdo 2001, 522). But this doesn't seem to be the case at *Herdonia* where the holes could have been used for tying the shells together and packing them in ice or snow for transport, or they could be the result of raising them in oyster beds, as suggested for oysters from Otranto and Egnazia in Apulia (Reese 1992, 349) and San Giovanni di Ruoti in Basilicata (Reese 2002, 189). The collected oysters might have come from the coasts near *Herdonia*; it is not known whether they were cultivated, but is interesting to note that the fishing-port of Lesina on the Gargano coast developed in the second half of the 8th century and continued to be important until the 9th century, for eels as well as shellfish. In a deed of gift of goods, dating to 788, Grimoaldo III, Prince of Benevento, speaks about the fishing-port of Lesina (*tota piscaria de civitate Lesina*) and about its developed activity (Martin 1993, 201–202). Furthermore the *Donax trunculus*, typically found in sandy terrain, could come from Lesina, while the *Unio elongatulus*, a typical fresh-water clam (still eaten today in many parts of Mediterranean and Near East) probably comes from the river Carapelle, not far from *Herdonia*. Besides their use as food for humans, the soft part of *Unio* can be eaten by domestic animals or used as bait, while the shells can be used as containers, or, if pulverised and crushed, for degreasing and thickening ceramics (Di Martino, Girod, Di Giancamillo 2001, 212–214). This clam could also be collected for its nacre (mother-of-pearl).

Bone working

Worked bone objects have been found at the site. Some unfinished worked bones representing manufacturing waste seem to confirm that this area of the city was probably the focus of craft activities. Three objects are personal female ornaments, interpretable as hat or dress pins. One of them is intact, while the others consist of only the head and part of the stem (fig. 14.10:1). The complete hat pin, belonging to the Late Antique period, has an ovoid undecorated head linked by a small neck, finely worked, with three different sizes of reels decorating the upper part of the shank. It has a circular stem in section and is little faceted, tapering gradually towards the end. The stem shows traces of primary working of the raw material and is not highly polished. Similar well-made bone objects were found in Milan (Tosatti 1991, 64, 5th–7th centuries AD; Bianchi 1995, 68), at S. Giovanni di Ruoti in Basilicata dating to the end of 4th–5th century AD (Simpson 1994, 72, tab. 58, n. 88). Anyway, pins like these were found also in more antique contexts.

The other hat-pins found in early middle age layers in *Herdonia* are similar: they consist of a conical head (of differing sizes) ending with three reels and a circular-section stem (fig. 14.10:2–3). In some cases, it has been possible to distinguish between pins with decorated heads, produced in specialized workshops from those with undecorated ones, produced in a domestic context (Martin 1999, 443; Di Giovanni 1994, 364). At *Herdonia* the pins seem to belong to the second category; however, the

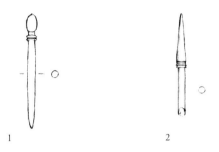

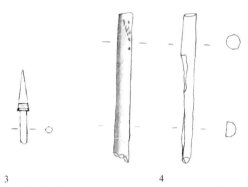

Fig. 14.10 Herdonia: *worked objects (1, 2, 3, 4).*

ones shown in figs. 14.10:2 and 14.10:3 could have been produced by more sensitive and technical workers, probably indicative of a more complex and specialized bone working process in the Early Middle Ages with respect to Late Antiquity. The fourth object (7th–10th century), probably obtained from a sheep/goat tibia (fig. 14.10:4) is not represented in the distal part, while in the proximal it is evident it was smoothed and the shaft seems highly polished. Its function is not clear: it could be the shaft of a stylus or, less likely, a knife-handle. The stylus was used to write on wax tablets and generally had a flat spatula or conical head to erase writing and re-model the tablet. Though fragmentary, the bone shows some affinity with objects found in Milan interpreted as styli (Tosatti 1991, 66), and with a similar worked bone from imperial layers at Carminiello ai Mannesi at Napoli (Di Giovanni 1994, 363) and from Otranto (Hicks 1992, 310–311, n. 185). The stylus from *Herdonia* probably had a pointed end for writing and a blunt one for erasing. Indeed, the hat-pins with the conical head could be interpreted as styli, if one thought of the conical heads as pointed ends for writing and the blunt ones for erasing.

Canusium – San Pietro

The excavation in Canosa di Puglia (2001–2004) uncovered a religious complex

Fig. 14.11 Canosa di P.-San Pietro: aerial view by G. Volpe (2001–2004).

situated in a suburban area of the actual city (hill of San Pietro) consisting of a large church with an atrium and a narthex and the Episcopal palace dating to the 6th century AD (fig. 14.11). In the following centuries (the end of 7th–10th centuries), some parts of the complex were despoiled, others were reoccupied with simple domestic architectures including a fireside and holes, probably for foodstuffs or with hats until they were left after the 10th century (Volpe *et al.* 2002, 133–190; Volpe *et al.* 2003, 107–164, Volpe *et al.* in press).

The bones collected in 2001–2002 were analysed from two periods: a), period I (the end of 7th/8th–9th–10th centuries) and b) period II (post 9th–10th century). All the skeletal bones were recovered. Sheep/goat bones showed many butchery marks not dissimilar from those identified at *Herdonia*, related to skinning and disarticulating the carcass. More relevant are the saw marks on horns separating them from the head to obtain the horn for working or for processing the hide (fig. 14.12). Marks on cattle and pig bones are few and similar, although there are none on equids.

In total 4911 bones were collected, of which only 37.4% could be ascribed to species and element; many bones were fragmented and this account for the high percentage of unidentified finds. There were 3118 fragments from period II, of which 1298 could be identified (41.6%); sheep/goat is prevalent in terms of NISP among domestic animals, followed by domestic fowl, pig and cattle. There were few wild animal remains (table 14.3). 42.5% of sheep/goat was still alive after 48–60 months, suggesting an adult pattern associated with wool production; 37.5% slaughtered in 36 months reveals a significant interest in meat production, while interest in producing milk was limited (only 20% died before 12 months; fig. 14.13). As far as pigs are concerned, only 17.6% were younger than one year at the time of slaughter, while the rest were killed after 12 months: this pattern is supported by tooth wear evidence, many

Table 14.3 Canosa di P.-San Pietro: species represented by fragment count (NISP; %NISP) and by minimum number of individuals (MNI; %MNI) for the end of 7th–10th centuries.

Domestic animals	NISP	% NISP	MNI	% MNI
Equus caballus L.	13	1	6	3.61
Equus asinus L.	2	0.15	2	1.2
Bos taurus L.	124	9.5	18	10.8
Ovis vel *Capra*	595	45.8	45	27.1
Sus domesticus Erx	240	18.8	41	24.6
Gallus gallus L.	279	21.49	50	30.1
Wild animals				
Cervus elaphus L.	4	0.3	2	1.2
Fishes				
Pisces ind.	7	0.53		
Raja clavata L.	10	0.77		
Shells				
Ostrea edulis L.	6	0.46		
Glycimeris glycimeris L.	1	0.07		
Murex trunculus L.	2	0.15		
Unio elongatulus	1	0.07		
Lutraria lutraria L.	14	1.07		
Total ID	1.298		164	
Small ribs	335			
Large ribs	114			
Small vertebrae	47			
Large vertebrae	20			
UNID fragments	1.304			
Total UNID	1.820			

belonging to pigs, mostly males, who died after 35 months when their bodies had reached an optimum in terms of meat and fat quality (fig. 14.14). Ageing data for cattle indicated that adults were not so dominant; they were probably raised for traction, but also provided high quality meat (fig. 14.15).

Among fowl, the proportion of adult chickens to juveniles indicates that adult ones (mostly hens) were better represented (90% on 50 MNI). Many bird bones come from pits relative to habitats built in the Early Middle Ages in the area of San Pietro (Volpe

Fig. 14.12 Canosa di P.-San Pietro: saw marks on a horn.

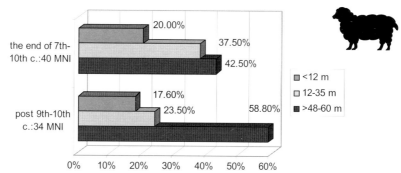

Fig. 14.13 Canosa di P.-San Pietro: sheep/goat mortality data.

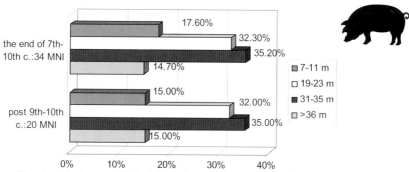

Fig. 14.14 Canosa di P.-San Pietro: pig mortality data.

et al. 2002, 154–156; 164–166) where bones from different animals were discarded (fig. 14.16). In pits 2087–2088 (fig. 14.17) fowl bones (belonging mostly to adult individuals) are distributed in the section of wing and lower limbs, while skull, vertebrae and extremities are absent. This may represent a selected fowl sample identifiable as consumption waste (with the heads and necks removed and discarded elsewhere during slaughtering) or could suggest that poultry were imported from elsewhere. It

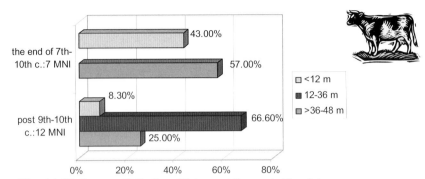

Fig. 14.15 Canosa di P.-San Pietro: cattle mortality data.

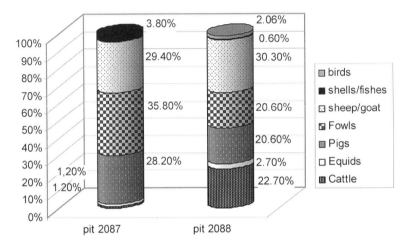

Fig. 14.16 Canosa di P.-San Pietro: bone distribution in the pits 2087 (ID= 78) and 2088 (ID=245).

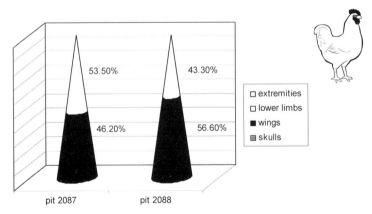

Fig. 14.17 Canosa di P.-San Pietro: fowl bone distribution in the pits 2087 (NISP= 78) and 2088 (NISP=52).

Fig. 14.18 Canosa di P.-San Pietro: the holed Glycimeris.

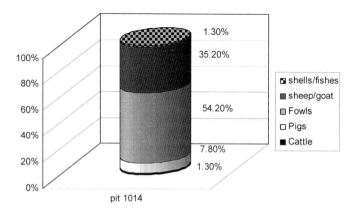

Fig. 14.19 Canosa di P.-San Pietro: bone distribution in the pit 1014 (ID= 178).

is different for sheep/goats: all body parts are present, belonging to at least 11 MNI, among which some juveniles, probably slaughtered for meat. Pig and cattle bones represent waste rather than food remains, with skulls and limbs prevalent.

Pit 2087 contained shell remains belong to *Murex Trunculus* (two) and to *Glycimeris* sp. (one). Both species have a hole in the valve; in the case of the former, it may have been a way of removing the liquid used for the purple-dye (Tyrian purple) from the hypobranchial gland in the mantle cavity of the *Murex trunculus* (Cretella 1994, 428), although it was more often obtained by breaking the superior part of the shell, evident from its extreme fragmentation (Becker 1996, 11; Minniti 1999, 182). The *Glycimeris* (fig. 14.18) has a polished hole, which could be due to natural causes or to its use as a necklace – as with examples recovered from Settefinestre in central Italy (King *et al.* 1985, 303). However, these shells were also often consumed as food.

Ribs and vertebrae recovered from the pits make up 16% and 27.8% of the sample and some ribs shows butchery marks; the presence of these bones, the kind of butchery marks and shells suggest that the pits were probably used as middens or for storage by a butcher. These buildings, together with others, such as pit 1014 containing numerous chicken remains (fig. 14.19) and in which probably four whole chickens

Table 14.4 Canosa di P.-San Pietro: species represented by fragment count (NISP; %NISP) and by minimum number of individuals (MNI; %MNI) for post 9th–10th centuries.

Domestic animals	NISP	% NISP	MNI	% MNI
Equus caballus L.	15	2.61	7	5.83
Equus asinus L.	11	1.91	2	1.66
Bos taurus L.	96	16.72	26	21.66
Ovis vel *Capra*	268	46.68	44	36.66
Sus domesticus Erx	104	18.11	22	18.33
Felis domestica L.	8	1.39	2	1.66
Gallus gallus L.	37	6.44	12	10
Wild animals				
Cervus elaphus L.	3	0.52	2	1.66
Lepus europaeus Pall.	3	0.51	1	0.83
Vulpes vulpes L.	3	0.51	1	0.83
Reptiles				
Testudo hermanni Gml.	7	1.21	2	1.66
Shells				
Ostrea edulis L.	8	1.39		
Mytilus galloprovincialis L.	1	0.17		
Donax trunculus L.	4	0.69		
Tapes decussatus L.	1	0.17		
Lutraria lutraria L.	4	0.69		
Cerastoderma edule P.	1	0.17		
Total ID	574		121	
Small ribs	32			
Large ribs	19			
Small vertebrae	20			
Large vertebrae	7			
UNID fragments	1.141			
Total UNID	1.219			

were thrown in (fig. 14.20), indicate the use of a system of waste disposal employing pits, at present little known in Italy during the Early Middle Ages (Gelichi 2000, 17).

Equid bones are, unsurprisingly, infrequent in the sample; they don't have butchery marks, but we can't exclude the possibility that they were eaten as well as being used for transport. Equally unsurprising is the low percentage of wild animals, represented

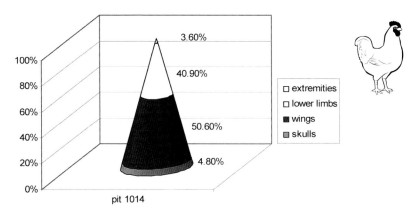

Fig. 14.20 Canosa di P.-San Pietro: fowl bone distribution in the pit 1014 (NISP= 95).

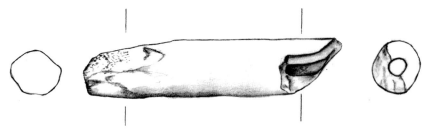

Fig. 14.21 Canosa di P.-San Pietro: the hide chisel.

by antlers of red deer; it is likely this species contributed little to the diet but it was hunted and butchered elsewhere, with, as the evidence suggests, only antler transported to the site for working. 3.1% of the assemblage is represented by fish and shell remains.

In the post 9th–10th centuries assemblage (only 32% identified), sheep/goat is the most commonly represented *taxon*, based on NISP and MNI, followed by pig, cattle, chicken and equid (table 14.4). The husbandry pattern doesn't seem to change much for the three principal domestic species, except for cattle, only for 25% slaughtered after 36–48 months (figs. 14.13–14.14–14.15). Also in this period, the percentage of wild animal bones is low, but more so than in the previous period. Not only red-deer, but also hare and fox are present in the sample, again with bones relative to antlers and limbs, except one scapula from a red-deer. The presence of tortoise is interesting, represented by the remains of carapace and one humerus, an animal often consumed in the Middle Ages and almost absent in earlier samples. The percentage of common shells is similar to the previous one (3.2%); the *Cerastoderma edule* could have been used as a recipient or object of adornment, besides food (Becker 1996, 12). These shells indicate different exploitation areas: the *Cerastoderma* lives in the sand and saltish water, while the *Mytilus galloprovincialis* is typical of coastal cliffs.

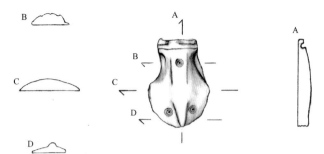

Fig. 14.22 Canosa di P.-San Pietro: the pendant.

Bone working

The zooarchaeological evidence indicates that in *Canusium* pastoral activities and transhumant breeding were important from the 7th to 10th century and beyond. According to a few historical sources, the city was famous for related manufacturing activities, particularly in the 4th century; the situation is more complex by the end of the 4th–5th century when a probable crisis of wool production began, but this does not mean that transhumant breeding vanished in Apulia (Volpe 1996, 279–299). Interestingly a rectangular bone comb found in a rich female burial dating to the end of the 6th century (Volpe *et al.* 2002, 135) belonged to a woman probably still engaged in textile manufacture in this period. The comb (cm 19 × 6) has teeth on its short sides rather than on its long ones, as is common in hair combs; it could be used to comb wool or flax or cotton, but it seems more likely for wool, judging by the traditional activities of the city. Another object that is related to the manufacture of textiles is an unfinished hide chisel (7th–10th century; fig. 14.21) with signs of use, probably obtained from a long bone, similar to one from Carminiello ai Mannesi in Napoli (Di Giovanni 1994, 364).

One particular object reflects specialized craft activity after the 10th century: it is decorated with zoomorphic features and its form, and the presence of a small grove for the insertion of a wire seems to indicate its use as pendant. It is smoothed on the posterior face, whilst two eyes and a beak are engraved on the other face; features resembling an owl (fig. 14.22). Some fragments of antlers show cut marks and are polished on the surface.

Faragola

The Faragola site is situated in the territory which currently belongs to the town of Ascoli Satriano, near the Carapelle River. The excavations (2003–2004) brought to light a large rural settlement with a large and sumptuous *villa*, with present investigations focusing on its Late Roman phase (4th–6th century) consisting of a *cenatio*, residential and artisanal rooms (fig. 14.23). The *villa* probably went out of use during half of the 6th century, but it wasn't entirely abandoned, probably being occupied by a village (Volpe, De Felice, Turchiano 2005A and 2005B). The faunal assemblage is mostly derived from the ruin layers of the late Roman *villa* (second half

Table 14.5 Faragola: species represented by fragment count (NISP; %NISP) and by minimum number of individuals (MNI; %MNI).

Domestic animals	NISP	% NISP	MNI	%MNI
Equus caballus L.	7	0.83	4	2.94
Bos taurus L.	188	22.3	20	14.7
Ovis vel *Capra*	386	45.8	42	30.8
Sus domesticus Erx	112	13.3	39	28.67
Gallus gallus L.	37	4.39	18	13.23
Wild animals				
Cervus elaphus L.	7	0.83	3	2.20
Capreolus capreolus L.	3	0.35	2	1.47
Sus scrofa ferus L.	1	0.11	1	0.73
Aves ind.	26	3	6	4.41
Reptiles				
Testudo hermanni Gml.	1	0.11	1	0.73
Fishes				
Pisces ind.	2	0.23		
Shells				
Ostrea edulis L.	68	8.07		
Spondylus gaederopus L.	2	0.23		
Murex trunculus L.	2	0.23		
Total ID	842		136	
UNID Fragments	800			
Small ribs	100			
Large ribs	66			
Small vertebrae	125			
Large vertebrae	124			
Total UNID	1.215			

of the 6th century) and from the layers relating to the subsequent occupation of the area (the end of 6th–7th centuries). The sample here considered was made up of 2057 bones of which 842 (41%) were identifiable in terms of element and species.

The identified bones belong predominantly to domestic animals (table 14.5); in general, the most common species was sheep/goat, followed by cattle, pig and

Fig. 14.23 Faragola: *aerial view by M. Attademo (2003–2004).*

Fig. 14.24 Faragola: *sawn horse's tibia.*

Fig. 14.25 Faragola: *sheep/goat skull with chops.*

poultry; there are a few bones (1.3%) belonging to roe-deer (ulna and shoulder), red-deer (metapodial and tibia ends, antlers) and wild boar (humerus). Meatier parts of the body were probably butchered or disposed elsewhere and their skins subsequently used in manufacturing.

Aside from the more common cut marks observed on the bones of cattle, sheep and goats, it is interesting to note a perfectly straight, smooth sawn distal epiphysis from a horse's tibia (fig. 14.24), and a fifth metapodial cut. It seems more likely, especially in the case of a tibia, that this is the result of bone working activity (see after). In any

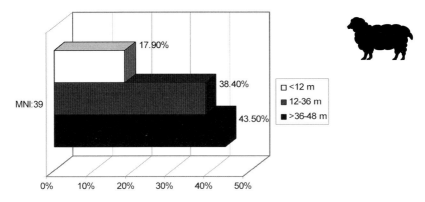

Fig. 14.26 Faragola: *sheep/goat mortality data.*

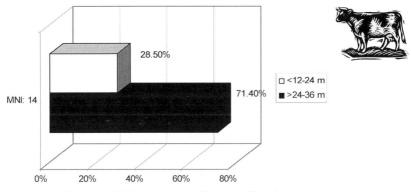

Fig. 14.27 Faragola: *cattle mortality data.*

case, one cannot completely rule out the possibility that these marks indicate that equids were used as food (Wilkens 2001, 194 with regard to equid butchered tibia at Montetorto, 3rd–5th century). However it is not usual to find marks of butchery on equid bones from other sites in Italy; some marks have only been observed in a few rural settlements such as Faragola, for example in the late-Roman cemetery connected to the *villa* at Poggio Gramignano in Umbria (MacKinnon 1999, 541) and on metapodials from a 5th century context at San Giacomo degli Schiavoni (Albarella *et al.* 1993, 207). In Apulia, it is thought that equids were used as food at the Masseria Quattro Macine (10th–11th century), although there is no direct evidence of this; it is likely that, in rural areas, the prohibition of hippophagy by Pope Gregory II (732) was unknown (Albarella 1996, 222).

As regard to the other domestic animals, the butchery marks were probably caused by light choppers and knives, with marks on sheep and goat bones being the most common. A cranium had chop marks at the base of the horn reflecting the removal of horns, suggesting that horn working was probably practised (fig. 14.25). Cutting meat away from bone results in very fine marks on long bones such as the middle shaft of the radius, tibia, in many cuts on the distal and lateral shoulders, in ventral and lateral

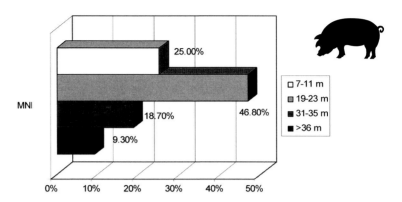

Fig. 14.28 Faragola: *pig mortality data.*

chops on the pelvis probably made by a knife or due to a light blow. Also for sheep/ goat the head of the femur was often butchered to remove the legs. Long bones such as the tibia were probably split longitudinally to enable marrow to be extracted. Only a few cattle bones display clear cut marks, predominantly on proximal femurs and extremities and on pelvis, near the *acetabulum*, probably to cut the meat. It seems that cattle vertebrae were consumed as whole bodies, cut on the spine. Marks on pig bone and poultry are fewer, located on the humerus, ulna and femur. Two chopped metapodial distal epiphyses of a red-deer probably represent manufacturing waste. The graphs show the preliminary and not final results of the estimated age of death for the three principal domestic species: for sheep and cattle it seems to reflect an adult husbandry pattern (figs. 14.26–14.27–14.28).

Shell finds are dominated by *Ostrea edulis* (94.4%), followed by two *Spondylus gaederopus* (eaten or used as a recipient: Becker 1996, 11) and two *Murex trunculus*. At Faragola there is also an example of a holed oyster.

Bone working
Fragments of worked bone objects confirm that the site could be the centre of manufacturing activities relating to the processing of bone. The smooth sawn distal epiphysis from the horse's tibia is probably the result of bone working activity (fig. 14.24). Long bones like the tibia and metapodials were often used for manufacturing objects and they would be sawn to obtain the mid-shaft area, leaving the sawn ends as waste. Another example is an equid metapodial (fig. 14.29), worked on the outside and smoothed off at both ends. The marrow-cavity of the shaft and its size could suggest it may have been prepared to serve as a hinge (De Tommaso, Famà 1985, 54; De Grossi Mazzorin, Minniti 1995, 374) and less likely as a handle of some implement: however, as a hinge, it would be an unfinished object, lacking holes on the shaft. As regards to bone artefacts, "by far the greatest portion are made from the bones of domestic cattle and equids and craftsmen often choose horse bones from slaughterers because metapodial bones on the one hand grow more regularly and on the other don't have the suture that cattle metapodials have and along which artefacts can

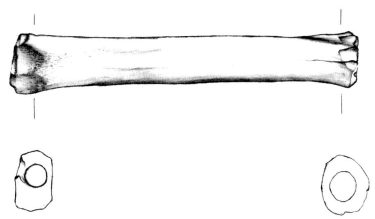

Fig. 14.29 Faraola: *the equid worked metapodial.*

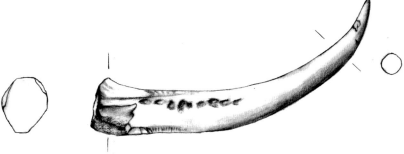

Fig. 14.30 Faragola: *the deer worked antler.*

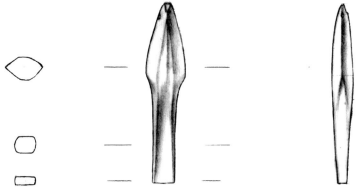

Fig. 14.31 Faragola: *the arrow end.*

break in manufacture" (Deschler-Erb 1997, 75). However, metapodial shafts were usually used for hinges (Lepetz 2003, 212). The second object is a red deer antler (fig. 14.30) highly polished, with cut marks (from a saw or knife) on the smoothed-off end. It could have been used as a handle upon completion. The working of deer antler is

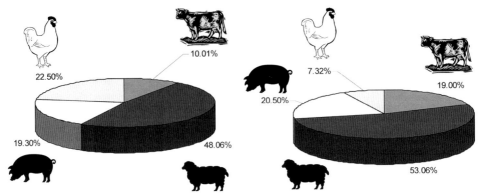

Fig. 14.32 Canosa di P.-San Pietro: principal
species used as food (end of 7th–10th centuries:
NISP= 1238).

Fig. 14.33 Canosa di P.-San Pietro: principal
species used as food (post 9th–10th century:
NISP= 505).

a well attested activity whether in prehistoric or in historical periods, in funerary and living contexts, especially for the construction of instrument handles (see Alhaique, Cerilli 2003 for Northern Italy). This object resembles one recovered from medieval layers at *Herdonia* (Buglione, De Venuto in press, and De Venuto in this volume) and a sophisticated handle recovered at *Crypta Balbi* from the 7th century AD (Ricci 2001b, 549). Another hypothesis is that the antler could be have used as a bow point and in this case it would have had two holes on the extremity to anchor and fix the cord, such as from *Crypta Balbi* (Ricci 2001a, 399).

Another interesting object is an arrow point, made of smoothed bone or ivory, probably used for hunting (fig. 14.31). The arrow consists of a shaft with a rectangular section, very well worked, and an elliptical point, lightly faceted, inserting thinned tang with flattened end. Bone could be used for this function, as it was resistant to crushing and piercing. It seems to be the product of specialized artisans, rather than as a result of an empirical experience, and it is interesting that arrows like this have been found in Italy only at San Antonino di Perti, a Late Antique military settlement in the North (De Vingo, Fossati, Murialdo 2001, 531–540). Iron arrows on the other hand are very common at many sites. Finally, two deer antlers showed working marks.

Conclusion

In the sites considered in this paper, different but also similar in many respects, sheep/goats seem to have been extremely important in domestic animal breeding in Late Antiquity and the Early Middle Ages. Percentages of sheep/goat remains, age of death and some worked bone object found in the sites, situated in an area of the region where transhumance was practiced in Antiquity, suggest that this practice did not completely disappear but was only reduced and changed in form (perhaps involving shorter distances) from the 6th–7th century. Furthermore secondary

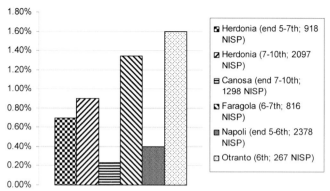

Fig. 14.34 Wild percentages among Herdonia, Canosa di P., Faragola *and other sites in South of Italy respect to the total NISP in the legend.*

activities, such as wool-production (for which Northern Apulia had been famous before) were important, but probably reduced, reflecting new political and economic realities, until they were reorganized in the medieval period (Volpe 1996, 279–299; Buglione 2006).

The recovery of bones from all parts of the domestic animal skeleton suggests that individuals were probably slaughtered and eaten in close proximity; butchery patterns don't vary significantly, suggesting a uniform trend. Vertebral bisection, more common from the Middle Ages onwards in many Roman sites in Italy, but already evident before, especially in rural sites, does not seem to be commonplace, also perhaps suggesting that a "non standardized butchery blueprint for a market oriented scheme" was developed (MacKinnon 2002, 117).

In the diet, fish and common shells, with a high nutritional value, were not lacking, indicating a good exchange whilst domestic fowl represented a significant part of the meat supply, especially at *Canusium* from the 7th to 10th century (figs. 14.32–14.33). This could indicate the presence of a developed chicken-farm in this period, besides an interesting relationship between the status and the food of the inhabitants of the new early medieval settlement who preferred this kind of meat. Caprines also probably provided good quality meat better than cattle which were more often used as work animals; pigs were above all important for meat and fat. Equids were probably not a frequent source of meat; at Faragola equid bones were worked.

Hunting did not appear as a developed activity in any site; carcasses were probably butchered where they were hunted and only the bone required for manufacturing was transported to the sites. However, the wild animal data reflects a comparable situation in many urban and rural settlements in Italy (MacKinnon 2001, 654–655; Clark 1997, 34), where the percentages of NISP for wild animals are very low with respect to the total in late antique and early middle age contexts (fig. 14.34). The post-10th century wild sample from Canosa is more varied, perhaps indicating quite a dynamic landscape. In all the sites processing bone activities seem to have developed to a fairly good level, but, judging by the limited number of finished objects and the absence of much manufacturing waste from workshops, probably remained small and local scale.

Acknowledgments

I would like to thank Prof. G. Volpe for the opportunity he gave me to start and convince Zooarchaeological Studies. Also I thank Professor De Grossi Mazzorin and C. Minniti for their support in my studies. The English was corrected by Colin Gorlon; photographs of bones were taken by M. Attademo; the authors of bone drawings are V. Acquafredda (for *Herdonia*), M. Lo Muzio (for the others) and N. Mangialardi of figure 14.1. I sincerely thank them.

Bibliography

Albarella, U. (1996) The faunal remains. In P. Arthur, U. Albarella, B. Bruno, and S. King (eds.) "Masseria Quattro Macine" a deserted medieval village and its territory in Southern Puglia: an interim report on field survey, excavation and document analysis. *Papers of the British School at Rome* LXIV, 222–224.

Albarella, U. Ceglia, V. Roberts, P. (1993) San Giacomo degli Schiavoni: an early fifth century A.D. deposit of pottery and animal bones from central adriatic Italy. *Papers of the British School at Rome* LXI, 157–230.

Alhaique, F. and Cerilli, E. (2003) Handicraft, Diet and Cult Practices in the late antique Villa Rustica of Brega (Rosà, Vicenza, Northeast Italy), *Archeofauna*, 12, 2003, 95–111.

Baker, P. (1999) The vertebrate remains from the Longobard and IX–X occupations at S. Giulia, Brescia. In G. P. Brogiolo (ed.) *Santa Giulia di Brescia, gli scavi dal 1980 al 1992,* 425–487. Firenze, All'Insegna del Giglio.

Barone, R. (1974) *Anatomia comparata dei mammiferi domestici. Vol. I. Osteologia.* Bologna, Ed. agricole.

Becker, C. (1996) Nourriture, cuillères, ornements…les témoignages d'une exploitation variée des mollusques marins à Ayos Mamas (Chalcidique, Grèce). *Anthropozoologica* 24, II, 3–17.

Bianchi, C. (1995) Spilloni in Osso di età romana. Problematiche generali e rinvenimenti in Lombardia, Milano, Edizioni ET.

Boessneck, J. Müller, H. H. and Teichert, M. (1964) Osteologische Unterscheidungsmerkmale zwischen Schaft (Ovis aries LINNÉ) und Ziege (Capra hircus LINNÉ). *Kühn-Archiv* 78, H. 1–2.

Buglione, A. (2006) Ricerche Archeozoologiche in Puglia centro-seccentrionale: Primi dati sullo sfruccamenco della risorsa animale fra tardoantico e altomedioevo. In A. Gravina (ed.) *26th Convegno Nazionale di Preistoria, Protostoria e Storia della Daunia,* San Severo, 495–532, San Severo.

Buglione, A. and De Venuto, G. (in press). I reperti archeozoologici dell'area delle terme di Herdonia in età tardoantica e medievale. Campagne di scavo 1997, 1998, 2000. In G. Volpe (ed.) *Ordona XI. Ricerche archeologiche a Herdonia.* Bari, Edipuglia.

Bull, G. and Payne, S. (1982) Tooth eruption and epiphisial fusion in pigs and wild boar. In B. Wilson, C. Grigson and S. Payne (eds.) *Ageing and Sexing Animal Bones from Archeological Sites,* 55–81. British Archaeological Reports, British Series, 109, Oxford, Archeopress.

Bullock, D. and Rackham, J. (1982) Epiphysial fusion and tooth eruption of feral gotas from Maffatdale, Dumfries and Galloway, Scotland. In B. Wilson, C. Grigson and S. Payne (eds.) *Ageing and Sexing Animal Bones from Archeological Sites,* 73–80 British Archaeological Reports, British Series, 109, Oxford, Archeopress.

Clark, G. (1997) Monastic economies? Aspects of production and consumption in early medieval central Italy. *Archeologia Medievale* XXIV, 31–54.

Cretella, M. (1994) Molluschi. In P. Arthur (ed.) *Il complesso archeologico di Carminiello ai Mannesi, Napoli (scavi 1983–1984)*, 423–428. Galatina, Congedo Editore.

Davis, S. J. M. (1987) *The Archaeology of Animals*, London.

De Grossi Mazzorin, J. Minniti, C. (1995) Gli scavi nell'area della Meta Sudans (I sec. d. C.): l'industria su osso. *Atti del secondo Convegno di Archeozoologia (Rovigo 1993)*, Padusa Quaderni, 1, Stanghella (Padova), 371–374.

De Tommaso, G. Famà M. L. (1985) *Elementi e rifiniture di infissi e di mobili*. In A. Ricci (ed.) *Settefinestre 3. Una villa schiavistica nell'Etruria meridionale. La villa e i suoi reperti.* 50–54 Modena, Ed. Panini.

De Vingo P. Fossati A. and Murialdo G. (2001) Le armi: punte di freccia. In T. Mannoni and G. Murialdo (eds.) *S. Antonino: un insediamento fortificato nella Liguria bizantina*, II, 531–540. Firenze, Artigrafiche.

Deschler-Erb, S. (1997) Bone, antler, tooth and ivory: raw materials for Roman artifacts. *Anthropozoologica*, 73–77.

Di Giovanni, V. (1994) *Osso lavorato*. In P. Arthur (ed.) *Il complesso archeologico di Carminiello ai Mannesi, Napoli (scavi 1983–1984)*, 363–365. Galatina, Congedo Editore.

Di Martino S. Girod A. and Di Giancamillo M. (2001) La fauna. In P. Frontini (ed.) *Castellaro del Vhò. Campagne di scavo 1996–1999. Scavi delle civiche raccolte archeologiche di Milano*, 203–214. Milano.

Favia, P. Giuliani R. and Leone D. (2000) L'area delle terme (Saggio III. 1997–1998). In G. Volpe, (ed.) *Ordona X. Ricerche archeologiche a Herdonia (1993–1998)* 127–201. Bari, Edipuglia.

Gelichi, S. (2000) L'eliminazione dei rifiuti nelle città romane del Nord Italia tra antichità ed altomedioevo. In X. Dupré Raventos and J. A. Remolà (eds.) *Sordes urbis. La eliminación des residuos en la ciudat romana*, Actas de la reunión de Roma (15–16 de noviembre de 1996), 13–23. Roma, Erma di Bretschneider.

Halstead, P. Collins, P. and Isaakidou, V. (2002) Sorting the sheep from the goats: morphological distinctions between mandibles and mandibular teeth of adult ovis and capra. *Journal of Archaeological Science* 29, 545–553.

Hicks, A. J. (1992) The small objects. In F. D'Andria and D. Whitehouse (eds.) *Excavations at Otranto, The Finds*, II, 310–312. Galatina, Congedo Editore.

King *et al.* (1985) I resti animali. In A. Ricci (ed.) *Settefinestre 3. Una villa schiavistica nell'Etruria meridionale. La villa e i suoi reperti*, 278–299. Modena, Ed. Panini.

Lepetz, S. (2003) Gérer les rejets de boucherie et les cadavres animaux dans les villes de Gaule romaine. *La ville et ses déchets dans le monde romain: rebuts et recyclages*, Actes du Colloque de Poitiers (19–21 Septembre 2002), 209–217. Monique Mergoil, Montagnac.

Lignereux, Y. and Peters J. (1996) Techniques de boucherie et rejets osseux en Gaule Romaine, *Anthropozoologica* 24, 45–98.

MacKinnon, M. (1999) Animal bone remains. In D. Soren and N. Soren (eds.) *A Roman Villa and a Late Roman Infant Cemetery. Excavation at Poggio Gramignano, Lugnano in Teverina*, 533–594. Roma, L'Erma di Bretschneider.

MacKinnon, M. (2001) High on the hog: linking zooarcheological, literary and artistic data for pig breeds in Roman Italy. *American Journal of Archaeology*, 105, 649–673.

MacKinnon, M. R. (2002) *The Excavations of San Giovanni di Ruoti, The Faunal and Plant Remains*, Toronto, Buffalo, London.

MacKinnon, M. R. (2004) *Production and Consumption of Animals in Roman Italy: Integrating the Zooarchaeological and Textual evidence*. Porthsmouth, Rhode Island.

Martin, A. (1999) Additional small finds. In D. Soren and N. Soren (eds.) *A Roman Villa and a Late Roman Infant Cemetery. Excavation at Poggio Gramignano, Lugnano in Teverina*, 443–445. Roma, L'Erma di Bretschneider.

Martin J-M. (1993) *La Pouille du VI au XII siècle,* (Coll. Ecole Française de Rome, 179). Rome.

Minniti, C. (1999) L'utilizzazione dei molluschi nell'età del Bronzo di Coppa Nevigata. *19th Convegno sulla Preistoria-Protostoria e Storia della Daunia. San Severo 1998,* 177–195. San Severo.

Murialdo (2001) Gli elementi da parure in osso o corno e gli amuleti. In T. Mannoni and G. Murialdo (eds.) *S. Antonino: un insediamento fortificato nella Liguria bizantina,* II. 521–523. Firenze, Artigrafiche.

Nobis, G. (1954) Ur- und frühgeschichtliche Rinder Nord- und Mitteldeutschlands. *Zeitschr. f. Tierzüchtg. u. Zücthgsbiol* 63, 155–194.

Payne, S. (1973) Kill-off patterns in sheep and goats: the mandibles from Aşvan Kale. *Anatolian Studies* XXIII, 281–303.

Payne, S. (1985) Morphological distinctions between the mandibular teeth of young sheep, Ovis, and goats, Capra. *Journal of Archaeological Science* 12, 139–147.

Prummel, W. and Frisch, H. J. (1986) A guide for distinction of species, sex and body side in bones of sheep and goat. *Journal of Archaeological Science* 13, 567–577.

Reese, D. S. (1992) The marine and fresh-water shells. In F. D'Andria and D. Whitehouse (eds.) *Excavations at Otranto, The Finds,* II, 349–351. Galatina, Congedo Editore.

Reese D. S. (2002) Marine and freshwater shells. In M. R. MacKinnon, *The Excavations of San Giovanni di Ruoti, The Faunal and Plant Remains,* 189–193. Toronto, Buffalo, London.

Ricci, M. (2001a) Armi. In M. S. Arena, P. Delogou, L. Paroli, M. Ricci, L. Saguì and L. Venditeli (eds.) *Roma, dall'Antichità al Medioevo. Archeologia e Storia,* 395–402. Milano, Electa.

Ricci, M. (2001b) Elementi in osso per rivestimento di cassette in legno. In M. S. Arena, P. Delogou, L. Paroli, M. Ricci, L. Saguì, and L. Venditeli (eds.) *Roma, dall'Antichità al Medioevo. Archeologia e Storia,* 543–550. Milano, Electa.

Silver, I. A. (1969) The ageing of domestic animals. In D. Brothwell and E. Higgs (eds.) *Science in Archaeology, a Survey of Progress and Research,* 283–302. Bristol.

Simpson, C. J. (1994) Small finds. In A. Small and R. J. Buck (eds.) *The Excavations of San Giovanni di Ruoti, I, The Villas and their Environment.* 72, 108–109, 399. Toronto, Buffalo, London.

Tosatti, A. M. (1991) Materiali in osso e corno. In *MM3. Scavi della MM3. Ricerche di archeologia,* 63–69. Milano.

Volpe, G. (1996) *Contadini, pastori e mercanti nell'Apulia tardoantica.* Bari, Edipuglia.

Volpe *et al.* (2002) Il complesso episcopale paleocristiano di san Pietro a Canosa. Prima relazione preliminare. *Vetera Christianorum* 39, 133–190.

Volpe *et al.* (2003) Il complesso episcopale paleocristiano di San Pietro a Canosa. Seconda relazione preliminare (campagna di scavi 2002). *Archeologia Medievale* XXX, 107–164.

Volpe, G. De Felice, G. and Turchiano, M. (2005A) I rivestimenti marmorei, i mosaici e i pannelli. In *opus sectile della villa tardoantica di Faragola (Ascoli Satriano, Foggia). Atti del X Colloquio dell'Associazione Italiana per lo Studio e la Conservazione del Mosaico, Lecce, 18–21 febbraio 2004,* 61–78. Tivoli, Edizioni Scripta Manent.

Volpe, G. De Felice, G. and Turchiano, M. (2005B) Faragola (Ascoli Satriano). Una residenza aristocratica e un villaggio altomedievale nella valle del caraelle: Primi dati. In G. Volpe and M. Turchiano (eds.) *Paesaggi e insediamenti rurali in Italia meridionale fra tardoantico e altomedioevo,* Atti del I Seminario sul Tardoantico e l'Altomedioevo in Italia meridionale (12–14 febbraio 2004), 265–297. Bari, Edipuglia.

Volpe *et al.* (in press) Il complesso sabiano di S. Pietro a Canosa, in *La Cristianizzazione in Italia fra Tardoantico e altomedioevo: Aspetti e problemi, atti del IX Congresso di Archeologia Cristiana,* Agrigento 20–25 Novembre 2005.

Wilkens, B. (2001) I reperti faunistici. In G. Pignocchi (ed.) *Monte Torto di Osimo. L'impianto produttivo,* 193–202 Ancona, Soprintendenza Archeologica Delle Marche.

Chapter 15

Animals and Economic Patterns in Medieval Apulia (South Italy): Preliminary Findings

Giovanni De Venuto

Introduction

Until the beginning of 1970s, in Italy, zooarchaeology was mostly applied to prehistoric studies (Tagliacozzo 1993, 7–13). Thanks to the pioneering results of English and French experiences related to 'the archaeology of lost villages', the discipline became employed as a tool for reconstructing the rural medieval economy. The first analysis in southern Italy was made by Graeme Barker and David Whitehouse, focusing on three sites: Santa Maria in Città (Molise; Barker 1980), Santa Maria d'Anglona (Basilicata; Whitehouse 1969, 72–74) and Satriano (Basilicata; Whitehouse 1970, 216–217). In Sicily, Corinne Bossard-Beck (1984; Bossard-Beck and Maccari-Poisson 1980) studied the fauna of Brucato, a Norman-Swabian village, and used the faunal assemblage to explore *"la culture matérielle des habitants"* – i.e. alimentation and culinary practices. During the 1980s and 90s, in southern Italy, zooarchaeological applications to medieval contexts remained isolated cases and, with the exception of Otranto (Apulia), the only example of a faunal assemblage from an urban context (Cartledge *et al.* 1992), there have been no programmes of extended research.

In Apulia, medieval zooarchaeological research should make it possible to explore the economic and cultural differences between newly occupied territories and those districts under Roman-Byzantine administration during the 10th and 11th centuries. Zooarchaeology will also enable us to establish economic and cultural hierarchies of production and consumption sites directly managed by the Crown. It is interesting and useful to demonstrate with material culture the alternation between animal breeding (transhumance) and cereal growing: this dichotomy has been indicated by some historians as a cultural constant of the region from the Roman period to the Middle Ages (Del Treppo 1984).

Archaeological Context: Ordona, Canne della Battaglia, Apigliano (fig. 15.1)

Ordona (Foggia, North Apulia)

The faunal assemblage comes from the 1998 and 2000 excavations of the medieval occupation phases (11th – first half of 15th century) of the Roman thermal quarter

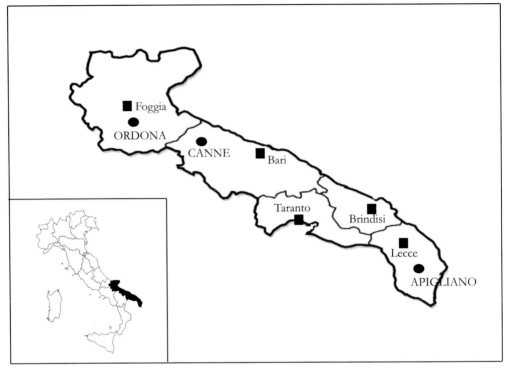

Fig. 15.1. The geographical distribution of the three medieval sites in Apulia (by dott.ssa N. Mangialardi)

(Favia *et al.* 2000, 176–197). The sample was obtained from occupation layers of an house that was situated within the ancient *calidarium* (second half of 12th century–15th century; Volpe *et al.* 2003, 41–43), from structural collapses and from the fillings of abandoned pits used for cereal storage (14th–15th century). It is possible to recognize two archaeological periods: one dates to the re-foundation of the town by Norman and Swabian conquerors, when it assumed the character of a *casale* (a rural, not fortified, village, usually in a plain, designed to repopulate and plough deserted territories) and, most probably, the construction of a royal farm (11th–second half of 13th century); the other to the village desertion, coinciding with the Aragonese institution of the Sheep's Royal Customs (14th–15th cenutry; Volpe 2000, 541–554).

Canne della Battaglia (Bari, Central Apulia)

Between 1999–2000 the Apulian Archaeological Superintendence made two borings on the *cittadella* of Canne. The stratigraphic analysis uncovered some buildings composed of single-room houses provided with water drainage canals, as well as contexts relating to the use of castle. This evidences can be dated to the last occupation phase of the *castrum* (fortified town), in the 13th century (Postrioti 2003).

Apigliano (Lecce, South Apulia)

During the Byzantine occupation (from the 8th to 11th century) Apigliano was probably a *'chorion'*: a nucleated village of farmers, collectively managing the land but fiscally controlled by the State (Arthur 1999). Archaeological investigations have indicated sporadic 11th or 12th century occupation levels: the site was repopulated between the 13th and 14th century when it was founded as a hamlet around a small church (Bruno 1999). The faunal remains have been found in occupation (beaten earth floors, hearths) and desertion (fills of grain storage pits used as garbage dumps, artificial accumulation) layers.

The data

8051 fragments have been analysed: 4790 from Ordona (3113 identified), 2943 from Apigliano (802 identified) and 318 from Canne (244 identified). Fig. 15.2 shows the percentages referring to the number of remains (N.I.S.P.) of the four principal domestic animals. Taking a long term perspective, from the Byzantine (8th–10th century) to the first Aragonese Age (first half of 15th century), we observe a large presence of sheep/goat in all three contexts, with the only exception being Ordona's Norman occupation phase, when there are higher numbers of cattle. In Canne the

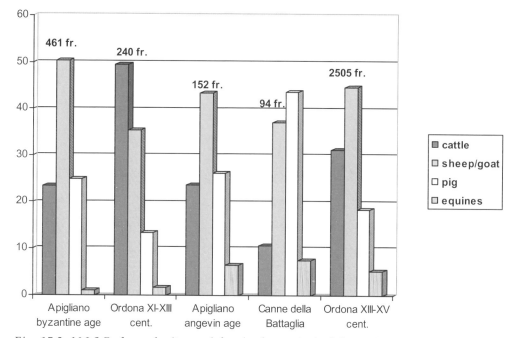

Fig. 15.2. N.I.S.P. for each sites and for the four principal domestic animals (cattle, sheep/goat, pig, equids)

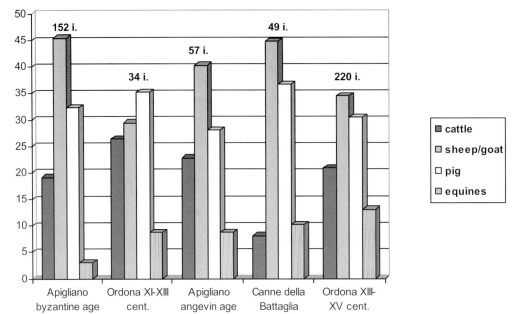

Fig. 15.3. M.N.I. for each sites and for the four principal domestic animals (cattle, sheep/goat, pig, equids)

percentage of pigs is a little higher than of sheep/goats. Equines, horses and donkeys, tend to increase from the first centuries to the latter ones of the Late Middle Ages. If we consider each site, the percentages are rather similar for Apigliano, from 8th/10th century to 13th/14th century, with ovines and caprines remains more numerous than those of pig and cattle. An interesting quantitative inversion between cattle and ovines can be noticed in the two samples from Ordona, where pig numbers are always below 20%.

The M. N. I. (minimum number of individuals) in part confirms this data (fig. 15.3). There is more evidence for pigs than cattle; during the historical period considered in this paper, ovines are clearly prevalent in Apigliano, while during the Norman phase, in Ordona, the number of ovines equals that of cattle and continues to increase until the Angevin and first Aragonese occupation phase. In the case of Canne it is interesting to note that ovines dominate and that numbers of equines exceed those of cattle. The general increment of pigs at all sites can probably be explained with the relatively poorer preservation of the bones of these animals compared to those of the other domestic species. Hence the number of pig remains calculated for the estimated N.I.S.P. may well be an underestimate.

The mortality data confirms that cattle were mostly used for agricultural work: these animals were frequently killed when they were more than four/five years old and had become useless for the plough. But with the exception of an arthritic scaphoid from Apigliano (dating to the Byzantine age), there is no evidence of traction pathologies on the bones. In the last centuries of the Middle Ages, as can be observed

Table 15.1 – Ordona, C11th – first C13th: cattle's, sheep/goat's and pig's age of death (estimated on the basis of the M.N.I.) (after Barone 1974)

Species			Age				Tot.
	Fetus	≤6 m	6-12 m	1-2 y	2-4 y	≥5 y	
Bos taurus				1		4	5
	≤3 m	3-6 m	6-18 m	1-2 y	2-4 y	>4 y	
Ovis vel Capra			1		2	2	5
	Fetus	≤6 m	6-12 m	1-2 y	2-4 y	≥5 y	
Sus domesticus		1	2	1	7		11

Table 15.2 – Ordona, second half C13th – first C15th: cattle's, sheep/goat's and pig's age of death (estimated on the basis of the M.N.I.) (after Barone 1974)

Species			Age				Tot.
	Fetus	≤6 m	6-12 m	1-2 y	2-4 y	≥5 y	
Bos taurus			1	6	8	15	30
	≤3 m	3-6 m	6-18 m	1-2 y	2-4 y	>4 y	
Ovis vel Capra	6	1	11	7	10	9	44
	Fetus	≤6 m	6-12 m	1-2 y	2-4 y	≥5 y	
Sus domesticus		4	10	11	4		29

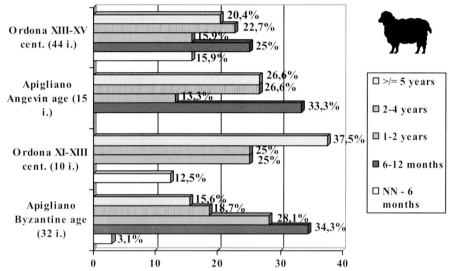

Fig. 15.4. *Sheep/goat age of death (estimated for the M. N. I.) on the basis of the epiphisial fusion and of the teeth eruption (after Barone 1974)*

in Ordona (Tables 15.1–15.2), there was probably differentiation in cattle breeding: some animals may have been destined for alimentary use when they were still young.

The sheep/goat bones epiphysial fusion and dental eruption indicate that Apigliano's inhabitants relied on dairy products (especially during the Byzantine age), whereas at Ordona we note a marked tendency towards milk and wool (fig. 15.4): mature individuals (over five years) represent nearly two quarters of the entire sample (37,5%), while newly-born animals represent one of the highest percentages among all sites (12,5%). During the 14th–15th century the mortality curve, based on the registration of Ordona's sheep/goat teeth wear, shows a high prevalence in the consumption of ovine meat, with nearly 50% of individuals killed when they were two and three years old (figs 15.5–15.6). This trend is also evident in Apigliano between 8th and 10th century (figs 15.7–15.8).

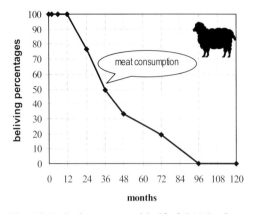

Fig. 15.5. Ordona, second half of C13th- first of C15th: sheep/goat mortality curve (after Payne 1973)

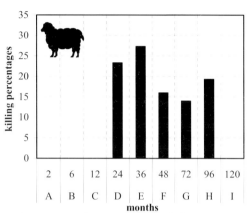

Fig. 15.6. Ordona, second half of C13th- first of C15th: sheep/goat killing diagram (after Payne 1973)

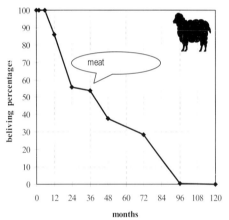

Fig. 15.7. Apigliano, C8th-C10th: sheep/goat mortality curve (after Payne 1973)

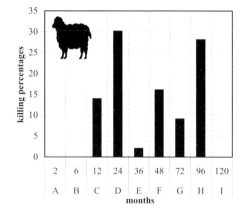

Fig. 15.8. Apigliano, C8th-C10th: sheep/goat killing diagram (after Payne 1973)

Between the 13th and 14th century the estimated age of death for pigs seems indicates similar levels of stock keeping at the three sites (fig. 15.9). In the 14th century, in Apigliano, a higher demand for young individuals is evident. During the Angevine and the first Aragonese period, in Ordona, the noticeable change in pig raising (it become convenient to keep pigs until their first or second year of life) could indicate the utilisation of a better meat supply and a local economic rise. During the 13th century, the town and castle of Canne also demanded good quality products.

The distribution of pig skeletal elements indicates a difference between Apigliano and Ordona in the breeding purpose of these animals (Table 15.3; fig. 15.10). If we consider, for both sites, a clear over valuation of cranial elements for the presence of

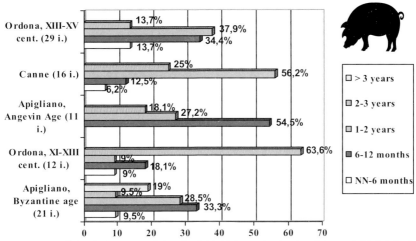

Fig. 15.9. Pig age of death (estimated for the M.N.I.) on the basis of the epiphisial fusion (after Barone 1974) and of the teeth eruption (after Bull and Payne 1982)

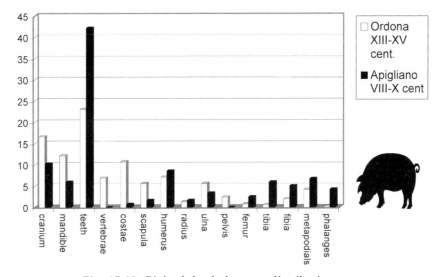

Fig. 15.10. Pig's skeletal elements distribution

teeth, in the sample from Apigliano it is possible to note a substantial balance amongst the skeletal elements, while in the sample of Ordona we can observe that forelimbs are more frequent than hind limbs. This could be explained both in terms of a *chorion* propensity to self production/consumption and with a *casale* or *massaria* inclination to a market economy. For the Byzantine age, in Apigliano, we also find higher numbers of very old animals, mostly females, probably raised for reproductive aims (fig. 15.9). We cannot exclude the possibility that Ordona was a specialized centre

Table 15.3 – Pig's skeletal elements distribution in the Ordona (C13th–C15th) and Apigliano (C8th–C10th) sample.

Pig's skeletal elements		Ordona XIII-XV cent.	Apigliano VIII-X cent
head	cranium	74	12
	mandibles	54	7
	teeth	103	49
rachis	vertebrae	31	-
	costae	48	1
forelimb	scapula	25	2
	humerus	32	10
	radius	6	2
	ulna	25	4
hindlimb	pelvis	11	-
	femur	4	3
	tibia	3	7
	fibia	9	6
extremities	metapodials	19	8
	phalanges	1	5
Total		445	116

producing salted pork which was not consumed by its inhabitants, who instead were satisfied with the poorer forelimbs.

We assume, from written and artistic sources, that pig killing and the consumption of its salted or roasted meat must have been a widespread alimentary custom of rural and powerful people (figs 15.11–15.12). The Frederician-Swabian Statute concerning the management of regal farms (*Constitutio sive encyclica super massariis Curie*) dedicated long passages to pig keeping: "Control if they make the animals fat for the regal table or, when we are out of the reign, to procure a profit to the Crown from their sale" (Huillard-Bréholles 1854, 214–216). The laws

Fig. 15.11. Otranto (Le), Southern Italy. Cathedral mosaic floor (C11th): december, the pig/wild boar killing

Fig. 15.12. Otranto (Le), Southern Italy. Cathedral mosaic floor (C11th): february, the pig roasting

controlled the pig's births and their nourishment: "Each fertile sow has to drop four pigs; one *salma* of barley must be prepared for their nourishment" (Winkelmann 1880, 754). Among the goods owned by the regal farms was salted pork. There was probably a real cultural inclination amongst the Angevin ruling class to eat this type of meat as suggested in a sumptuary law dated to 1290, which stated that during the Vespers Wars, lunch must be restricted "to eat *salted meat* with soup in accordance with *ultramontano* (i.e. Angevin) custom" (Licinio 1994, 319).

Alimentary uses

Comparing the faunal assemblages of Apigliano and Ordona we notice a marked increase in the number of tortoises (*Testudo hermanni*), from the first to the last human occupation phases (figs 15.13–15.16). This pattern may be explained in terms of a local interest in the consumption of this animal only in the last centuries of the Middle Ages, also found in other sites with evidence for tortoise consumption, such as at the village of Brucato in Sicily (Beck-Bossard 1981a, 314–319). This new alimentary trend was accompanied by a greater availability of the little reptile, probably due to environmental changes (perhaps an increase in wetlands) or to habitat modification as a

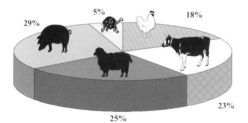

Fig. 15.13. Ordona, C11th–first C13th: the principal alimentary animal resource (on the basis of M.N.I.)

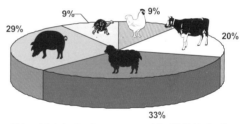

Fig. 15.14. Ordona, second half C13th–first C15th: the principal alimentary animal resource (on the basis of M.N.I.)

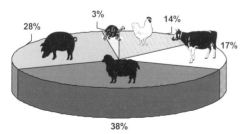

Fig. 15.15. Apigliano, C8th–C10th: the principal alimentary animal resource (on the basis of M.N.I.)

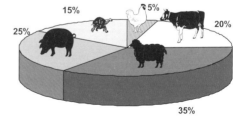

Fig. 15.16. Apigliano, C13th–C14th: the principal alimentary animal resource (on the basis of M.N.I.)

result of human activity. In fact, one of the tortoise's behavioural traits is feeding on other animal droppings (Arnold, Burton 1985, 85–86): an increase in pastoral activity could therefore have in turn attracted more tortoises. In the first half of the 15th century Ordona became a pasturable area managed directly by the Aragonese Crown in the organization of the Sheep's Customs. There is no evidence for the modification of tortoise carapace or plastrons, but we cannot exclude the possibility that after the animal's beheading the shell could have been broken up to enable meat to be removed and boiled; a number of Renaissance cookery-books refer to hulled tortoise soup (De Grossi Mazzorin, Minniti 2000, 337).

During the last centuries of the Middle Ages (14th–15th centuries), in the sample from Ordona, some butchery marks on horse bones (chops on the proximal extremity of an ulna and on the proximal extremity and diaphysis of two metatarsus) could indicate the practice of eating horse meat (fig. 15.17). In southern Italy, archaeological evidence of this practice from medieval contexts is extremely rare (Beck-Bossard 1981b, 545) and it can only be supposed on the basis of the animal's killing age (Albarella 1996, 222): hence a sample of young horse bone would suggest it was used for food. In the first half of the 8th century it is known that this animal was the object of Church attention: it was forbidden to eat its meat because the horse was considered a useful military tool (Baker, Clark 1993, 59). Many of the 14th century hippology treatises, written for the Angevin and Aragonese specialized regal farms, prescribed that taking care of a horse was the same as taking care of a man; as someone wrote, to eat a horse was the same as eating a man (Porsia 1995, 128). Did all respect this prohibition? The poorest classes probably ate infirm or very old horses (Harris 1990, 90–94). The status of the horse could be the real discriminant: only when it was used as a working instrument or as a useful means of transport, could it be eaten. This is probably what happened in Ordona, which increasingly became a destination for transhumance. Until the first decades of the last century, ethnographic sources indicate that horses were used to transport food-stuffs and were also employed in the construction of sheep pens (Marino 1988, 84).

Fig. 15.17. Butchery marks on two horse metatarsals from Ordona (first C15th; photo by M. Attademo)

Table 15.4 – NISP and MNI for the wild animals in the Apigliano, Canne and Ordona sample.

Species	Apigliano VIII-XI cent.				Apigliano XIII-XIV cent.				Canne XIII cent.				Ordona XIII-XV cent.			
	NISP	%	MNI	%	NISP	%	MNI	%	NISP	%	MNI	%	NISP	%	MNI	%
Cervus elaphus L.	2	0,3	2	1,5	-	-	-	-	7	2,8	3	4,3	15	0,5	5	1,6
Capreolus capreolus L.	2	0,3	2	1,5	-	-	-	-	1	0,4	1	1,4	-	-	-	-
Sus scrofa ferus L.	1	0,1	1	0,7	2	0,7	1	0,01	8	3,2	3	4,3	1	0,03	1	0,3
Vulpes vulpes L.	1	0,1	1	0,7	-	-	-	-	-	-	-	-	-	-	-	-
Erinaceus europaeus	2	0,3	2	1,5	-	-	-	-	-	-	-	-	-	-	-	-
Lepus europaeus Pall.	1	0,1	1	0,7					-	-	-	-				
Totale	**9**	**1,6**	**9**	**6,7**	**2**	**0,7**	**1**	**0,01**	**16**	**6,4**	**7**	**10**	**16**	**0,53**	**6**	**1,9**

Table 15.5 – Deer skeletal elements distribution in Apigliano, Canne and Ordona sample.

Deer bones	*Apigliano 11th cent.*	*Canne*	*Ordona 13th-15th cent.*
antler	-	7	2
scapula	2	-	2
humerus	-	-	1
radius	-	-	2
ulna	-	-	1
metapodials	-	-	5
phalanges	-	-	2
Total	**2**	**7**	**15**

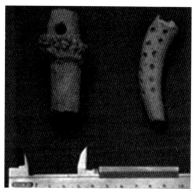

Fig. 15.18. Canne, C13th: two antler object, part.

Game and its products

The few wild animal remains from Ordona, Canne and Apigliano indicate that game played a relatively minor role in the regional economy or diet. Red deer and roe deer are the most recurring species, followed by wild boar, hedgehog, fox and hare. Their total percentage (N.I.S.P.) is little over 1% (Table 15.4). In the case of Canne, the distribution of deer anatomical elements indicates that cervid exploitation was limited to collecting antlers (Table 15.5: all the fragments are antlers!): it is possible to trace the integral working process of this material, from the breaking and sawing of the extremities to the polishing and decoration of the final object (fig. 15.18). Working scraps are also present in Ordona (fig. 15.19): the production of antler tools was, probably, a widespread activity in medieval Apulia, particularly in North Apulia, where environmental conditions (the proximity of the South Appennino Mountains and higher numbers of streams than in South Apulia) could favour the spread of the deer, today extinct in this region.

Handicraft

The working of domestic animal horns is attested: a high number of male sheep horns

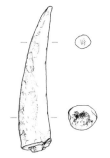

*Fig. 15.19. Ordona,
C14th: a semi-worked
deer antler (by V.
Acquafredda)*

from Canne present saw marks at their lower ends.
Unlike deer antlers, these remains do not have working marks on their surface. Perhaps this reflects the
limitations of research, but it is more probable that
they are the result of other activities. Antlers are more
suitable for working than sheep or cattle horn; moreover it was also necessary to cut off the horns before
skinning the carcasses. The Swabian royal statutes
concerning farm management include the values of
dressed or raw leather obtained from domestic
animals: a cattle hide was worth between 10 and 15
tarì and a horse hide 4 *tarì* (Winkelmann 1880, 755–
756). Domestic animal long bones were also worked
(fig. 15.20).

Unusual use

Hedgehog remains are rarely recovered from medieval
contexts in Italy. They normally display no cut marks
and an alimentary use of this animal is excluded in
most cases. At Apigliano, a hedgehog's mandible
(dating to the 9th century) presents clear butchery
marks (fig. 15.21): these do not confirm that the animal
was consumed by people, but this is a probable
scenario. Perhaps it was necessary to disarticulate the
mandible from the skull with a knife, before manually
skinning the little animal's body. Was hedgehog meat
regularly consumed? It was certainly considered
disgusting by some European Renaissance dietary
authors (Albala 2002, 71); indeed, there is so little meat
on a hedgehog that it could not have represented a
significant contribution to human diets. Nonetheless,

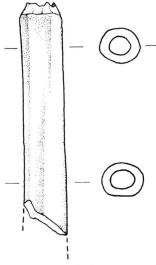

*Fig. 15.20. Ordona, second
half C13th-C14th: a sheep/
goat polished and worked
tibia (by V. Acquafredda)*

when combined with ethnographic studies, the rural
archaeological context may support this possible
interpretation (Moreno-García 2004, 332).

The faunal sample from the filling of a hypogean
structure in the house quarter of Canne (layer 196) is
composed of, with the exception of domestic and wild
animal bones (sheep/goat, pig, wild boar and domestic fowl), a high number of cat
remains (Table 15.6). Figure 22 shows that 85% of the identifiable fragments must be
attributed to at least five cats. The distribution of skeletal elements indicates a high
presence of cranial remains, perhaps as a result of their predisposition to fragmentation; the percentage of vertebra is also high (Table 15.7). Epiphysial fusion and
teeth eruption attest the presence of one young individual (less than 7 months), 3 sub
adults (between 7 and 12 months) and one adult (older than 1 year). The mandibula

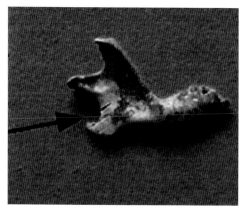

Fig. 15.21. Apigliano, C11th: hedgehog
mandible with butchery marks

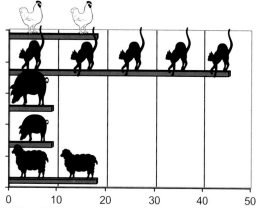

Fig. 15.22. Canne, C13th: layer 196, M.N.I.

Table 15.6 – Canne C13th, layer 196: NISP and MNI of the faunal sample.

Species	N.I.S.P.	%	M.N.I.	%
Ovis vel Capra	5	3,9	2	18,1
Sus scrofa dom.	4	3,1	1	9
Gallus gallus	4	3,1	2	18,1
Felis sylvestris f. dom.	107	84,9	5	45,4
Sus scrofa ferus	6	4,7	1	9
Total	**126**	*100*	**11**	*100*

and cranium measurements (Tables 15.8–15.9) are compared with that of other North-European medieval sites, reported by R. Luff and M. Moreno García (1995, 103). Assuming our sample is smaller than others, the individuals of Canne should be bigger than those reported from Cambridge (a high number of Bene't Court individuals are young or sub adult) and more similar to individuals recovered from medieval contexts at Colchester, Höxter or Odense.

This zooarchaeological sample does not appear to reflect accidental preservation, given the taxonomic homogeneity and a number of cut/chop marks on the surface of the bones. The 'knife' cuts are localized on the cranium nasal and frontal portions (fig. 15.23), on a mandibula (fig. 15.24), on a proximal femoral epiphisis (fig. 15.25) and around the acetabulum of a pelvis; fissures are also present on the dorsal surface of a last lumbar vertebra (fig. 15.26). These marks can be interpreted as the result of a skinning and

Table 15.7 – Canne C13th (layer 196): cat skeletal elements distribution

Cat's bones	n.	%
cranium	28	26,1
mandibles	4	3,7
vertebras	46	42,9
ribs	3	2,8
scapula	2	1,8
humerus	4	3,7
radius	3	2,8
ulna	3	2,8
pelvis	6	5,6
sacrum	3	2,8
femur	3	2,8
tibia	1	0,9
fibula	1	0,9
Total	**107**	**100**

Table 15.8 – Comparison among some cat mandible measurements from Canne and from others North Europe sites

Mandible	Total lenght *(1)*			Height of vertical ramus *(8)*		
	n	r	x	n	r	x
Haithabu C9th – C11th	56	48.9-61.6	55	56	20.0-26.6	23.5
Canne C13th	**4**	**48.4-55.8**	**52.5**	**4**	**20.0-22.5**	**21.0**
Höxter C13th	13	50.6-56.7	53.9	12	19.2-23.2	21.3
Bene't Court C13th	59	44.9-54.1	49.5	57	17.3-21.7	19.5
Colchester	11	47.7-57.9	52.7	10	19.0-25.7	21.8
Castle Mall C15th – C16th	9	49.7-60.1	53.9	10	19.8-25.4	21.7

Table 15.9 – Comparison among some cat cranium measurements from Canne and from others North Europe sites

Cranium	Condylobasal length *(2)*			Greatest mastoid breadth *(18)*			Greatest breadth of the occipital condyles *(19)*		
	n	r	x	n	r	x	n	r	x
Odense C11th	4	71.0-79.2	75.6	8	34.8-38.6	36.9	8	17.9-21.5	19.5
Canne C13th	**1**	**81.4**	**81.4**	**3**	**36.9-38.6**	**37.7**	**3**	**19.5-20.7**	**20.2**
Höxter C13th	7	70.2-78.8	75.6	7	36.1-38.0	36.8	7	17.2-20.7	19.3
Bene't Court C13th	5	71.6-74.5	72.9	50	31.6-37.3	34.3	50	16.7-21.1	18.7

dismemberment action. In Italy they represent an *unicum* in medieval zoo-archaeological research: the only evidences come from Brucato (Sicily; represented by chop marks on a cranium temporal portion: Bossard-Beck 1984, 626) and from the castle of Montaldo di Mondovì (Piedmont; represented by stripes on a mandibula and a chop on the ventral surface of an epistropheus: Aimar *et al.* 1991, 239). The most convincing comparisons are those with Norman, Saxon (Luff, Moreno García 1995, 108–110) and Viking sites (Hatting 1990) in northern Europe. In particular the examples from Cambridge and Odense highlight the question: was it possible to breed a cat for its fur? Documentary sources consider cat pelts as a useful material for dress production as much as fox and squirrel fur. The alimentary use of this feline is attested only during famines: it is known that in the 9th century, the inhabitants of Salerno were forced to eat cats and mice as a result of a heavy siege; the same happened at Monteccassino Abbey in 1163 (Bobis 1998, 75).

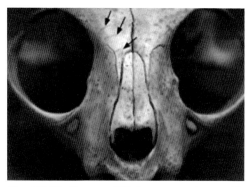

Fig. 15.23. Canne, C13th: cat cranium with cuts on the frontal portion

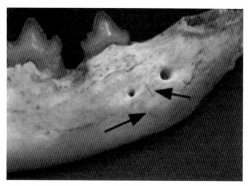

Fig. 15.24. Canne, C13th: cat mandible with cut marks

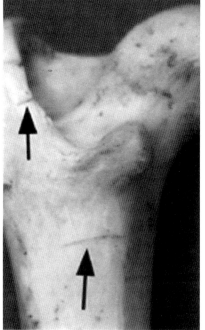

Fig. 15.25. Canne, C13th: cat femur with cuts on the proximal epiphisis and on the diaphisis

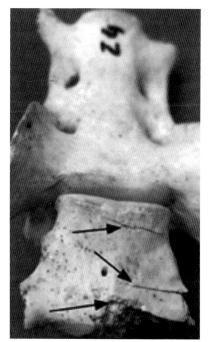

Fig. 15.26. Canne, C13th: cat last lumbar vertebra with chop marks

The cats of Canne represent a probable case of a new habit of wearing clothes incorporating fur. Originating from northern Europe, this practice changed the dress mode of a population usually reliant on wool. Between the 12th and the 13th century, cat fur does not appear in the southern Italian diploma of *mercatura* (Nada Patrone 1989). We cannot exclude the possibility that it was difficult to supply Canne.

Fishes and Shells

Mollusc and fish remains are scarce at all three sites. The only exceptions are some valves of *Unio elongatulus* (unio), a freshwater clam, in Ordona and Canne. Of course, we cannot exclude that people could breed these clams in suitable basins or catch them directly in the river courses of Ofanto and Carapelle. This species is usually edible, but their breeding may also have been aimed at providing a source of pearly shell. Finally, a number of fossil teeth of shark (*Carcharias taurus*) were recovered from Apigliano's Byzantine and Angevin layers. The archaeological context (the filling of an abandoned cereal pit, a cinereous accumulation and red compact earth) prevents a clear interpretation.

Some Considerations

The study of animal bones can partially contribute to reconstructing the regional economy when considering the differences of status for each site. This analysis focused on a comparison of two rural centres (Apigliano and Ordona), one of Byzantine colonization and one of Norman-Swabian re-foundation; the last occupation phases of both coinciding with the 14th–15th century (Angevin age). Throughout its many historical phases, the region was widely exploited for pasture; besides the keeping of sheep/goat, pigs represented an important source of protein. The main economic characteristics of the two villages emerge as follows: Apigliano appears to have assumed a connotation of auto-consumption during the 8th–10th century. In the ovine population mortality was high among young individuals and only old pigs (over three years) have been recorded. Ordona demonstrates an even greater diversification in the pattern of ovine killing, with a more marked tendency to meat production. The 14th century represented a turning point: in Apigliano and Ordona the demand for meat products increased and this was probably due to an improvement or to a specialization in stock keeping methods. This is particularly evident in Ordona with the institution of the Aragonese Sheep's Customs. In the first occupation phases of Ordona, nearly 50% of cattle remains may represent animals used for ploughing. In the case of Canne, the absence of a diachronic sample does not allow us to understand the major possible variations in the appropriation of animal resources, although it is clear that the status of town/castle influenced the composition of the faunal assemblage. This is the only situation in which pig remains outnumber those of sheep/goat and where cattle hardly reach 10%. Canne was therefore almost certainly a consumption site provisioned by its own rural hinterland.

Acknowledgements

I want to thank Professor De Grossi Mazzorin of the University of Lecce for having accepted my request for a specialization thesis. Professors Volpe and Arthur gave me the opportunity to study the faunal assemblages of Ordona and Apigliano; I would like to note that in 1999 Simon Davis studied a sample of one hundred bones from Apigliano. Dott.ssa M. Corrente (Apulia Archaeological Superintendancy) permitted the study of the sample of animal bones from Canne. I would also like to thank dott.ssa A. Tritto for having revised my article.

Bibliography

Aimar, A. D'Errico, F. and Giacobini, G. (1991) Analisi dei resti faunistici. In E. Micheletto and M. V. Gambari (eds.) *Montaldo di Mondovì. Un insediamento protostorico. Un castello. Quaderni di Archeologia del Piemonte, Monografie* 1, 237–244.

Albala, K. (2002) *Eating Right in the Renaissance*. Berkeley-Los Angeles-London, University of California Press.

Albarella, U. (1996) The faunal remains. In P. Arthur, U. Albarella, B. Bruno and S. King "Masseria Quattro Macine" a deserted medieval village and its territory in Southern Puglia: an interim report on field survey, excavation and document analysis. *Papers of the British School at Rome* 64, 222–224.

Arnold, E. N. and Burton, J. A. (1985) *Guida dei Rettili e degli Anfibi d'Europa*. Padova, Mursia Edizioni.

Arthur, P. (1999) Un Chorion bizantino? In P. Arthur (ed.) *Da Apigliano a Martano. Tre anni di archeologia medievale (1997–1999)*, 14–20. Galatina, Congedo Editore.

Baker, P. and Clark, G. (1993) Archaeozoological evidence for medieval Italy: a critical review of the present state of research. *Archeologia Medievale. Cultura materiale. Insediamenti. Territorio* 20, 45–77.

Barker, G. (1980) Stock keeping at D85 (Appendix 4). In R. Hodges, G. Barker and K. Wade (eds.) *Excavations at D85 (Santa Maria in Città): an early medieval hilltop settlement in Molise. Papers of the British School at Rome* 48, 123–124.

Barone, R. (1974) Anatomia comparata dei mammiferi domestici. Bologna, Edagricole.

Beck-Bossard, C. (1981) Le ossa. In Flambard, A. M., Noyé, G., Beck-Bossard, C., Finetti, A. and Gareri, E. *Nuovi scavi nel castello di Scribla in Calabria. Archeologia Medievale. Cultura materiale. Insediamenti. Territorio* 8, 544–546.

Beck-Bossard, C. (1981a) L'alimentazione in un villaggio siciliano del XIV secolo, sulla scorta delle fonti archeologiche. *Archeologia Medievale. Cultura materiale. Insediamenti. Territorio* 8, 311–320.

Bobis, L. (1998) Trappola per topi. In «Medioevo» 21, 72–76.

Bossard-Beck, C. (1984) Le mobilier ostéologique et botanique. In J.-M. Pesez (ed.) *Brucato. Histoire et archéologie d'un habitat médiéval en Sicile. Collection de l'École Française de Rome* 38, 615–671.

Bossard-Beck, C. and Maccari-Poisson, B. (1984) L'alimentation. In J.-M. Pesez (ed.), *Brucato. Histoire et archéologie d'un habitat médiéval en Sicile. Collection de l'École Française de Rome* 38, 749–773.

Bruno, B. (1999) Il casale medioevale: fonti ed archeologia. In P. Arthur (ed.) *Da Apigliano a Martano. Tre anni di archeologia medievale (1997–1999)*, 21–24. Galatina, Congedo Editore.

Bull, G. and Payne, S. (1982) Tooth eruption and epiphysial fusion in pigs and wild boar. In B. Wilson, C. Grigson and S. Payne (eds) *Ageing and sexing animal bones from archaeological sites*. British Archaeological Reports, British Series, 109, 55–71.

Cartledge, J., Clark, G. and Higgins, V. (1992) The animal bones: a preliminary assessment of the stock economy. In F. D'Andria, D. Whitehouse (eds) *Excavation at Otranto. Volume II: the finds*, 317–336. Galatina, Congedo Editore.

De Grossi Mazzorin, J. and Minniti, C. (2000) Alimentazione e pratiche religiose: il caso di due contesti monastici a Roma tra il XVI e il XVIII secolo. In *Convegno Nazionale di Archeozoologia II – Atti del 2° Convegno Nazionale di Archeozoologia (Asti, 1997)*, 327– 339.

Del Treppo, M. (1984) Agricoltura e transumanza in Puglia nei secoli XIII–XVI: conflitto o integrazione?. In A. Guarducci (ed.) *Agricoltura e trasformazione dell'ambiente. Secoli XIII–XVIII.* Atti della "Undicesima settimana di studio" (25–30 Aprile 1979, Firenze), 455–460.

Favia, P., Giuliani, R. and Leone, D. (2000) L'area delle terme (Saggio III. 1997–1998). In G. Volpe (ed.) *Ordona X. Ricerche archeologiche a Herdonia (1993–1998)*, 127–201. Bari, Edipuglia.

Harris, M. (1990) Buono da mangiare. Enigmi del gusto e consuetudini alimentari. Torino, Einaudi.

Hatting, T (1990) Cats from Viking Age Odense. In *Journal of Danish Archaeology* 9, 179–192.

Huillard-Bréholles, J. L. A. (1854), Historia Diplomatica Friderici secundi, IV/1. Paris, Plon Fratres.

Licinio, R. (1994) Castelli medievali. Puglia e Basilicata: dai Normanni a Federico II e Carlo I d'Angiò. Bari, Edizioni Dedalo.

Luff, R. M. and Moreno García, M. (1995) Killing cats in the medieval period. An unusual episode in the history of Cambridge, England. In *Archaeofauna* 4, 93–114.

Marino, J. A. (1988) L'economia pastorale nel Regno di Napoli. Napoli, Guida Ed.

Moreno-García, M. (2004) Hunting practices and consumption patterns in rural communities in the Rif mountains (Morocco) – some ethno-zoological notes. In S. Jones O'Day, W. Van Neer and A. Ervynck (eds) *Behaviour Behind Bones. The zooarchaeology of ritual, religion, status and identity*, 327–334. Oxford, Oxbow Books.

Nada Patrone, A. (1989) Pelli e pellami. In G. Musca (ed.) *Uomo e ambiente nel Mezzogiorno Normanno-Svevo.* Atti delle ottave giornate normanno-sveve (Bari, 20–23 ottobre 1987), Bari.

Payne, S. (1973) Kill-off patterns in sheep and goats: the mandibles from Aşvan Kale. In *Anatolian Studies. Journal of the British Institute of Archaeology at Ankara* 23, 281–303.

Porsia, F. (1995) Umanità e arroganza dell'alimentazione equina medievale. In *Alimentazione animale nella storia dell'uomo*, 117–133. Bologna, Edagricole.

Postrioti, G. (2003) Barletta (Bari), Canne della Battaglia. F. 176 IV NE I. G. M. *Taras. Rivista di Archeologia* 21. 1, 132–139.

Tagliacozzo, A. (1993) L'archeozoologia: problemi e metodologie relativi all'interpretazione dei dati. *Origini* 17, 7–88.

Volpe, G. (2000) Herdonia romana, tardoantica e medievale alla luce dei recenti scavi. In G. Volpe (ed.) *Ordona X. Ricerche archeologiche a Herdonia (1993–1998)*, 507–554. Bari, Edipuglia.

Volpe, G., Annese, C., De Felice, G., Favia, P., Turchiano, M., Leone, D. and Rocco, A. (2003) Ordona (Foggia), Cacciaguerra. F. 175 IV NE I. G. M. *Taras. Rivista di Archeologia* 21. 1, 39–44.

Whitehouse, D. (1969) Animal bones. In D. Whitehouse and R. Whitehouse *Excavations at Anglona. Papers of the British School at Rome* 37, 72–74.

Whitehouse, D. (1970) The animal bones. In D. Whitehouse (ed.) *Excavations at Satriano: a deserted medieval settlement in Basilicata. Papers of the British School at Rome* 38, 216–217.

Winkelmann, E. (1880) Acta Imperii inedita saeculi XIII et XIV. Urkunden und briefe zur Geschichte des Kaiserreichs und des Königreichs Sizilien, I. Innsbruck, Verlag der Wagner'shen Universitäts-Buchhandlung.

Chapter 16

Breaking and Shaping Beastly Bodies: Animals as Material Culture in the Middle Ages: Final Discussion

Pam Crabtree

Introduction

It is both a privilege and an honor to replace Annie Grant as the discussant for this important conference. I first met Annie Grant in 1976 when I was a post-graduate student at the University of Pennsylvania about to begin the analysis of the faunal remains from the Anglo-Saxon village of West Stow. Annie was wonderfully supportive of my research and has continued to be a valued colleague and friend for nearly 30 years. Grant has made many important contributions to the zooarchaeology of Iron Age, Roman, and medieval sites in Europe, but two of her contributions are especially relevant for this conference. First, Grant (1982) developed the techniques that are used by most zooarchaeologists to measure dental wear on the teeth of cattle, sheep, and pigs. These methods are crucial to the study of animals as material culture in the Middle Ages because they allow researchers to identify the uses of domestic mammals for secondary products such as wool production and traction. Second, Grant was one of the first medieval archaeozoologists to focus on the importance of hunting in medieval society and culture. Grant's work on hunting (see, for example, Grant 1981) was an important challenge to the then-dominant paleoeconomic school of archaeology, which focused on the economic uses of the most common domestic mammal species. The use of domesticates for secondary products and the role of hunting in European medieval society are two themes that are woven through many of the papers in this volume. As the discussant for this conference, I have tried to identify a number of other themes that are common to several papers.

The Middle Ages as a different culture

In his keynote address, Terry O'Connor reminded us that the past is a foreign country. While all archaeologists need to avoid making the past a mirror of the present by, for example, inappropriately using ethnographic analogies, the recognition that the past was a different material and symbolic world is particularly important when attempting to reconstruct day-to-day life in the Middle Ages. It is entirely too easy to assume that medieval archaeology is the archaeology of "us" and that modern economic, social, and ideological practices can be used to reconstruct medieval behavior. However, the Agricultural and Industrial Revolutions, as well as the many political, social, and religious changes that have taken place over the past five hundred years, have created a modern world that is technology, socially, and ideologically remote from the medieval world. To give just one example from this conference, Bloxam examined the use of parchment and skins in the production of medieval belt books. The appearance of the printing press led to the substitution of paper for parchment in the production of books, and the medieval technologies of book production virtually disappeared in the early modern period. O'Connor notes, however, that we can use documents, iconography, along with archaeology and taphonomy, to get a glimpse of the medieval mindset. This is underlined by Wells in her survey of animal representation on medieval English misericords, enabling us to access a different value system where the fantastic were placed alongside the exotic, wild and domestic. The papers presented in this volume provide an important window into the world of the Middle Ages through an examination of the role of hunting in medieval society, the role of animals and animal products in ritual and in the definition of personal identity, and the roles of animal primary and secondary products in medieval economy and culture.

Hunting in the Middle Ages

The examination of the written, artistic and zooarchaeological evidence for hunting is one way that archaeologists can get a glimpse of the medieval mind. Several of the papers presented at this conference investigated different aspects of hunting in the European Middle Ages. Bejenaru examines Byzantine hunting in the region between the Danube and the Black Sea and notes that the goal of Byzantine hunting in this region was food procurement. Other authors examine the social and ideological contexts of medieval hunting. Valenti and Salvadori identify hunting in central and northern Italy as a military aristocratic prerogative developing with the rise of castle sites. Thomas, focusing on England, also notes that medieval hunting served as preparation for warfare and was restricted to certain members of society. He explains that the hunt is a form of ritualized activity. His data indicate that there was an increasing adherence to hunting manuals from the 13th to the 14th century and that this adherence was an attempt to reinforce social boundaries. This use of animals to construct and maintain exclusive identities is underlined by Pluskowski, demonstrating the centrality of hunting and hunted animal bodies to Western aristocratic visual display.

Sykes takes a somewhat different approach to medieval hunting, noting that the hunt was a central part of medieval popular culture. She uses zooarchaeological data to trace the distribution of hunted meat through medieval society. Sykes finds that keepers' residences can be identified by the high proportions of deer remains, and particular the high proportion of left forelimb elements. Rural sites include larger numbers of mandibles and scapulae, especially right side elements, and these may represent hunters' portions. Deer remains on urban sites do not conform to the rigid patterns called for in hunting manuals, and Sykes suggests that some of the urban venison may have been obtained though illicit means, specifically poaching.

These data are important because they show that individual actions may not always conform to social rules and that we can identify these actions archaeologically. One of the main tenets of the post-processual critique of processual archaeology is that processual theories paid little attention to individual actions (Hodder 1986, 26). The careful use of historical sources and archaeological data in the study of medieval hunting can allow us to begin to discuss the role of individual actors in medieval society.

Animals and medieval identity

A second, related theme is the question of the way in which animals and animal products can be used to define personal identity. As already noted above, a number of papers draw attention to the link between aristocratic status and faunal exploitation; a connection that appears to have been re-forged particularly in Western Europe in the second half of the first millennium AD: for example, Crabtree notes that animals such as peregrine falcons may have served as markers of social status at Middle Saxon Brandon. The continuing use of animal products to define social identity is similarly explored by Pluskowski, who notes that the appropriation of animal bodies by aristocratic groups during the course of the Middle Ages was focused on provisioning, visual display and access to exotica. The material expression of identity is another way that archaeologists can explore the role of individual actors in medieval society.

Medieval animals and ritual

Questions of personal identity are part of the broader archaeology issues of ideology and ritual. The growing interest in the use of zooarchaeological data to study ritual activity has been an important consequence of the post-processual movement in archaeology. A number of the papers in this volume address the roles of medieval animals in ritual life. Crabtree notes that a horse skull was found in a door pit leading to the chancel of the timber church that was constructed around 700 AD at the Middle Saxon site of Brandon in East Anglia. Stallibrass explores rosary production in medieval England. She notes that a traditional taphonomic approach would focus on the depositional history of the fish and cattle bones that were used to make the rosary. Her research shows that it is equally important to examine the social and ritual context in which these rosaries were produced and deposited. Stallibrass's focus on the social and ritual context of bone rosary production allows us to begin to understand medieval minds.

Bone, hide, skins, antler, and horn as raw materials

As Stallibrass's study of bone rosaries shows, bone served as an important raw material for the manufacture of medieval artifacts. Archaeological and historic research has shown that bone served as a raw material for artifacts and tools from the early Pleistocene (Blackwell and d'Errico 2001; d'Errico and Blackwell 2003) to the invention of plastic in the middle of the 20th century. De Venuto provides zooarchaeological evidence for antler- and horn-working in medieval Apulia. His data on cat marks on cut bones suggest that these animals were being raised for their skins. Helen Leaf's data indicate that bird and mammal bones were frequently used for the manufacture of flutes, and Buglione describes the evidence for the manufacture of bone pins in Apulia. Bloxam demonstrates how parchment and skins were used in the manufacture of belt books whilst Pluskowski considers the role of bone and fur in both household and personal ornamentation. Finally, Yeomans provides a comprehensive overview of the use of skin, horn, antler, and bone in medieval and post-medieval London. The growing interest in the use of bone, skin, horn, and antler is an important development in medieval zooarchaeology. Earlier zooarchaeological studies focused on the use of animals for meat and a number of secondary products including milk, wool, and traction. The collection of papers presented here shows that medieval animals were sources for a wide range of *primary* products in addition to meat.

Animals as sources of meat and secondary products

While many of the papers in this volume address the symbolic and social roles of animals in medieval life, a number address more traditional paleoeconomic concerns, including the uses of animals for meat and secondary products. As noted above, Bejenaru maintains that although deer antlers served as sources of raw materials for medieval hunters in the region between the Danube and the Black Sea, the primary goal of deer and boar hunting in that region was food. Seetah examines the archaeological and historical evidence for the establishment of the Guild of Butchers in London. His research clearly demonstrates that butchery differs from the dis-articulation of a carcass after a hunt, since the goal of butchery is to produce specific joints and cuts of meat. Particular tools are used for specific tasks in butchery. As noted above, after the hunt, a series of social rules governed the partition and distribution of the animal carcass. Hunting and butchery also seem to have played very different roles in the medieval worldview. While hunting is commonly represented in art, butchery is not. De Venuto presents evidence for the production of salt pork at medieval Ordonna in Apulia. He notes that the body part distributions for pigs from medieval Ordonna include far fewer hindlimb elements than forelimb elements and suggests that the hindlimbs may have been removed for the production of salt pork. Finally, Crabtree examines the archaeological evidence for wool production at Middle Saxon Brandon. The sex and age profiles from this extensively excavated East Anglian site indicate that many of these animals were kept to advanced ages and that a majority of the adult animals were males. This pattern is consistent with the specialized production of wool for textiles.

Conclusion

Medieval animals were biological entities whose bodies were transformed by a distinctive range of cultural processes. The products that resulted from these transformations served a wide range of social, ritual, and economic uses in the European Middle Ages. By examining the ways in which beastly bodies were broken and re-assembled during the Middle Ages, archaeologists can obtain a window into medieval minds.

Bibliography

Backwell, L. R. and d'Errico, F. (2001) Evidence of termite foraging by Swartkrans early hominids. *Proceedings of the National Academy of Sciences* 98 (4), 1358–1363.
d'Errico, F. and Backwell, L. R. (2003) Possible evidence of bone tool shaping by Swartkrans early hominids. *Journal of Archaeological Science* 30, 1559–1576.
Grant, A. (1981) The significance of deer remains at occupation sites of the Iron Age to the Anglo-Saxon period. In M. Jones and G. Dimbleby (eds.) *The Environment of Man: the Iron Age to the Anglo-Saxon Period*, 205–213. British Archaeological Reports, British Series 87, Oxford, Archeopress.
Grant, A. (1982) The use of tooth wear as a guide to the age of domestic ungulates. In B. Wilson, C. Grigson, and S. Paynes (eds.) *Ageing and Sexing Animal Bones from Archaeological Sites*, 91–109. British Archaeological Reports, British Series 109, Oxford, Archeopress.